The devil's highway

Manchester University Press

STUDIES IN POPULAR CULTURE

General editor: Professor Jeffrey Richards

There has in recent years been an explosion of interest in culture and cultural studies. The impetus has come from two directions and out of two different traditions. On the one hand, cultural history has grown out of social history to become a distinct and identifiable school of historical investigation. On the other hand, cultural studies has grown out of English literature and has concerned itself to a large extent with contemporary issues. Nevertheless, there is a shared project, its aim, to elucidate the meanings and values implicit and explicit in the art, literature, learning, institutions and everyday behaviour within a given society. Both the cultural historian and the cultural studies scholar seek to explore the ways in which a culture is imagined, represented, and received, how it interacts with social processes, how it contributes to individual and collective identities and world views, to stability and change, to social, political, and economic activities and programmes. This series aims to provide an arena for the cross-fertilisation of the discipline, so that the work of the cultural historian can take advantage of the most useful and illuminating of the theoretical developments and the cultural studies scholars can extend the purely historical underpinnings of their investigations. The ultimate objective of the series is to provide a range of books which will explain in a readable and accessible way where we are now socially and culturally and how we got to where we are. This should enable people to be better informed, promote an interdisciplinary approach to cultural issues and encourage deeper thought about the issues, attitudes and institutions of popular culture.

To buy or to find out more about the books currently available in this series, please go to: https://manchesteruniversitypress.co.uk/series/studies-in-popular-culture/

The devil's highway

Urban anxieties and subaltern cultures in London's sailortown, *c.* 1850–1900

Brad Beaven

MANCHESTER UNIVERSITY PRESS

Copyright © Brad Beaven 2024

The right of Brad Beaven to be identified as the author of this work has been asserted in accordance with the Copyright, Designs and Patents Act 1988.

Published by Manchester University Press
Oxford Road, Manchester, M13 9PL

www.manchesteruniversitypress.co.uk

British Library Cataloguing-in-Publication Data
A catalogue record for this book is available from the British Library

ISBN 978 1 5261 7792 6 hardback

First published 2024

The publisher has no responsibility for the persistence or accuracy of URLs for any external or third-party internet websites referred to in this book, and does not guarantee that any content on such websites is, or will remain, accurate or appropriate.

Typeset by Newgen Publishing UK

Contents

List of illustrations	*page* vi
General editor's foreword	vii
Acknowledgements	viii
Introduction: Seaports and sailortowns	1
1 The curse of Ratcliffe Highway: Its reputation and its people in the nineteenth century	16
2 The imagined geography of Ratcliffe Highway	40
3 From Jolly Jack and Moll to proletarian Jack and Jill: The depictions of sailors and women in a nineteenth-century sailortown	62
4 Leisure in a sailortown	86
5 The inner world of the seafaring boarding house	110
6 Sex work and Ratcliffe Highway: Brothels, crime, and matriarchal networks	136
7 Male violence, class, and ethnicity in sailortown	161
Conclusion	184
Bibliography	188
Index	197

List of illustrations

Figures

1.1	Smith's new map of London, 1860	page 27
2.1	Palmers Folly/Place and Perseverance Place, c. 1870	51
4.1	Ratcliffe Highway, early 1900s	88
7.1	German and English sailors fighting, 1892	165
7.2	Monthly categories of offences: Thames Magistrates Courts, 1891	167
7.3	The sex of offenders and victims of assault: Thames Magistrates Courts, 1891	168

Tables

1.1	Occupations of male workers on Ratcliffe Highway in 1861 and 1891	33
6.1	Sex and occupation of the residents of Palmers Folly, 1861 and 1871	146
6.2	Sex and occupation of the residents of Perseverance Place, 1861 and 1871	147
7.1	Male-on-male knife fights in St George's in the East and Whitechapel between 1850 and 1900	170
7.2	Districts with the most serious knife crime compared with St George's in the East and Whitechapel between 1881 and 1900	170

General editor's foreword

By the middle of the nineteenth century, London's port was the largest in the world and at the centre of a global trade network with a floating multi-ethnic population of seafarers. Like other big ports, it had its own distinctive area of settlement known as sailortown. At the heart of London's sailortown was Ratcliffe Highway. Ratcliffe Highway became a mythic location in the Victorian imagination as a synonym for criminality, depravity, and, with its complement of Indian, Chinese, and later Jewish inhabitants, exotic 'Otherness'. With the aid of the vivid analyses provided by popular journalists, slum novelists, philanthropic reformers, and the ubiquitous social explorers, Brad Beaven recreates the popular image of sailortown and then digs beneath its surface to discover the reality of life on the ground in the pubs, brothels, lodging houses, music halls, and opium dens of the area. He also considers the drive by societies, institutions, and individuals to eradicate the perceived evils associated with the area, notably drink, violence, and sex work. He concludes that Ratcliffe Highway was more socially heterogeneous than contemporaries imagined and that sailortown, rather than being a single moral abyss, consisted of functional working-class communities. Taking the various aspects of the negative image, he establishes the actual nature and function of the violence and the varied role of sex work in the economy. This is a thoughtful, multi-layered, and eminently readable study which along with its carefully argued interpretation of the abundantly detailed evidence evokes the sights, sounds, and smells of a cosmopolitan neighbourhood.

Jeffrey Richards

Acknowledgements

This book has taken some time to come to fruition, but of the books I've written, this one has been the most enjoyable to write. Nineteenth-century Ratcliffe Highway had everything a twenty-first-century historian could wish for: class, gender, racial dynamics, cultural conflict and appropriation, moral panics, with a large dose of gothic horror thrown in for good measure. My enthusiasm for the book was matched by the team at Manchester University Press, who ensured that the peer-review and publication process progressed smoothly and efficiently. To help me understand the Highway, I have been fortunate to call upon a fantastic set of colleagues at the University of Portsmouth and beyond. My thanks to Dave Andress, Jodi Burkett, Rob James, Rudolph Ng, Katy Gibbons, Maria Cannon, Alexandra Ortolja-Baird, Tom Rodgers, Mike Esbester, Guy Collender, Zack White, Matthew Heaslip, Fiona McCall, Lee Sartain, and Cathy Pearce. In addition, my nineteenth-century colleagues Mel Bassett, Karl Bell, and Mathias Seiter have provided me with critical feedback on various chapters. This book was written while Karl and I set up a new research centre, and I'm grateful to James Ryan (Head of School) and Anne Murphy (Executive Dean) for supporting our endeavours and granting me a research sabbatical to finish the book.

Thanks also to my fellow urban and maritime historians Tomas Nilson, James Davy, Elin Jones, Graeme Milne, Valerie Burton, and Isaac Land, who have all commented on or discussed papers I've given. Thanks also to John Griffiths, a historian and academic whom I've known since our undergraduate days and whose entertaining take on life puts everything into perspective. I've also enjoyed discussions with fellow Coventrian Peter Bailey, not only about nineteenth-century leisure but also about the trials and tribulations of Coventry City, which until very recently had come to resemble a music hall joke.

I have been fortunate to present aspects of this research around the world, including at the International Congress of Maritime History, Perth,

Australia; at Hong Kong Baptist University; Kobe University, Japan; the University of Gothenburg; the Institute of Historical Research, London; National Maritime Museum seminars; the Centre for Urban History, University of Leicester; the Centre of Maritime History, University of Exeter; the Blaydes Maritime Centre, University of Hull; and the Centre for Port and Maritime History at the University of Liverpool and John Moores University.

My thanks to staff of the many archives I've visited, including Tower Hamlets Local History and Archives; London Metropolitan Archives; the National Archives; the Sailors' Society; and the Modern Records Centre, University of Warwick.

Thanks to my parents, Martin and Gail. Not only have they always given me moral support, but my dad briefly came out of retirement to help with some Ratcliffe Highway census work.

Finally, thanks to my wife, Becky, and our sons, George and Sam. While they are sceptical that my international travel and writing retreats were necessary to write the book (note to my funders – they were), they are at the centre of my world, and I dedicate this book to them.

Brad Beaven
Centre for Port Cities and Maritime Cultures,
University of Portsmouth
www.port.ac.uk/portcities
March 2024

Introduction: Seaports and sailortowns

From the mid-nineteenth century to the early twentieth century, Ratcliffe Highway was the infamous 'sailors' playground' in London. It was a place that sailors longed for while on a lengthy voyage, a place of work and entertainment for the local working-class community, and for the bourgeois social investigators, it was a laboratory to examine 'exotic' and heathen communities. It was also a place of excess, and sailors remembered it as 'a world of sordid pleasure, unlimited vice, and lashings of booze'.[1] As a pleasure district, Ratcliffe Highway shared a key characteristic to London's West End as, according to Rohan McWilliam, the Haymarket was a 'self-mythologizing dimension, a place that created fantasies, utopias, but also anxieties about morality and respectability'.[2] This is perhaps where the similarities end as overshadowing almost everything else on Ratcliffe Highway was its reputation for harbouring a dangerous underbelly of impulsive violence and criminality. In the Victorian popular imagination, this mysterious district, with its strange maritime traditions and 'exotic peoples', was a lawless place located in the extremities of the east and impervious to civilising influences.

This book examines two broad issues – Ratcliffe Highway's external representation, and the subaltern cultures that developed in an urban–maritime community. First, the book will investigate the Victorian cultural construction of Ratcliffe Highway and explain how Victorian anxieties relating to urbanisation, class, race, and gender triggered a reimagining of the district and its people in the mid-nineteenth century. Second, the book will peer beneath the Victorian rhetoric of sailortown and recover the subaltern cultures that flourished in this waterfront community. It is argued that, far from being anarchic and lawless abysses, sailortowns were *functional* working-class communities that exhibited a distinctive international *urban–maritime culture*. Sailortowns were important contact zones enabling this urban–maritime culture to flourish and provide an environment that fostered self-regulating traditions, which were recognised by both international seafarers and the local subaltern community alike.

While the Victorians of all different social backgrounds were drawn to Ratcliffe Highway, historians have often overlooked the significance of waterfront communities. In reviewing the literature on port towns, Isaac Land has noted that 'urban history – for all its sophisticated debates about the meaning of theatres, towers, and temples – has offered surprisingly few insights into the forest of masts in the harbour'.[3] Instead, historians have tended to explore ports through tracking their urban and commercial development. Indeed, ports have presented an opportunity to analyse global business and trade networks and the importance of imperial systems. This approach was encapsulated in Gordon Jackson's authoritative survey of the historiography of ports between 1700 and 1840. Jackson identified the development of port facilities, port-based industries, trade, labour, and urban elites as the key areas that historians have focused upon.[4] More recently, ports have taken a greater prominence in imperial, Atlantic, and global histories.[5]

The significant breadth of literature on merchant ports has provided the context for the few studies that have focused on sailortowns. Over fifty years ago, Stan Hugill, a former sailor, explored sailortowns from across the world through a part historical and part memoir perspective. He noted that 'Sailortown was a world in, but not of, the landsman' and that it exuded a sense of 'Otherness' for those who visited the district.[6] During the 1980s, professional historians began to explore the sailortown economy and its consequences for sailors and coastal communities. For example, Judith Fingard's *Jack in Port* focused on the merchant shipping industry in Canada's eastern seaports and broke the mould by making ordinary sailors the focus of the story. However, even this study was taken to task by one critic for failing to analyse the sailors' culture as the book did 'not purport to explain their appearance, experience and demise' nor 'identify the real sailors within their actual, boarding-house society ashore'.[7]

In the early 2000s, Valerie Burton advanced a sophisticated account of sailortown through contextualising it within changing economic and industrial relations. She explained how, during the nineteenth century, merchant ports became an important centre of industrial disciplining and labour reorganisation as the British Empire expanded and commercial interests grew overseas. Burton noted that for the transient sailor and casually employed dockyard worker, the ideals of the liberal classical economy, with its associated values of individualism, prudence, and respectability, had little to commend it. Burton argued that for these people, 'there were other means of getting by when the future was one of uncertainty'.[8] Thus, the commercial activities of lodging houses, crimps, and brothels, while on the margins of legitimate trade, 'were important in the circulation of the products of capital'.[9] Graeme Milne's *People, Place and Power on the Nineteenth Century Waterfront* makes a significant contribution to the literature on international sailortown. In this macro study of sailortown, he convincingly argues that it is better understood as a frontier district rather than a rigid border that was defined by its fluidity rather than barriers.[10] Moreover, he suggests that 'sailortown now offers us a laboratory for studying important historical tensions and transformations'.[11] While Malte Fuhrmann's recent study on port cities did not focus on sailortown, his research investigated the formation of urban culture in the eastern Mediterranean during the nineteenth and twentieth centuries. His book is an exploration of the process of urban cultural production in ports and argues that many pastimes were a stage for exchange rather than a transference of an undiluted imperial culture. Thus, Fuhrmann argues that his selected ports were not subject to simple Europeanisation but rather were sites of cultural blending, exchange, and appropriation.[12]

The geographical focus for this book is London's sailortown, which formed part of the world's largest port and was a key component in Britain's imperial infrastructure during the nineteenth century. London's sailortown consisted of Ratcliffe Highway and the alleys and courts that ran off it, and was located north of Wapping, close to the newly built docks. It lay at the heart of Britain's Empire trading system but also attracted seafarers from beyond the Empire, making it one of the most cosmopolitan places on earth during this period. Conversely, this part of the East End was one of the poorest districts in Britain where a working-class population mixed with a transient and cosmopolitan sailor workforce.

This study will go beyond existing analyses of sailortown that have broadly conceptualised it as an imperial or economic hub in the shipping industry and advance our understanding of the distinct subaltern cultures that evolved in the second half of the nineteenth century. The book will focus on the class, gender, and racial dynamics within these communities and the cultural negotiation, appropriation, and conflicts that occurred in these dynamic urban spaces. The waterfront urban space was a crucible for a distinctive fusion of domestic and transnational influences comprising interactions between seafarers, locals, and external actors within the port hinterland. Indeed, sailortowns were sites where domestic and far-flung foreign cultures from overseas met and cross-fertilised. To this end, this book will deploy the concept of 'contact zones' to reveal new perspectives on the production of subaltern cultures within a waterfront setting during the nineteenth century.

Urban–maritime cultures and the sailortown contact zone

In recent years there has been a growth of historiography exploring the globalisation in the nineteenth and twentieth centuries that has emphasised the importance of imperial networks and new transport technologies. Central to these studies are the new railway and steamship routes that were forged, extending commerce and imperial networks around the globe. However, as Lasse Heerten points out, most historians 'let their gaze pass rather quickly through port cities, focusing on the flows running through them'. Ports are deemed as nothing more than 'nodes' or 'hubs' of globalisation as the historians' main interest has been to map the flow of goods and the imperial networks that emerge when the ports are connected. Few historians have taken an actual interest in how these imperial and commercial networks impact upon the port's urban space. Heerten suggests that this oversight reflects the dominance of the non-urban containerised shipping ports of the mid-twentieth century that have ensured a clear separation between port and city. Historians have mistakenly read this separation between port and city back into the nineteenth and early twentieth centuries.[13]

This examination of port transnationalism in isolation from their broader social and cultural contexts aligns with more general trends in transnational history. As Dietz and Naumann have pointed out, transnational historiography has tended to focus on the 'transnational sphere', rather than the actors who not only connect spatial boundaries but also possess an ability to produce various kinds of cultures and environments.[14] The sailor perhaps represents the best example of a subaltern transnational actor who regularly crossed borders and connected cultures. The sailor was engaged in, reproduced, and appropriated a variety of subaltern urban cultures, and yet, until recently, few historians had turned their gaze from the sea to the land. The historians who have focused on sailors in port have tended to explore the socio-economic structures that *impacted upon* the seafaring community.[15] For example, Milne's use of the concept of 'entanglements' to understand the sailor experience has led him to conclude that seamen were 'well aware of the dangers of sailortown and the threats that awaited them there, but valued its relative freedom with a mix of resignation, fatalism and optimism'.[16]

In mapping out the *dangers* of sailortown, the concept of 'entanglement' can be useful as the cultural theorist Sarah Nuttall has argued that it 'signals a relationship or set of relationships that is complicated, ensnaring, in a tangle'.[17] However, it will be argued here that viewing sailortown *solely* through a series of entanglements can somewhat limit our understanding of the agency that sailors, locals, and external actors wielded as they negotiated their way through a distinct and functional subaltern cosmopolitan community. While sailortown could undoubtedly prove dangerous to the uninitiated, sailors were generally aware of the risks. Emily Cuming has shown that sailors were more 'worldly' wise than Victorian commentators would have us believe and were 'inveterate travelers and observers of places, and accumulated essential survival skills in order to navigate their lives in precarious conditions both at sea and on land'. Indeed, she has convincingly argued, sailors fostered an internal culture that promoted 'a common language of transnational affiliation and a complex sense of being at home in the world'.[18]

Anthropologists and cultural historians have long identified the importance of a transnational 'maritime culture', which Brigitte Reinwald has summarised as 'the combining and overlapping of transoceanic, littoral and interior flows in the mediation of culture on the one hand, and to people's appropriation and blending of diverse cross-bordering cultural elements on the other'. It is argued here that within the context of sailortown, this maritime culture became adapted to an urban setting by seafarers and those living in the district.[19] Sailortown institutions, then, were not just places to become ensnared or entangled but spaces where sailors could shape a shared urban–maritime culture that functioned to their own advantage.[20] Sailortown was the site in which the maritime and the urban came into contact with one another and was a space of intensive social interaction. These waterfront spaces nurtured a hybrid urban–maritime culture that was fluid and transnational. Thus, to capture these subcultures, we will conceptualise sailortown as a *contact zone* as it better explores the *broader process* of cultural transference, appropriation, and clashes that occurred in these acutely cosmopolitan districts.

The port was also a key site for the collision and negotiation of relations between and within social classes. While Ratcliffe Highway was descended upon by an army of middle-class urban explorers, the sailortown neighbourhood encompassed a surprising number of 'middling sorts' and a more settled demographic than sensational reporting would admit.[21] With its transient international sailor workforce, the district was undoubtedly a space where cultures of class, gender, and ethnicity were negotiated, collided, challenged, and appropriated. The concept of the contact zone was developed in Area Studies by Mary Pratt, who employed it to decolonise imperial travel writing. According to Pratt, employing contact zones enables researchers to view the relations between colonisers, the colonised, or travellers 'not in terms of separateness, but in terms of co-presence, interaction, interlocking understandings and practices and often within radically asymmetrical relations of power'.[22] Significantly, a contact zone perspective emphasises *transculturation*, a process which recognises that while subjugated actors cannot control the transition of the dominant culture upon them, they can decide upon what to appropriate, reinvent, and what it means to them.[23]

This book offers a new approach in investigating sailortown in two important areas. First, we shall argue that sailortown hosted an *urban–maritime culture* that was recognisable to international seafarers and residents of waterfront districts alike. In adapting the model of 'transnational maritime cultures' to include waterfront urban spaces, we can better understand subaltern experiences in sailortown.[24] Second, the book broadens the concept of 'contact zone' from exploring the power relations between imperialists and their subjects, to explore the relations between differing groups *within* subaltern communities. As Fuhrmann has argued, contact zones were essentially 'spaces of heightened interaction', and therefore they should not be perceived as sites exclusive to the imperial and colonised relationship.[25] Just as the power relations between imperialists and their subjects were unequal, so too were the power relations within subaltern communities, with white, English, working-class men often holding the most (albeit limited) social capital. In this contact zone, sailors of different ethnicities negotiated their customs and cultures with each other, and the local working-class community. This could include sailors navigating sailortown institutions such as the boarding house or ultimately defending their masculinity through learned sailortown combat rituals.

The contact zone is a particularly powerful tool of analysis in deciphering relations between differing ethnic subaltern groups as it enables the recovery of agency and negotiation within transient communities. Sailortown provides an ideal location to study this process – a multi-ethnic space that is embedded in a maritime community during a period when scientific racism was increasingly becoming influential in wider European society. As we shall see, viewing sailortown as a contact zone adds greater nuance to cultural conflicts within subaltern cultures. For example, while Chinese sailors successfully negotiated their way through aspects of subaltern leisure, they were often unable to find private accommodation on Ratcliffe Highway due to racist ideas that linked south-east Asian seafarers with disease and immorality. Thus, the deployment of contact zones to analyse sailortowns should not obscure the class, gender, and imperial relations that were embedded in European society during the nineteenth century. Thus, Jung Lee has rightly criticised the growing body of literature on contact zones that has emphasised the 'mutuality' between centres and peripheries at the expense of imperial, class, and gender power relations.[26] Thus, while sailortown was socially fluid and often unsettling for bourgeois observers and the authorities, the choices available to subaltern actors remained limited by asymmetric power relations.

Broader connections with social and cultural history

The book's subject matter also cuts across several broader historiographical themes in social and cultural history such as the craze for 'slumming', moral panics, and crime and society. A key actor in 'uncovering' the story of the urban poor on Ratcliffe Highway was the Victorian social investigator. In recent years, historians have rightly shown how British 'slum explorers' of the mid-nineteenth century were significantly influenced by contemporary imperial expeditions. The language of exploration had become interchangeable, with terms such as 'civilising', 'heathens', and 'savagery' liberally employed by explorers in both imperial and domestic settings. For example, Joseph McLaughlin's research on literary sources such as Conan Doyle, William Booth, and Jack London amply demonstrated how 'the imperial mission' was as important in Britain as was the Empire.[27] Likewise, Jonathan Schneer described the docks as a physical manifestation of empire on British soil as it was a 'cross roads' for imperial goods, people, and culture.[28] However, recently, Oliver Betts has questioned whether historians have overemphasised the imperial overtones of slum writing and has argued that explorers were also attempting to understand Britain's shifting urban landscape and the people who resided in it.[29] Certainly, as Seth Koven has argued in his seminal study on slumming, we must acknowledge the complexities and nuances that drove middle-class men and women into 'discovering' the dark underworld of Victorian life. His study is a subtle analysis of private conscience and public policy where humanitarian goals, sexual desires, and the accumulation of personal wealth and cultural capital all potentially had a part to play in motivating an individual into engaging in slum philanthropy.[30] This is an important corrective as we should not imagine that slum writing conformed to a universal imperial template since important local, contextual issues undoubtedly influenced the explorer's narrative and assessment of the district.

While the middle class's reimagined city has been deconstructed by historians, some of the key infrastructure that allowed the poor to function in the city has been largely overlooked. The lodging house was an essential institution for the very poor as it allowed them a degree of security and short-term relief from the street. On Ratcliffe Highway, sailor boarding houses were an integral component to sailortown as they allowed seafarers a level of comradeship, safety, and maritime intelligence in a crowded and unfamiliar port. Nevertheless, both the common lodging house and the sailor boarding house were at the centre of bourgeois moral panics and acquired a reputation for immorality and criminality. Indeed, according to Milne, the sailor would become 'entangled' in the boarding house as they were 'a battleground between crimps and their opponents', and while 'some sailors enjoyed comforts and safety … others were essentially imprisoned'.[31]

However, while there were undoubtedly sailor boarding houses that operated as criminal enterprises, many of the sensational reports of sailor boarding houses came from the social explorers who sought to civilise the urban poor. Tom Crook has argued that the lodging house imbued a sense of mystery, fear, and disgust as the transient population and unconventional living arrangements seemed to break Victorian codes on morality, decency, and respectability.³² Thus, common lodging houses were places of 'alternative ordering' and spaces of freedom that defied norms but crucially comprised their own rules and rituals.³³ Conceptualising the sailor boarding house as an 'othered' space not only enables an examination of the rituals and customs but also assists us in exploring its role as a significant contact zone.

Perhaps the most significant broader historiographical theme that is perpetually associated with sailortown is impulsive male violence and criminality. However, this discussion has run counter to some of the key mainstream historiography that suggests that the state's 'civilising mission' successfully ushered a steady decline in male-on-male violence during the nineteenth century. Martin Wiener has claimed that during the first quarter of the nineteenth century, the English judicial system pursued a 'civilising offensive' that no longer tolerated street violence as a way of settling disputes. At the heart of this shift was the justice system's attempt at reframing masculinity. He argued that the courts 'set out a more self-disciplined and pacific ideal of male violence' that was eventually accepted by the working class.³⁴ Wiener added that along with rising incomes, education, and welfare reform, 'English life by the outbreak of the First World War was nearing culmination of the long process of pacification'.³⁵

Writing in a similar vein, John Carter Wood argued that as the nineteenth century progressed, the police and courts were far less tolerant to extra-legal street violence in working-class communities. This 'pacification of public spaces' saw working-class men grudgingly accept that manhood could be preserved through legal rather than violent fighting traditions. Like Wiener, Carter Wood concluded that widespread societal changes, such as political inclusion, consumption, and education, were also important in forging the decline in male-on-male violence.³⁶ Both of these accounts identify the courts and the police as major drivers in shifting a rough street culture and working-class masculinity towards a more civilised and less violent path. The debate on whether the justice system was civilising English masculinity and street violence is somewhat more complicated in cosmopolitan port towns. John E. Archer has estimated that in the 1870s, over 100,000 sailors from all nationalities annually stepped ashore in Liverpool.³⁷ Foreign sailors brought to seaports their own ethnic traditions that defended masculine honour.³⁸ Indeed, the changing British justice system had very little leverage on the transient foreign seafarer who would not have been subject to the state's sustained 'civilising conditioning' that Carter Wood and Wiener described. Certainly, the idea that the foreign sailor brought violence to British shores was a common assumption among civic port authorities.³⁹

Clive Emsley has shown that foreign men arrested for fighting on British soil were often marked out as uncivilised by the British press. The press's desire to foster the English characteristics of fairness, gentility, and restraint compared favourably against the foreigners' use of knives to settle disputes.[40] Similarly, Steve Poole has noted of Bristol that the local and national press vilified knife-carrying foreign seamen as they provided a convenient scapegoat for violent incidents that continued to occur on the city's waterfront in the late nineteenth century. However, in exploring the 'foreign devils' moral panic in Bristol, Poole concluded that 'urban coastal histories have so far offered little in the way of corrective evidence, and we still know all too little about the multi-cultural politics of British ports'.[41]

The book is divided into seven chapters that explore the external cultural construction of London's sailortown and the subaltern cultures that flourished within Ratcliffe Highway and its surrounding district. Chapter 1, 'The curse of Ratcliffe Highway', examines how the Victorians 'imagined' Ratcliffe Highway through tracing how the Ratcliffe Highway murders of 1811 left an indelible stain on the district's reputation. By the mid-nineteenth century, the press and social observers had conflated the bloody murders of 1811 with the perceived vice and violence of sailortown. However, this chapter employs census material to uncover a rather different picture of Ratcliffe Highway, one that is more socially heterogeneous than contemporaries imagined. By the 1860s, it was a cosmopolitan contact zone where sailors, the local working class, and trades people contributed to, and found support from, cultures and sailortown institutions of Ratcliffe Highway. Sailortown, however, was not only a contact zone for those who lodged, worked, and leisured in the district; it was also a site targeted by a legion of religious evangelists, social explorers, and journalists where they could observe and interact with the urban poor.

Chapter 2, 'The imagined geography of Ratcliffe Highway', argues that while these social explorers imbued many similarities of the traditional slum tourists of the nineteenth century, Ratcliffe Highway's 'sailortown' status unsettled researchers in very different ways from the 'orthodox' land-locked slum. For the modern social explorer, the district's remoteness and isolation from 'civilisation' had allowed sailortown to evolve unchecked by religious and civic intervention. Indeed, sailortown's seclusion had fostered a malign and degenerate maritime culture that was ingrained in its geography, buildings, commerce, and people. However, these lofty assessments of the people and the environs of Ratcliffe Highway clashed with realities of an emerging and independent working-class community and, with a notable number of local business people, challenged the dominant narrative that stigmatised the people and the district.

Chapter 3, 'From Jolly Jack and Moll to proletarian Jack and Jill', explores how Victorians explained Ratcliffe Highway's slide into a perceived depravity and violence through focusing on an apparent moral degeneration of the sailors and women of the district. On making contact with the populace of the sailortown district, the social explorers searched in vain for 'Jolly Jack and lusty Moll' and were instead confronted with a modern, urbanised, waterfront people. The chapter interrogates the texts of a range of social commentators who recast the sailors and women they met from their benign eighteenth-century caricatures, that had been largely invented by Dibdin's ballads, to dangerous, urban, proletarian seamen and degraded prostitutes who stalked the streets of sailortown.

While Chapters 1–3 largely investigate the external construction of Ratcliffe Highway, Chapter 4 embarks on an exploration of the subaltern cultures of sailortown. In this chapter, titled 'Leisure in a sailortown', it will be argued that leisure institutions were important contact zones that hosted an urban–maritime material culture that both visiting and returning sailors recognised, shared, transmitted, and reproduced. Indeed, while acknowledging the dangers that lurked in sailortown, the chapter demonstrates that subaltern maritime cultures could function effectively to equip sailors with navigational skills to avoid entanglement with a criminal fraternity.

Another pillar in the sailortown urban–maritime culture was the seamen's boarding house. Chapter 5, 'The inner world of the seafaring boarding house', argues that these institutions provided a familiar and welcoming maritime environment for the transnational sailor and an important contact zone in the heart of Ratcliffe Highway. Contrary to the enduring stories of boarding houses being run by exploitative crimps, established keepers were often valued and trusted members of the onshore maritime community. They held important information on the locality and the latest news on shipping voyages. Moreover, as this chapter demonstrates, foreign seamen's boarding houses were ethnically diverse and afforded spaces where cultural negotiation was learned and exercised. However, by the 1890s, such was the intense institutional racism within the shipping industry and wider society that the experiences of the Chinese and Indian sailors proved exceptional, and they were compelled to carve out their own lodging house arrangements further east in Limehouse.

Chapter 6 focuses on the women of Ratcliffe Highway, a group much maligned by the Victorian press, as reporters were keen to sensationalise the district's sin and vice. In 'Sex work and Ratcliffe Highway', we shall explore how ports became locations for women living on the margins of even subaltern societies. This chapter, then, will investigate how micro-matriarchal networks evolved in the streets and alleys off Ratcliffe Highway and how women adopted survival strategies that gave themselves a degree of agency in environments that bordered on destitution.

The final chapter, 'Male violence, class, and ethnicity in sailortown', challenges the notion that Ratcliffe Highway was overrun with lawlessness and viciousness. This chapter demonstrates that despite the sensational press stoking fears of knife-wielding foreign sailors, there were relatively few serious acts of violence that went before the Old Bailey during this period. Indeed, it is argued that sailortown's important role as a contact zone often mitigated against extreme incidents of violence as male aggression was relatively self-regulated through recognised fighting customs. British and foreign sailors proved adept in recognising the different customs of upholding masculinity in densely populated working-class districts and, in some cases, aligned themselves with the local working-class population in opposing the police.

Approaches and sources

During the nineteenth century, Ratcliffe Highway attracted a great deal of comment from the growing band of local London newspapers, the national press, social observers, and the religious evangelists who were keen to save the poor. Sources, then, on the sin, vice, and poverty of the district were not hard to come by but represented a rather skewed view of London's largest sailortown. The challenge was to uncover a more authentic voice of sailortown that provided some experiential dimension of living, working, and being entertained there. This came often in the form of memoirs of those people who had embedded themselves in the community and were able to often retell the mundane nature of life on Ratcliffe Highway and, albeit inadvertently, reveal the characteristics of the district's subaltern cultures. This form of 'reading against the grain' proved fruitful as although the sailors and the working-class women and men of Ratcliffe Highway were not speaking directly, their behaviours and conversations were retrievable. A few men and women did speak directly in the Thames police court, the Old Bailey, and, on occasion, through the letters in the local press.[42] While this working-class voice was mediated through press reporting and Old Bailey transcription, there were occasions when an authentic challenge to authority or some attempt to assume a degree of agency was evident.

The Census proved invaluable in mapping out the district's demographic and urban geography, and it became apparent that Ratcliffe Highway's social and cultural make-up was more complicated than the standard land-locked Victorian slum. The Census of 1861 captured the Highway at its most infamous, while the 1891 Census revealed the district's subsequent changes within the chronology of the book. Every individual living on Ratcliffe Highway who appeared in the 1861 and 1891 Censuses was logged, and their name, position in the household, sex, age, occupation, and place of birth were recorded. The same procedure using the 1861 and 1891 Censuses was carried out for the thirteen streets, alleys, and courts that ran off Ratcliffe Highway. Broadening my research into the alleys and courts that surrounded Ratcliffe Highway was rewarding as it became apparent that many of the lurid reports about 'Ratcliffe Highway' were in fact of the Blue Gate Fields area that adjoined it. With the help of spreadsheets, it was possible to reconfigure the social structure of the Highway and its surrounding alleys and trace the maritime and urban cultural networks that were forged by sailors, and working-class men and women.

I have also attempted to quantify the numbers and categories of crime by using the St George's in the East court records, the Old Bailey records, and the Parliamentary Papers. The statistical analysis of crime is fraught with problems as contextual issues that could influence crime rates are often absent from the historical record. For example, certain districts could well have had more police assigned to them than other areas, which has the potential to distort the crime figures. Conversely, if there was a local culture of settling issues without recourse to the police, crime rates would be artificially low since they would not appear in the criminal justice system. Given these problems, I have used this data to complement and inform qualitative material drawn from newspapers, memoirs, contemporary pamphlets, and government reports.

I have drawn and quoted from Victorian sources that are, at times, racist and misogynist and which, of course, do not represent my views. This material, however, does provide us with an insight into the Victorian ideas and discourse that influenced their understanding of a changing urban and maritime environment. Finally, despite its change to St George's in the East in the mid-nineteenth century, I have persisted with the name Ratcliffe Highway as it was an appellation that was continually used in the popular vernacular until the dawn of the twentieth century. These sources and approaches, then, have helped produce an alternative picture of London's sailortown and an insight into a transient, ethnically diverse, working-class community in the nineteenth century.

Notes

1 S. Hugill, *Sailortown* (London, Routledge and Kegan Paul, 1967), xviii.
2 R. McWilliam, 'Man about town: Victorian night life and the Haymarket Saturnalia, 1840–1880', History, 103(358), 2018, 758–76, 776.
3 I. Land, 'The humours of sailortown: Atlantic history meets subculture theory', in G. Clark, J. Owens, and G. Smith (eds), *City Limits: Perspectives on the Historical European City* (Montreal, McGill-Queen's University Press, 2010), 325.

4 G. Jackson, 'Ports 1700–1840', in P. Clark (ed.), *The Cambridge Urban History of Britain: Volume II, 1540–1840* (Cambridge, Cambridge University Press, 2000), 705–31.
5 S. Haggerty, A. Webster, and N.J. White (eds), *Empire in One City? Liverpool's Inconvenient Imperial Past* (Manchester, Manchester University Press, 2008).
6 Hugill, *Sailortown*, xviii.
7 J. Fingard, *Jack in Port: Sailortowns of Eastern Canada* (Toronto, University of Toronto Press, 1982); see also C. Dixon, 'The rise and fall of the crimp', in S. Fisher (ed.), *British Shipping and Seamen, 1630–1960: Some Studies* (Exeter, University of Exeter, 1984), 49–67. For a critique of Fingard's approach, see R. Rice, 'Sailortown: Theory and method in ordinary people's history', *Acadiensis*, 13(1), 1983, 154–68, 156.
8 V. Burton, 'Boundaries and identities in the nineteenth century English port: Sailortown narratives and urban space', in S. Gunn and R.J. Morris (eds), *Identities in Space: Contested Terrains in the Western City since 1850* (Aldershot, Ashgate, 2001), 137.
9 Burton, 'Boundaries and identities in the nineteenth century English port', 142.
10 G. Milne, *People, Place and Power on the Nineteenth Century Waterfront: Sailortown* (Basingstoke, Palgrave Macmillan, 2016), 8.
11 Milne, *People, Place and Power*, 2.
12 M. Fuhrmann, *Port Cities of the Eastern Mediterranean: Urban Cultures in the Late Ottoman Empire* (Cambridge, Cambridge University Press, 2018), 24.
13 L. Heerten, 'Mooring mobilities, fixing flows: Towards a global urban history of port cities in the age of steam', *Journal of Sociology*, 34, 2021, 350–74, 351.
14 A. Dietze and K. Naumann, 'Revisiting transnational actors from a spatial perspective', *European Review of History: Revue européenne d'histoire*, 25(3–4), 2018, 415–30, 419.
15 For example, see Fingard, *Jack in Port*, Chapters 1–3.
16 Milne, *People, Place and Power*, 5.
17 S. Nuttall, *Entanglement: Literary and Cultural Reflections on Post-Apartheid* (Johannesburg: Wits University Press, 2009), 1.
18 E. Cuming, 'At home in the world? The ornamental life of the sailors in Victorian sailortown', *Victorian Literature and Culture*, 47(3), 2019, 463–85, 466.
19 B. Reinwald, 'Space on the move: Perspectives on the making of the Indian Ocean seascape', in J. Deutsch and B. Reinwald (eds), *Space on the Move: Transformations of the Indian Seascape in the Nineteenth and Twentieth Century* (Berlin, Klaus Schwarz, 2002), 14. For the original discussion on 'maritime culture', see A.H.J. Prins, *Sailing from Lamu: A Study of Maritime Culture in Islamic East Africa* (Assen, Netherlands, Van Gorcum, 1965).
20 Land has shown how a distinctive sailor subculture in the early nineteenth century was characterised by its visual display that separated them from society's norms and constituted a resistance to the city and its authorities. See Land, 'The humours of sailortown', 325–47, 326, 333.

21 Margarette Lincoln found a similar mixed social structure in the eighteenth century. See M. Lincoln, *Trading in War: London's Maritime World in the Age of Cook and Nelson* (New Haven, CT, Yale University Press, 2018).
22 M.L. Pratt, *Imperial Eyes: Writing and Transculturation* (London, Taylor & Francis, 2007), 9.
23 Pratt, *Imperial Eyes*, 9.
24 For a subaltern twentieth-century anthropological study of seafaring and sailing ships, see Prins, *Sailing from Lamu*.
25 Fuhrmann, *Port Cities of the Eastern Mediterranean*, 24.
26 J. Lee, 'Mutual transformation of colonial and imperial botanizing? The intimate yet remote collaboration in colonial Korea', *Science in Context*, 29(2), 2016, 179–211, 181.
27 J. McLaughlin, *Writing the Urban Jungle: Reading the Empire in London from Doyle to Elliot* (Charlottesville, VA, University Press of Virginia, 2000), 132.
28 J. Schneer, *London 1900: The Imperial Metropolis* (New Haven, CT: Yale University Press, 1999), 39; F. Driver, *The Geography Militant: Cultures of Exploration and Empire* (Oxford, Blackwell, 2001); J. Marriott, *The Other Empire: Metropolis, India and Progress in the Colonial Imagination* (Manchester, Manchester University Press, 2003).
29 O. Betts, '"Knowing" the late Victorian East End', *The London Journal*, 42(3), November 2017, 257–72, 258. On the importance of local contexts shaping the imperial message, see B. Beaven, *Visions of Empire: Patriotism, Popular Culture, and the City, 1870–1939* (Manchester, Manchester University Press, 2012).
30 S. Koven, *Slumming: Sexual and Social Politics in Victorian London* (Princeton, NJ, Princeton University Press, 2005), 286.
31 Milne, *People, Place and Power*, 146.
32 T. Crook, 'Accommodating the outcast: Common lodging houses and the limits of urban governance in Victorian and Edwardian London', *Urban History*, 35(3), 2008, 414–36, 422.
33 Crook, 'Accommodating the outcast', 425.
34 M. Wiener, *Men of Blood: Violence, Manliness and Criminal Justice in Victorian England* (Cambridge, Cambridge University Press, 2004), 289.
35 Wiener, *Men of Blood*, 289.
36 J. Carter Wood, *Violence and Crime in Nineteenth Century England: The Shadow of Our Refinement* (London, Routledge, 2004), 141.
37 J.E. Archer, *The Monster Evil: Policing and Violence in Victorian Liverpool* (Liverpool, Liverpool University Press, 2011), 23.
38 T.W. Gallant, 'Honor, masculinity, and ritual knife fighting in nineteenth-century Greece', *American Historical Review*, 105(2), April 2000, 359–82, 361.
39 Archer, *The Monster Evil*, 83.
40 C. Emsley, *Hard Men: Violence in England since 1750* (London, Hambledon Press, 2005), 93.

41 S. Poole, 'More like savages than men: Foreign sailors and knife crime in nineteenth century Bristol', in S. Poole (ed.), *A City Built upon the Waterfront* (Bristol, Redcliffe Press, 2013), 174.
42 For an excellent discussion on 'reading against the grain', see J. Seed, 'Did the subaltern speak? Mayhew and the coster-girl', *Journal of Victorian Culture*, 19(4), 1 December 2014, 536–49, 536. For more on recovering subaltern voices, see T. Hitchcock, 'The new history from below', *History Workshop Journal*, 57, spring 2004, 294–8.

1

The curse of Ratcliffe Highway: Its reputation and its people in the nineteenth century

> *Mr Quincey remarks that much of the peculiar and contagious horror excited throughout the metropolis by the Ratcliff-highway murders, half a century ago, arose from the fact that they seemed prompted by no motive except the mere love of murder.*
>
> Daily News, 13 November 1863

In the Victorian popular imagination, Ratcliffe Highway was the sailor pleasure-seeking capital, a thoroughfare packed with public houses, beer shops, music rooms, lodging houses, and brothels. The sensational journalist's gas-lit foray into the bustling Highway and its night-time entertainments brought sin, vice, and hints of murder into the respectable living rooms of their avid readers. However, while sensational journalists made it their mission to seek out the 'dangerous classes' and the 'dens of iniquity', more serious journalists who visited the district throughout this period were surprised at the Highway's 'dullness' and that its fearsome reputation and sailor revelry was in terminal decline. This chapter will explore the context of how Ratcliffe was imagined and explain how these two apparent inconsistent narratives of Ratcliffe Highway developed side by side from the mid-nineteenth century. As part of this investigation, we will explore the census material and reconstruct the social structures and networks that were fostered in the district. Thus, while there is no mistaking that the Highway was *perceived* by the popular press as the sailor's entertainment mecca, the thoroughfare was also home to a surprisingly socially diverse population.

The chapter will first explore the cultural construction of Ratcliffe Highway that began with the 'Ratcliffe Highway murders' of 1811. These horrific murders cast the district as a 'mysterious' and dangerous space, and its 'strange' urban–maritime culture further 'Othered' its people from civilised society. However, the opacity and mysterious nature of the district was also cultivated by sections of the maritime community who used these tropes to their own advantage. The second half of the chapter will excavate beneath the veneer of these sensational narratives and stereotypes in an attempt to retrieve experiences and cultures of those living on Ratcliffe Highway and its environs. It will draw on census material, memoirs, and the press to explore the demographic changes in the second half of the nineteenth century and its implications for sailortown culture. The chapter will identify the social and occupational backgrounds of the people of Ratcliffe Highway and its surrounding streets, courts, and alleys to explore how they contributed to the district's urban cultures. It will be argued that Ratcliffe Highway's lawless reputation obscured a relatively diverse population and an important international contact zone. While this proved dull for the serious journalists expecting a riotous bacchanalia, what they were effectively witnessing was a functioning working-class sailortown.

Ratcliffe Highway: the search for horror

Throughout the nineteenth century, Ratcliffe Highway was undoubtedly tainted by a series of unexplained gruesome murders that took place in the thoroughfare in 1811. Known as the 'Ratcliffe Highway murders', seven people, including an infant, were killed in two separate properties in the space of twelve days. The only firm evidence the police found at the scene was the murder weapon, a long-handled shipwright hammer, or maul, covered with blood. Panic and outrage not only consumed the district but also spread across the nation to such an extent that Richard Ryder, the Home Secretary, intervened and appointed Aaron Graham, a Bow Street magistrate, to oversee the enquiry. Just over two weeks after the last murder and with few leads, the authorities arrested John Williams, a sailor, who had come into money and was suspected of stealing the murder weapon from another sailor boarding at his lodgings. The evidence was flimsy and there seemed little in Williams's character or actions that indicated his guilt or would have led to him committing such horrific crimes. However, while in prison, Williams appeared to have taken his own life, which led to the magistrates presuming his guilt, though a sense of mystery and intrigue about the whole affair stubbornly persisted.[1]

Significantly, the grisly notoriety of the Ratcliffe Highway murders, and its association with a barbarous seafaring community, became embedded in both popular and elite literary cultures to such an extent that, by the mid-nineteenth century, London's sailor district became a byword for murder and mayhem. In the first quarter of the nineteenth century, the thirst for accounts of sensational and gruesome murders in popular culture was quenched by ballads, broadsheets, and cheap pamphlets. One of the most popular outputs at this time was *The Newgate Calendar*, which was a record of crimes, testimonies, and executions. These reports were written in a sensational style and accompanied by often ghoulish woodcuts depicting murders or executions. Often criticised for glamorising crime, *The Newgate Calendar* was nevertheless read aloud to groups of men, women, and youths in pubs and lodging houses.[2] Over ten years after the murders, the authors of *The Newgate Calendar* felt it necessary to remind readers of the 'most horrible murders and suicide' on Ratcliffe Highway. It continued, 'the metropolis – we may correctly say the whole nation – was never before so completely horror struck at any private calamity, as those of the daring inhuman murders perpetuated in the very heart of the City of London, on the close of the year 1811'.[3]

Given its reputation for hyperbole, *The Newgate Calendar*'s contention to rank the murders as the most shocking and unprecedented must have been a powerful message to its avid readers. During the same period, the Ratcliffe Highway murders had also caught the imagination of those in more intellectual circles. For example, the English author Thomas De Quincey published 'On murder considered as one of the fine arts' in *Blackwood's Magazine*, which was a satirical account of a discussion in a gentleman's club on the aesthetic appreciation of murder. Published in 1827, De Quincey turned to the Ratcliffe Highway murders for a contemporaneous exploration of the 'art of killing':

> in 1812, Mr. Williams made his debut on the stage of Ratcliffe Highway, and executed those unparalleled murders which have procured for him such a brilliant and undying reputation. On which murders, by the way, I must observe, that in one respect they have had an ill effect, by making the connoisseur in murder very fastidious in his taste, and dissatisfied by anything that has since been done in that line. All other murders look pale by the deep crimson of his; and, as an amateur once said to me in a querulous tone, 'There has been absolutely nothing doing since his time, or nothing that's worth speaking of.' But this is wrong; for it is unreasonable to expect all men to be great artists, and born with the genius of Mr. Williams.[4]

De Quincey succeeded in transcending the Ratcliffe Highway murders from the tragedy of a series of unexplained killings in the backstreets of London to an otherworldly phenomenon where the murders were 'performed' by an artistic 'genius', or an artisan of murder. The article had a deep cultural impact in literary circles, and it was quoted and remained in print in various forms throughout the nineteenth century.[5]

However, until the Whitechapel murders in 1888, both the serious and the sensational press viewed the Ratcliffe Highway murders as the most shocking killings in Britain and a grisly marker from which other horrific crimes could be measured. For example, in 1839 the *Argus* reported that the murder of a family in the neighbourhood of Portsmouth was 'perhaps the most atrocious murder that has taken place since that of the families of Marr and Williams, some years ago, in Ratcliffe Highway'.[6] For the press, the Ratcliffe Highway murders symbolised the worst aspects of urban decay and degeneracy in working-class communities whose uncivilised behaviour was likened to the 'inferior races'. In 1848 a disturbing murder of an affluent family at Stanfield Hall in Norwich brought further comparisons with the 1811 killings. The *Northern Whig* noted that the English were not a 'red-handed' race, but there remained a significant proportion of the working-class population who were inflicted with 'ungovernable passion'. These people would not be out of place in Ireland where 'ruffians, with blackened faces, have surrounded a farmhouse, at the dead hour of night, and have shot or cut down the helpless occupants, the old and the young, without distinction of sex or age'.

The indiscriminate slaughter of the Marrs firmly placed the Ratcliffe murders in the urban savagery category where 'ruffian' attacks were like that of 'a party of New Zealanders or Red Indians, conceived and carried out with the cunning and tact of savages'. *The Times* compared the murders of Stanfield Hall and Ratcliffe and reassured readers that Stanfield was not robbery by a labouring man but a more sophisticated crime by someone out for revenge and 'will remain isolated in the annuls of English crime'.[7] Moreover, whenever murder occurred in the East End, the national press felt compelled to remind readers of the 1811 murders and the lawless nature of the district. For example, twenty-six years after the Ratcliffe Highway murders, the *Morning Post* reported that the killing of a respectable tailor, who had resided in the thoroughfare, brought back memories of the 'horrible murder of Mr Marr and his family'.[8] Likewise, after a brutal murder in Stepney in 1860, the *Morning Chronicle* claimed that 'the excitement in the eastern part of the metropolis ... has not been equalled since the massacre of the Marrs family in Ratcliffe Highway in 1811'.[9] In 1869, after a murder in Poplar, *The Sun* seemingly forgot about the Stepney homicide nine years earlier, and employed the familiar phrase that 'the excitement in the neighbourhood is intense, and has not been exceeded since the awful murder of the Marrs family in Ratcliffe Highway in the year 1811'.[10]

Predictably, when fear spread across the East End with the Whitechapel murders in 1888, the press immediately drew comparisons with the Ratcliffe killings. As early as 11 September and after the third murder, the press began to make parallels with the Ratcliffe and Whitechapel murders.[11] However, in the view of *The Graphic*, the Ratcliffe murders were more shocking as 'Jack the Ripper' had targeted 'a particular class, and that their object was certainly not robbery'.[12] Other newspapers used the Whitechapel killings to sensationally retell the Ratcliffe murders, recasting the murderer as a mysterious 'bestial' figure in the shape of 'Jack the Ripper'. The *Evening News* titled one report 'Jack the Ripper in 1811', and reported that:

> For a parallel to the crimes in Whitechapel, committed by a fiend to whom people have given the name of 'Jack the Ripper' we have to go back many years in the records of crime in London. The year 1811 was in London a year of terror. Horror and fright convulsed the public. A panic seized all classes of the community, for there was a large human tiger, thirsting for blood. Right and left his victims fell. He too, selected the hour of midnight for his fell work. He too, selected the East-end of London as the scene of his operations. He, also, never failed as in the present undiscovered crimes, to cut the throat of his victim.[13]

Thus, throughout most decades of the nineteenth century, the national press made a consistent association between Ratcliffe Highway and the 1811 murders. Ratcliffe Highway's connection with barbaric murder further entered the national consciousness as many of the provincial newspapers often carried verbatim the reports of shocking crime first published in the national press.[14]

While the sensational press was perhaps the most culpable in providing Ratcliffe Highway with an infamous reputation, it cannot take sole responsibility. The sailors themselves regaled their colleagues, families, friends, and especially journalists with tales of their seafaring adventures and sailortown escapades. However, within these communities, these stories were captured, preserved, and reimagined in broadside ballads, songs, and memoirs that were disseminated through maritime neighbourhoods via sailors voyaging on international shipping routes. Within this maritime network, iconic sailortowns such as Ratcliffe Highway became known and feared around the world. Stan Hugill, the former sailor, epitomised this tradition through his books *Sailortown* (1967) and *Sea Shanties* (1977), which drew on his experience of sailing ships in the first half of the twentieth century.[15]

However, these texts were more than a personal memoir; they were compilations of overheard stories and anecdotes that he had collected in his seafaring days. Hugill was almost certainly accurate when he mused in his *Sailortown* introduction that 'for the first time a book on sailortowns of the world has been offered to the reading public'.[16] However, while it was the first time such an extensive survey of sailortowns had been committed to text, the book in many ways resembles that oral tradition that had served sailors well over the centuries. Throughout the book, Hugill emphasised the danger to sailors of the excesses of sailortown at every opportunity and conveyed a vice-laden urban district that was continually teetering on the brink of violence. For example, he claimed that:

> A sailor ashore was anything but safe. He was far safer at sea, hanging on by his eyebrows and toenails to an upper tops'l yard, reefing sail in a Cape Horn snifter, than he was in Sailortown, where every boarding-house master, harpy, pub hanger-on, and wharf-rat was awaiting to skin or slug him, and where his useless corpse was often to be found, knife between the shoulder-blades lying sprawled in some dark alley, or coiled, obscenely, around a tide-washed, barnacle pile.

He added that sailors were 'foot loose men, Batchelors by choice, shore-likers, women likers, booze likers', who were 'wonderful men at sea' and were 'often deteriorated ashore'.[17] Through his books, Hugill faithfully provided readers with the familiar tropes of the dangers of sailortown and the womanising and drunken seafarer who was disoriented in this 'mysterious and sinister' environment.[18] However, in telling these stories, Hugill implicitly informs the reader that he was able to successfully navigate these dangers and temptations, much like the sailors who told their stories and sang songs about Ratcliffe Highway to a willing audience in the nineteenth century. Nevertheless, while these tall tales were a maritime tradition and a welcome form of entertainment, they also provided some agency for seafarers in periods of intensive change.

Karl Bell has argued that sailortowns were the site of competing constructions of Otherness in the nineteenth century. On the one hand, the press, philanthropists, and religious bodies had constructed a sailortown defined by its spatial separateness and an 'immoral typography', while on the other, the plebian seafaring community took advantage of this physical and moral estrangement to pursue unorthodox maritime folkloric traditions. Given the scrutiny placed upon maritime communities, and a suspicion of authority that characterised working-class communities in the period, it is perhaps no surprise that sailortown residents were keen to perpetuate an opaqueness that would disrupt external intervention. George Mitchell, a religious missionary, believed there were more 'mysterious people' in London's sailortown than in any other part of the world. He noted:

> Human, and apparently unhuman, beings, pass as ships in the night and are seen no more. Some are stationary and we see them every day. Men and women whose lives are a closed book find shelter in East London from curious eyes. Those whom I write emit uncanny and mysterious influences, not necessarily bad, and not either of necessity good ... silently they steel about, their footfall is as silent as their tongue.[19]

It was no accident that Mitchell described the residents as 'uncanny', as he undoubtedly was referring to the long tradition of seafaring communities holding both conventional religious and unorthodox belief systems. Bell has shown that in sailortowns, seafarers and their families drew upon maritime folklore and superstition as 'it connected the individual to the supernatural and natural worlds, and was oriented towards navigating the misfortunes that were liable to arise from any given environment'.[20] Thus, in such a dangerous profession, seafarers drew on un-Christian belief systems that potentially added another layer of personal protection while at sea.[21] For example, one religious mission in Plymouth reported that it had uncovered a community that preferred to rely on alternative spiritual guidance to that offered by the established church. The mission claimed that they had discovered a white witch who 'was in the habit of burning candles with pins stuck into them, and sitting up late at night to keep the evil-wishers down'. They also claimed that 'a man from Stonehouse [Plymouth], known as the white-witch, would frequently call to give her instructions in the art of witchcraft'. Clearly, for families anxious about their seafaring relatives, a spiritualist or white witch could offer more reassurance than the platitudes of a local priest.[22]

Similar stories about seances and witchcraft circulated on Ratcliffe Highway with the added dimension that 'heathen' practices were being introduced into Britain through foreign seamen. According to Mitchell, the sailortown district accommodated London's chief exponents of 'Black Magic', where 'pagan rites' would conjure up 'disembodied demons'.[23] Indeed, as late as the 1920s, one writer noted that 'the superstitions of bygone ages, of pagan antiquity and of Christian medievalism, are not yet extinct among the seafaring communities of our own days and have only been modified'.[24]

For social commentators, this folkloric maritime culture only confirmed their worst fears that the inhabitants of sailortown were fostering a premodern heathenism and were in desperate need of 'civilisation'.[25] While maritime superstition heightened sailortown's sense of Otherness, it was for its reputation for brutal violence and vice that it had entered the Victorian public consciousness. Indeed, Fox Smith commented that Ratcliffe Highway in the mid-nineteenth century was 'one of the toughest streets in the world', only rivalled in her opinion by other large sailortowns such as Liverpool, the Barbary Coast, and San Francisco.[26] Living and visiting such an infamous district did not, of course, harm a sailor's own masculine reputation. Seafarers were transient workers, often entering tough working-class waterfront communities, and what better way to prove your own masculine credentials than by regaling your success in navigating the dangers of sailortown the world over. As we shall see in Chapter 7, preserving one's masculinity in sailortown was essential, as failure to do so could often end in conflict and violence. However, in the late nineteenth century, the dwindling number of sailing seafarers began to feel under threat with the energy transition from sail to steam.

Valerie Burton has shown that the traditional sailing mariner's masculinity had been bound tightly to the craft and culture of sailing in the first half of the nineteenth century. This crisis of masculinity in the sailing fraternity was most pronounced between 1870 and 1914 when seafarers on sailing vessels declined from the majority to the minority of the British merchant marine. She argues that this generation of sailors, who were reduced to working for low wages, on long voyages, on old vessels, engaged with shore life very differently to their steamship counterparts. Burton argues they perpetuated the myth of the raucous sailortown as 'these crews found consolation in an escapist world of male bonding and they took to minimalizing their emotion, financial and psychological engagement with women by rejecting what was considered feminine in the social world'.[27] In sailortown legend, Jack was in control and free to squander his bounty on shore where the 'sexual connotations of "spending" are surely involved in these songs and tales'.[28] It was these sailors that Fox Smith and other journalists interviewed in an attempt to uncover the lost world of sail and the maritime culture that it fostered.

This form of anti-modernist writing was part of a wider folk revivalist movement among middle-class authors of the late nineteenth and early twentieth centuries who were keen to uncover the 'lost traditions' in rural and maritime England. However, there are very clear dangers of understanding mid-nineteenth-century sailortown through this generation of seafarers. Burton explains that:

> There was a difference between the 'bachelor' culture which gave rise to tales of whoring, drinking sailors around the mid-19th century and an equally ebullient, but more aggressively misogynist culture of seafarers in the early 20th century. That distinction should be kept in mind because much of what we think we know about life at sea before the last century comes, atypically, from the final days of sail.[29]

Thus, the ballads and broadsides we have at our disposal today were largely collected by the folklorists of the late nineteenth century and reflected the mentalities of the unrepresentative seafarers of the final days of sail. For example, the song 'Rolling down Ratcliffe Highway' describes a seaman disembarking from his ship and wandering into Ratcliffe Highway where he goes for a drink in a public house. After ordering his drink, the barmaid refuses to give him his change, and so he takes a violent revenge:

> The bottle and glass on the table,
> At her head I quickly let fly,
> Then down on the floor she did tumble,
> 'oh murder I'm killed' she did cry
> A gold watch hung over the chimney, For the change of my guinea I seized.[30]

The ballad goes on to celebrate the carefree, womanising, and spendthrift nature of the old-time sailor. 'Rolling down Ratcliffe Highway' would appear under different titles and lyric variations, but all had a deeply violent and misogynist core running through them and represented the canon of shanties disseminated by the twentieth-century sailing seafarers. And yet, as Burton has argued, most sailors at this point were engaged in steam vessels.

This promotion of a mythical, eighteenth-century, golden-aged sailor culture may have suited the sailors in the last vestiges of sail, but it often hid the family life of the Victorian sailor. Indeed, this rampaging bachelor seafaring life, that was so celebrated in the Ratcliffe Highway ballads, was hardly representative of a large proportion of the sailors living in Ratcliffe Highway district. Indeed, the 1891 Census returns show that 49 per cent of the sailors living in the St George's in the East district were married or were sons living with their families.[31] Furthermore, the land-starved sailor who, over a matter of days, would lose his entire wages earned over many months did not ring true in the age of steam where voyages of over six months were rare. A more typical account of a sailor's experience is A. Sherran's memoir of his seafaring days in the late nineteenth century. He described how careful he was with his wages, avoiding the motley crew of crimps when stepping ashore, and wrote movingly about the excitement of returning home to his family.[32] Indeed, evidence suggests that seafarers took their family responsibilities seriously, and spent more time at home than historians have previously thought.[33] In the late 1890s, Charles Booth's researchers discovered, to their surprise, that families living on Ratcliffe Highway regularly saved. In one interview, a religious missionary reported that 'many belong to sick benefit clubs and the children deposit money in the saving bank at the Board School'. The teacher noted that the bank was 'doing well: they have an enormous number of entries from very poor children'.[34]

Through its association with the 1811 murders and its reputation as a wild sailortown, Ratcliffe Highway had become, for the sensational press, shorthand for chaos, violence, and vice. However, when more serious journalists explored the district, they consistently found that London's sailortown did not meet with their expectations and so concluded that the Highway had entered into some form of decline. This much less celebrated body of journalism reported its findings from the 1850s, when Ratcliffe Highway was supposedly at the height of its infamy, to the early twentieth century when larger docks had been constructed further east. For example, in 1912 a correspondent to the local press noted that Ratcliffe was a shadow of the booming sailortown of the 1850s with its thousands of sailors, 'shady doings of crimps', and 'fallen women'.[35] Indeed, in the early twentieth century, there was a consensus that Ratcliffe Highway's most dangerous and infamous era was during the mid-nineteenth century. In 1902 the *East London Observer*'s editor commented that London port was in decline and that Ratcliffe's mid-nineteenth-century heyday was over. He called for action to revitalise the port as 'it is time something was done. Ratcliffe Highway is no longer the sailors' haunt, and poor poll had gone to the Wapping of Liverpool. The empty dock warehouses stand gaunt memorials of former greatness'.[36] Writing in the 1880s and 1890s, Charles Booth's observations of Ratcliffe Highway confounded his and his researchers' expectations as they consistently reported a quieter district that had failed to match its low and dangerous reputation. In 1898 George Duckworth, one of Booth's researchers, noted that while its key characteristics remained, Ratcliffe Highway's wild sailor reputation had all but disappeared. Walking east, he wrote that 'the notorious Ratcliffe Highway' was quiet, and 'its balmy days are over! many public houses, many beer houses, many lodging houses of a low class, many courts, and remnants of old wooden London, are its characteristics'.[37]

The consensus among late-nineteenth-century journalists and researchers, then, was that Ratcliffe Highway's heyday was the 1850s and 1860s. However, even mid-nineteenth-century journalists recorded their disappointment with what they found. Reporting for the *Daily News*, the journalist Joseph Parkinson endeavoured to uncover the horrors of Ratcliffe Highway when he explored the thoroughfare in 1864. To his surprise, and not just a little frustration, he unearthed what could only be described as a fairly mundane street that was adorned with orderly entertainment venues. He noted that:

> During an inspection of some hours, when we had ample opportunities of estimating the entertainments provided for Jack we failed to find a single oasis in the barren desert of unattractive dullness; and it is almost with a sensation of relief that the explorer finds himself conducted down the dark and sordid Bluegate-fields and Palmer's Folly, to sojourn for a while at the Chinese opium smoking-house in New-court.[38]

Moreover, sensation-seeking journalists in the 1850s were equally disappointed. One reporter noted that 'Ratcliffe Highway is growing more lethargic and moral – while in that locality street "shindies" are growing fewer and far between, and drunken revelries more and more exceptional'. The journalist speculated that it must have been thirty years ago when 'the bibulous thoroughfare became at once the Rue d'Enfer and the Rue d' Or of London'.[39] In each decade from the mid-nineteenth century, journalists who had sought out the infamous vice and crime of the Highway were often left disappointed and so assumed Ratcliffe Highway's reputation was based on a boom time that was always twenty or thirty years in the past. Dibdin's mythical Jack Tar and Poll, who rampaged down the Highway, were always one generation out of reach and were assumed to be fading figures of a lost era.

The sensational press's lurid depiction of Ratcliffe Highway was often a misreading of a working-class cosmopolitan district that functioned through cultural negotiation and social networks, which often transgressed bourgeois norms of gender, race, orderliness, and morality. Undoubtedly, Ratcliffe Highway did evolve, and it grew as a sailortown when the new docks were created in the first quarter of the nineteenth century. It also began to contract when the twentieth century dawned as larger docks were opened further east. However, the Census reveals that these changes were gradual and Ratcliffe Highway still operated as a major sailortown in the late nineteenth century. Journalists and social researchers were looking for the daily crime, mayhem, and lawlessness that in their eyes had defined Ratcliffe Highway. What they found but did not understand was a 'dull' functioning community that often strayed beyond the protocols of respectable communities but, nonetheless, was an important contact zone where cultural mores and traditions were learned, negotiated, and contested. This section, then, has explored Ratcliffe Highway's various cultural constructions that endured for much of the nineteenth and early twentieth centuries. The final part of the chapter will use the Censuses of 1861 and 1891, along with memoirs and newspaper reports, to investigate the people of Ratcliffe Highway. It will explore how the changing demographic patterns can help us retrieve the experiences of those living in the Highway that have since been obscured by the district's sensational and lawless reputation.

Ratcliffe Highway c. 1850 to 1900: an evolving sailortown

London had been Britain's largest port since Roman times. During the early modern period, London's port exported over 80 per cent of Britain's textile goods and imported 70 per cent of the nation's wine. While London lost trade to the west coast ports of Liverpool and Bristol during the eighteenth century, the port remained dominant in the North Sea trade.[40] It was in this period that the districts of Wapping and Ratcliffe became the focal point for sailortown and where maritime traditions and living patterns became culturally embedded.[41] As Leonard Schwarz has argued, 'the port had its own social structure and its own pattern of life', as 'until the advent of steam from about the middle of the nineteenth century, the pulse of the port beat to the trade winds and to foreign harvests'.[42] For example, while there was constant marine traffic throughout the year, the arrival of the American ships in the spring and autumn triggered intensive periods of activity. Moreover, the truly international character of the port meant that London's sailor population was continually changing with seafarers lodging temporarily in the many boarding houses located in the Wapping area.

By the mid-eighteenth century, Wapping High Street had become the unrivalled centre of sailortown as, due to its proximity to the water's edge,

The curse of Ratcliffe Highway 27

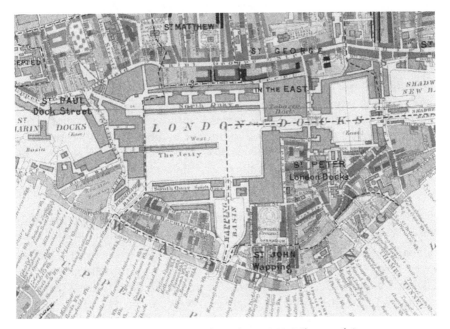

Figure 1.1 Smith's new map of London, 1860 (Library of Congress, Geography and Map Division)

a micro-economy of boarding houses, public houses, brothels, sail makers, and general marine trades had developed in the area. However, in the nineteenth century, Britain's imperial expansion and the development of larger ships merited the construction of London docks situated to the north and west of Wapping High Street. The newly constructed western and eastern docks occupied approximately thirty acres of land and lay close to Ratcliffe Highway, which ran through the three parishes of St George's, Wapping, and Shadwell (see Figure 1.1).[43] The docks' construction was a response to Britain's dominant imperial trading position and was not unrelated to London's rapid population and geographical expansion. Between 1861 and 1891, the population in greater London rose from 3.1 to 5.5 million.[44]

The London docks, built in the early nineteenth century, effectively killed off Wapping's sailortown. By the 1850s, sailors ashore made for the boarding houses and entertainment venues of Ratcliffe Highway, which was the main thoroughfare north of the docks. Indeed, by the mid-nineteenth century, Ratcliffe Highway was the principal sailortown in London and had gained worldwide notoriety.[45] Such was the Highway's reputation, the local authorities took the unusual decision to change its name to St George's in the East in the 1850s, though contemporaries continued to refer to it as Ratcliffe Highway well into the twentieth century.

However, with the building of larger docks further east, ships and sailors began to migrate out from Ratcliffe Highway towards Deptford in the late nineteenth century. The fall in trade undoubtedly damaged sailortown's notorious entertainment industry. Iconic public houses and music halls such as Paddy's Goose and the Mahogany Bar were taken over by religious and temperance groups who claimed that they were finally winning the war against sin and drunkenness.[46] Despite the closure of celebrated sailor entertainment venues, there was still a significant number of sailors residing in the Ratcliffe Highway vicinity as many seafarers continued to perceive the district as London's foremost sailortown.[47] Indeed, the Census figures for sailors residing on Ratcliffe Highway and the streets and alleys of its surrounding district are revealing.

In 1861, 256 men, or 20 per cent of the entire male working population living in these streets, were recorded as sailors.[48] These sailors lived mostly in boarding houses, though English sailors were more likely to have lodged in housing accommodation. The sailors were concentrated on Ratcliffe Highway and the streets and alleys that ran off it. Of the fifty-three seafarers residing on Ratcliffe Highway, 60 per cent were foreign and 95 per cent of them were lodging in a boarding house. However, the sensational newspapers' depiction of Ratcliffe Highway as a sailor slum consisting entirely of brothels, boarding houses, and entertainment venues does not bear up to closer scrutiny. Ratcliffe Highway's demographic was socially heterogeneous with an even split between male and female residents. The 1861 Census returns of almost 1,500 individuals living on Ratcliffe Highway themselves indicate that the street accommodated a mix of skilled and unskilled workers, and professionals. Indeed, sailors and labourers only accounted for 10 per cent and 34 per cent respectively of male workers on Ratcliffe Highway, which was lower than in most of the immediate surrounding streets (see Table 1.1). Undoubtedly, the significant property rents of Ratcliffe Highway explain the higher number of professional men and women (3 per cent) and skilled working-class men such as watchmakers and tailors who comprised 30 per cent of the male working residents. The large numbers of live-in general servants (33 per cent of working women) also indicate that larger and more affluent households were located in the highway. For example, William Howell, a solicitor, neighboured a large sailor boarding house, while Robert Lammiman, a general practitioner, lived with his wife Sarah and two domestic servants next to a tobacconist and a public house.

Alongside middle-class professions were owners of small businesses who could afford to employ servants. Abraham Harris was an outfitter and lived in a property that could accommodate his wife, two sons, a daughter, and two domestic servants. He lived next door to another small businessman, Solomon Davis, a corn dealer who lived with his wife and a domestic servant.

With a significant proportion of the Highway populated by 'respectable' residents, one would expect the sailortown institutions to be clustered together in a more run-down section of the Highway. However, the Highway was a curious mix of sailors, labourers, artisans, and the professional classes who lived cheek by jowl among sailortown institutions. This combination of the respectable and 'rough' was noted by social observers who strolled down the Highway. In 1878 one author wrote:

> It may be mentioned that what is commonly known as Ratcliffe Highway is a narrow thoroughfare of about a mile in length, containing a large number of shops, houses of business chiefly in the shipping interest, and all of respectable kind. Besides these, however, the Highway contains scores of public houses, to most of which either singing or dancing rooms are attached, and dozens of dirty little beer-shops (suggestive of the 'good dry skittle-ground' in the rear, and also of the confidence trick), with an equal number of 'cookshops' and coffee-shops, kept by persons of almost as many different nationalities as there are natives of other climes who, in the capacity of sailors, find temporary accommodation ashore here.[49]

An analysis of these entertainment venues also reveals that they were integrated among the 'respectable' businesses and residents. Significantly, the thirty-eight sailortown institutions identified in the 1861 Census, such as boarding houses, public houses, dance rooms, and coffee houses, were all spread relatively evenly along Ratcliffe Highway. Thus, the sailors who resided on the Highway, or boarded in nearby streets or on their ships, were not entertained in an enclave of Ratcliffe Highway but instead would have been visible throughout the thoroughfare and encountered the differing local social groups who lived there. Moreover, the assumption that sailortown was essentially a masculine environ also does not stand up to further scrutiny. Of the thirty-eight sailortown institutions, 40 per cent were run by women who between them managed boarding and public houses. Significantly, almost 40 per cent of all sailortown institutions were run by non-English men and women, a phenomenon that undoubtedly attracted the foreign sailor to the Highway. Indeed, Ratcliffe Highway's varied demographic social structure and the prominent and evenly spaced sailortown institutions ensured that the street itself was an important contact zone for sailors and the local people of the district.

The demographic picture changes once we examine the alleys and small streets that spun off the Highway. It was in these side streets that social observers based their most shocking accounts of 'Ratcliffe Highway', despite not being situated in the thoroughfare itself. In the Victorian imagination, Ratcliffe Highway was both the well-lit entertainment mecca and a dark and vice-laden working-class slum. It was the catch-all appellation for licentiousness, vice, and violence. Thus, when the social observers' journeys are traced, their encounters with working-class slums and 'dark mysterious figures' usually took place in the courts and alleys that ran adjacent to the Ratcliffe Highway itself. Places such as Neptune Street, Ship Alley, and Bluegate Fields or 'Tiger Bay', which comprised Brunswick Street, Palmers Folly, and Perseverance Street, were, in many accounts, conflated with Ratcliffe Highway. These courts and alleys hidden by the large buildings of the Highway or the towering edifice of the dockyard wall created a dark and mysterious setting and an added jeopardy for the bourgeois researcher.[50] These side streets also housed numerous sailor lodging houses that were deemed 'lower' than their Ratcliffe Highway counterparts.

In the mid-nineteenth century, contemporaries and subsequent chroniclers of sailortown consistently named Neptune Street as the worst side street that led off the Highway as it often comprised high concentrations of sailors in boarding houses. In 1861, 60 per cent of the male working population in Neptune Street were sailors, almost all of whom were foreign seafarers. Moreover, of these foreign sailors, 70 per cent of them originated from Southern Europe and the Philippines, regions that Victorians regarded as being 'uncivilised' as they were 'too free with the knife'.[51] The communities living in these side streets, alleys, and courts were, as one might expect, solidly working class. In streets such as Cannon Street, Princes Square, Wellclose Square, Denmark Street, and Betts Street, the male working population's occupations were concentrated in seafaring, and labouring in dock or sugar refineries located in the district. In these streets, where seafarers and labourers lodged in boarding houses and tenement buildings, men generally tended to outnumber the women.

However, in the 'notorious Tiger Bay' district, women were more numerous than men. In Brunswick Street, the highest occupational category for working men was seafaring (23 per cent) with labourers and tailors accounting for 16 per cent each. Census enumerators classified prostitution (23 per cent) as the most common occupation for women, with needle work (10 per cent) accounting for the second highest category of work. Women significantly outnumbered men in this street and accounted for 60 per cent of the adults who lived in the lane. Indeed, something like a matriarchal enclave had developed in Palmers Folly and Perseverance Place as women represented 78 per cent and 72 per cent respectively of the working population in these streets.[52] Of the men, sailors were the most important occupational group, comprising 44 per cent in Palmers Folly and 57 per cent of working males in Perseverance Street.

The transient nature of seafarers reinforced the notion that in spaces that Victorians labelled 'Tiger Bay' or 'Bluefields', matriarchal communities formed that helped shape the governance within boarding houses and brothels. Moreover, as we shall see in Chapter 6, these matriarchal networks informed the relationship dynamics between the women who managed and worked in the boarding houses and brothels. These networks also provided invaluable intelligence and surveillance on undesirable customers or unwanted interference from the authorities. For the mid-nineteenth-century bourgeois social explorer, Ratcliffe Highway was a socially cosmopolitan place where drunkenness and vice were paraded in the open and well-lit street. However, the side streets were an altogether different matter, an alien and enclosed space that unsettled the explorer. These were dark, slum-like places where the social investigator could stumble upon the 'roughest' working-class labourer or find himself in an alley or courtyard where he felt that women were in the ascendency and men were their 'prey'. One social explorer recalled Tiger Bay in its heyday in the 1850s, claiming that it was the headquarters of the 'savage' population. It was:

> a hideous network of courts and alleys, to which inebriated members of the mercantile marine were nightly inveigled and robbed and half murdered; and where, in cellars and dreadful backrooms, swarms of Lascars and Malays herded together to indulge in mad opium orgies.[53]

The disconcerting environment of Tiger Bay and the courts and alleys that led off the Highway added to the sense that Ratcliffe Highway was a lawless and immoral abyss, though as Chapter 7 will testify, the rate of male-on-male violence and murder was no different to other working-class districts in London.

The 1861 Census, then, provides a snapshot of a Highway that was surprisingly socially and ethnically diverse and evenly populated with sailor-town institutions. As we shall see in later chapters, while maritime cultures influenced the goods sold in shops, hospitality, entertainment, and even the décor of buildings, sailors were not geographically nor socially compartmentalised in the district, but instead they shared their living space with middle- and working-class locals. With the migration of sailors from Wapping to the Highway in the first quarter of the nineteenth century, this period was certainly known as the boom time for Ratcliffe's sailortown. The common assumption is that after the 1870s, and with the enlargement and creation of docks further east, sailors deserted the district and the Highway fell into perpetual decline. Contemporaries made much of the closure of iconic sailortown institutions such as Paddy's Goose and Wilton's Music Hall that were converted into evangelical religious missions. However, while these were very symbolic victories for church missionaries, Ratcliffe Highway's sailortown business, culture, and its significance as an international contact zone continued for the rest of the nineteenth century. The following section will explore the 1891 Census to demonstrate that far from a sailortown in decline, Ratcliffe Highway continued to attract sailors to a vibrant sailortown district.

The 1891 Census shows that the number of people living on Ratcliffe Highway had declined slightly to around 1,300 residents. On Ratcliffe Highway itself, sailors represented 15 per cent of all working men, a 5 per cent increase on the 1861 Census findings (see Table 1.1). However, there were 285 sailors residing in the Highway and the streets and alleys leading from it, and this represented a 10 per cent increase of seafarers from the 1861 Census.[54] The seafarers who were listed as living with partners or family were generally English and local to the area, most residing in streets further west and north such as the High Street and Cable Street. Moreover, a larger number were settling on Ratcliffe Highway itself as the larger town houses were increasingly being divided into tenement buildings. The English sailor, however, was largely invisible to the sensational journalist who often missed the cultural subtleties of sailortown. In failing to explore the wider district, the social commentators overlooked the more stable sailor communities. These sailor communities did not fit easily with the dominant narrative of fear and decadence that had begun to characterise Ratcliffe Highway and the wider neighbourhood.[55] These predominately English sailors, who lived with their wives and families close to Ratcliffe Highway, were socially and culturally integrated into London's urban life and well versed in the everyday life of urban working-class culture.[56] In addition to sailors living ashore, the Census enumerators captured a further 210 seafarers on ships docked in the district who would inevitably head for Ratcliffe Highway when they stepped ashore. Most of these sailors based on ships were from Scandinavia and Germany, though there were also seafarers from Greece, America, the West Indies, and Russia. In effect, Ratcliffe Highway continued to attract a concentration of foreign sailors who temporarily resided or visited when ashore.

Despite the loss of some infamous venues, in just a half-mile stretch, Ratcliffe Highway hosted at least thirty-two sailortown institutions, fifteen of which were licensed for music and dancing.[57] As was the case thirty years earlier, these venues were not concentrated within a 'sailortown enclave' but instead fairly evenly distanced from one another through Ratcliffe Highway. Moreover, interspersed between these licensed premises were the numerous beer and gin shops and 'low' drinking dens that are more difficult to track due to their quasi-legal status.[58] Women continued to manage a significant, though smaller, number of sailortown institutions than thirty years previously. In 1891 women accounted for 15 per cent of the heads of households for boarding houses, pubs, and coffee houses. Notwithstanding the actual increase in sailors in the Ratcliffe Highway district and evidence of a healthy sailortown economy, social commentators were convinced that the district was in terminal decline. Their sense that Ratcliffe Highway had become 'dull' may well have been partly due to a change in the district's

Table 1.1 Occupations of male workers on Ratcliffe Highway in 1861 and 1891

	1861	1891	Change
Professional /middle class	3%	< 1%	(1.5%)
Shopkeepers/public house landlords/coffee house keepers	23%	27%	3%
Skilled working class	30%	16%	(14%)
Labourers	34%	41%	(3%)
All sailors	10%	15%	5%
Foreign sailors as a percentage of all sailors on Ratcliffe Highway	60%	82%	12%

demography that witnessed the flight of the small but significant middle class from the grand villa housing on the Highway and a decline in skilled working-class residents. Table 1.1 illustrates the changing demography of Ratcliffe Highway between 1861 and 1891.

By 1891 the residents from the professional middle-class occupations had declined from 3 per cent to less than 1 per cent, and there is evidence that the large villas had become divided into tenement buildings or boarding houses. For example, by 1871 Robert Lammiman, the general practitioner, had moved from the Highway to the more prosperous Canon Street Road. Lammiman's former house on Ratcliffe Highway had become merged with a neighbouring boarding house by 1891. Indeed, there was over a 10 per cent decrease in women working as live-in domestic servants, and most of them by 1891 were employed in boarding houses, pubs, or coffee houses. Small businesses such as shops, bakers, tailors, and pawnbrokers were the only other employers of domestic servants by 1891. More worryingly for middle-class observers, between 1861 and 1891, the numbers of skilled working men living on the Highway had decreased by half and stood at just 16 per cent of the male working population. Indeed, for social observers such as Charles Booth, the skilled working man with his industriousness and respected social status was the exemplary role model for the lumpen proletariat.[59] In addition, the number of foreign sailors living on Ratcliffe Highway had increased by 12 per cent between 1861 and 1891 during a period when social Darwinism had produced heightened anxieties about threats to the 'Anglo-Saxon stock'.[60] Thus, a decline in the middle and respectable working classes and a significant increase in the unskilled labouring and foreign seafaring population would have, in the eyes of many social observers, cast Ratcliffe Highway as a downwardly mobile district.

The notorious 'dark and shadowy' streets and side alleys that surrounded Ratcliffe Highway had also undergone significant demographic change between the 1860s and the 1890s. The most important development was the slum clearances around the Bluegate Fields district, which, by 1891, had seen the demolition of the notorious 'rookeries' of Angel Court, Palmers Folly, and Perseverance Street. The clearances essentially removed the small boarding houses and brothels that dominated these thoroughfares and dismantled the matriarchal micro-networks that had flourished in this area. For example, while nearby Brunswick Street had survived destruction, its demographic make-up had changed considerably by 1891. In 1861 there were 30 per cent more women than men living in the street, most of whom were young and single and engaged in trades such as needlework and 'prostitution'. Almost a third of the males in the street were sailors, with the remaining working men employed in labouring or tailoring.[61]

Thirty years later, Brunswick Street had an even numerical balance between men and women, many of whom worked in family tailoring units employing children and extended family. An extensive number of these tailoring families were derived from the Jewish community who had fled to London in the 1880s to escape the pogroms in Eastern Europe and Russia.[62] Indeed, in the 1890s, journalists hoping to catch a glimpse of sailortown in the St George's in the East district were surprised to find that the backstreets contained few sailors. One journalist commented that, instead, a whole new Jewish community had formed and noted that he saw 'Jews of every age and of every condition of dirt. Yiddish advertisements of the best known soaps outside grocers' shops ... A Jewish wedding party had left one house in the main road in two coaches – even the drivers belonged to the race'.[63] Dock labourers and their families had also moved into these side streets, which dissipated the boarding houses and brothel culture that had exuded from the district. Thus, when a journalist charged with reporting on the 1899 dockers strike enquired where the strikers lived, he was informed by one local that:

> 'I expect there's more dockers lives down that street than any other in the East End', said a doleful-looking wight on Wednesday, nodding as he spoke to a deplorable dirty little thoroughfare not a thousand miles from Ratcliffe Highway. 'Pretty nigh all dockers there'. 'Yes' replied a couple of women seated on one of the doorsteps, 'we're all dockers here, wuss luck. There's 'ardly anybody as ain't down here.'[64]

The second major demographic shift was the drift of sailors from these side streets into Ratcliffe Highway itself. While the removal of large parts of Bluegate Fields had denied sailors a source of cheap boarding houses and brothels, seafarers also seemed to shun the 'low' boarding houses in streets untouched by Victorian slum clearances. For example, in the mid-nineteenth century, Neptune Alley had gained a disreputable reputation on account of its boarding houses for foreign sailors. In 1861 60 per cent of working men identified in the Census were sailors, and 96 per cent of these were foreign. However, by 1891 sailors accounted for less than 1 per cent of working men as they had been replaced by working-class families employed in the labouring and tailoring trades. Similar patterns of change occurred in Princes Square where the sailor population dropped from 15 per cent to 3 per cent of working men, while Wellclose Square, a well-known sailor quarter in the mid-nineteenth century, had no resident sailors by 1891. Former sailor boarding houses in these streets had been converted into tenements for labourers and dock worker families, a trend that further encouraged seafarers to find lodgings in the Highway or remain on their vessels at night.[65] Thus, social observers on a quest to experience the ill-famed sailortown district in the 1890s may well have been underwhelmed. It does appear that the sailortown district had mainly contracted to the Highway itself since significant parts of Bluegate Fields had been demolished, and the fewer number of sailor boarding houses ensured that sailors gravitated to the main thoroughfare from the infamous side streets. In 1875 the Reverend Harry Jones noted that 'The East London Railway has torn a great passage through the parish, on the edge of which lie Perseverance Place and Palmer's Folly, the courts in question. They must come down.'[66] While these notorious courts appear in the 1881 Census, Palmers Folly and Perseverance Place were demolished by 1881.

Sailors continued to live, lodge, and visit Ratcliffe Highway, and it continued as a sailortown well into the twentieth century. George Mitchell, the evangelist preacher, was as anxious to save the sailors from the evils of sailortown in the 1920s as his mid-Victorian counterparts.[67] Ships still moored at the nearby docks and wharfs until containerisation was introduced in the 1950s, which required larger sites further downstream. Containerisation dismantled urban–maritime cultures and effectively destroyed the sailortown micro-economies that had been fostered by the working-class community and the seafaring population. Sailors' working practices were transformed as containerisation sped up the shipping process, leaving little time for seafarers to spend ashore.[68] Ratcliffe Highway was not exempt from this shipping revolution, and, in the second half of the twentieth century, much of Wapping, Shadwell, and St George's in the East were cleared for the dockland redevelopment. The London docklands was part of an international waterfront regeneration movement that attracted affluent residents and customers to waterfront apartments and high-end retail and restaurant outlets. As Graeme Milne has noted, 'the idea of sailortown lurks in many of these changes, but albeit rarely with a sense of historical context'.[69] Ratcliffe Highway itself lies outside of this redevelopment and has simply been renamed 'the Highway', which unless you knew would appear to be just a rather anonymous and unremarkable through road. However, as this book will go on to explain, Ratcliffe Highway's past is anything but ordinary.

Conclusion

This chapter has explored how Ratcliffe Highway was reimagined in the nineteenth century and how its reputation was culturally constructed around the fascination and fear of the 'Othered' from civilised society. It has also shown that while the sensational press, authors, and social explorers were the key perpetuators of the Ratcliffe Highway reputation, sections of the subaltern community found some agency in preserving the opacity of London's sailortown. Meanwhile, seafarers at the tail end of the sailing era found solace in propagating the mythical 'Jack ashore' stereotype during a period of intense change in the shipping industry. However, such was Ratcliffe Highway's legendary infamy that more serious journalists, who were unable to witness a tirade of violence and lawlessness, concluded that it was a sailortown in terminal decline. These journalists, however, had misunderstood that sailortown was a functioning micro-economy and that the local working-class community and the maritime population's interests were interdependent. The chapter also argued that Ratcliffe Highway's surprisingly varied and cosmopolitan social milieu of the mid-nineteenth century puts a rather different complexion on the daily, residential, social, and business interaction that underpinned the culture of the district. It also draws into question the social explorers' common assumption that the Highway was a socially homogenous district that was dominated by the 'lowest and criminal classes'. Indeed, the Highway's rich social diversity continued to be obscured by the infamous Ratcliffe Highway murders in the early nineteenth century and its reputation as a dangerous sailortown.

In the 1860s, far from constituting a poverty-ridden abyss, the thoroughfare was a cosmopolitan contact zone where middle- and working-class residents, sailors, and local business people negotiated their way through a myriad of cultures on the streets, shops, and entertainment venues of Ratcliffe Highway. Furthermore, while the chapter acknowledged that the social character of the Highway had undoubtedly changed by 1900, the Victorian belief, and subsequent historiographical assumption, that Ratcliffe Highway was little more than a sailor-ghost-town is somewhat misleading. The Census evidence indicates there were more sailors in 1891 than in the middle of the nineteenth century and that key institutions such as pubs, singing saloons, and boarding houses continued to contribute to a vibrant sailortown economy. What had changed between 1861 and 1891 was the migration of the artisans and the middle class from the Highway district. In their place came dockyard workers and their families, seamstresses, and tailors, who set up home in the alleys and streets that led off the Highway. For social observers, the arrival of unskilled labourers, at the expense of the socially respectable artisan, and the immigration of Jewish tailors from Eastern Europe and Russia from the 1880s only confirmed their worst fears, that the Highway had finally sunk into a social and cultural abyss.

Notes

1. For an account of the Ratcliffe Highway murders, see '200th anniversary of the Ratcliffe Highway murders' blog, Londonist, https://londonist.com/2011/12/200th-anniversary-of-the-ratcliffe-highway-murders, accessed 30 September 2022; for a semi-fictional account, see P.D. James and T.A. Critchley, *The Maul and the Pear Tree: The Ratcliffe Highway Murders, 1811* (London, Faber and Faber, 1971).
2. www.bl.uk/collection-items/the-newgate-calender, accessed 12 March 2024; H. Mayhew, *London Labour and the London Poor* (London, Griffin, Bohn, and Company, 1861), Vol I, 416.
3. A. Knapp, *The New Newgate Calendar: Being Interesting Memoirs of Notorious Characters, Who Have Been Convicted of Outrages on the Laws of England, during the Seventeenth Century, Brought down to the Present Time* (London, J. and J. Cundee, 1826), 371.
4. T. De Quincey, 'On Murder Considered as One of the Fine Arts', in *The Works of Thomas De Quincey*, Riverside Edition, Vol IV (Boston: Houghton, Mifflin and Co., Cambridge, 1876), 535.
5. For example, see *Kings County Chronicle*, 11 February 1863.
6. *Argus*, 14 April 1839.
7. *Northern Whig*, 5 December 1848. *The Times* is quoted in the *Northern Whig*.
8. *Morning Post*, 13 January 1837.
9. *Morning Chronicle*, 19 September 1860.
10. *Sun*, 8 February 1869.
11. See, for example, *Dundee Courier*, 11 September 1888; *Angus*, 12 September 1888; *Sheffield Evening Telegraph*, 13 September 1888.
12. *The Graphic*, 13 October 1888.
13. *Evening News*, 19 July 1888.
14. See, for example, on the Poplar murder, *Cardiff and Merthyr Guardian*, 13 February 1869; *Newcastle Guardian and Tyne Mercury*, 12 February 1869.
15. S. Hugill, *Sailortown* (London, Routledge and Kegan Paul, 1967); S. Hugill, *Sea Shanties* (London, Barrie and Jenkins, 1977).
16. Hugill, *Sailortown*, xcvii.
17. Hugill, *Sailortown*, xix.
18. Hugill, *Sailortown*, 123.
19. G. Mitchell, *Down in Limehouse* (London, Stanley Martin and Co., 1925), 28.

20 K. Bell, '"They are without Christ and without hope": "Heathenism", popular religion, and supernatural belief in Portsmouth's maritime community, 1851–1901', in B. Beaven, K. Bell, and R. James, *Port Towns and Urban Cultures: International Histories of the Waterfront, c. 1700–2000* (Basingstoke, Palgrave Macmillan, 2016), 60.

21 See, for example, Tower Hamlets Library, Ref LC 6244, A. Sherran, 'Blackwall Pier and Sailor Memories of Sixty Years Ago', 1916, unpublished manuscript, 10–11.

22 B. Beaven, 'The resilience of sailortown culture in English naval ports, c. 1820–1900', *Urban History*, 43(1), 2016, 72–95, 88.

23 Mitchell, *Down in Limehouse*, 23.

24 A. Rappoport, *Superstitions of Sailors* (1928), 256, quoted in Bell, '"They are without Christ"', 57.

25 Bell, '"They are without Christ"', 54.

26 C. Fox Smith, *Sailor Town Days* (London, Houghton Mifflin, 1923), 27–8.

27 On how this period reimagined a toxic and masculine sailortown, see V. Burton, '"As I wuz a-rolling down the Highway one morn": Fictions of the 19th century English sailortown', in B. Klein (ed.), *Fictions of the Sea: Critical Perspectives on the Ocean in British Literature and Culture* (Oxford, Routledge, 2002).

28 Burton, '"As I wuz a-rolling down the Highway one morn"', 151.

29 Burton, '"As I wuz a-rolling down the Highway one morn"', 144.

30 University of Oxford, Broadside Ballads online, Roud Number V4683, 'Rolling down Ratcliffe Highway' (imprint London, 1877), collected between 1863 and 1885, http://ballads.bodleian.ox.ac.uk/search/roud/V4683, accessed 21 January 2019.

31 1891 Census returns for St George's in the East district.

32 Sherran, 'Blackwall Pier and Sailor Memories of Sixty Years Ago', 26–7, 1–3.

33 Burton, '"As I wuz a-rolling down the Highway one morn"', 152.

34 LSE, Charles Booth Archive, B/224, 'Missionaries on Ratcliffe Highway', 1896–98, 33.

35 *East London Observer*, 2 March 1912.

36 *East London Observer*, 28 June 1902.

37 LSE, Charles Booth Archive, BOOTH/B/350, 201, https://booth.lse.ac.uk/notebooks/b350#?cv=104&c=0&m=0&s=0&z=4150.889%2C-43.7976%2C1376.7641%2C818.8721, accessed 8 September 2022.

38 *Daily News*, 31 August 1864.

39 *East London Observer*, 6 August 1859.

40 L. Schwarz, 'London and the Sea', www.history.ac.uk/ihr/Focus/Sea/articles/schwarz.html, accessed 6 February 2014.

41 D. Morris and K. Cozens, *London's Sailortown 1600–1800: A Social History of Shadwell and Ratcliff, an Early-Modern London Riverside Suburb* (London, East London History Society, 2014).

42 Schwarz, 'London and the Sea'.

43 Hugill, *Sailortown*, 114.

44 www.demographia.com/dm-lon31.htm, accessed 2 February 2024.

45 *East London Observer*, 8 May 1858.

46 *East End Star*, March 1944, 4.
47 Hugill, *Sailortown*, 114–27.
48 The streets surveyed were Ratcliffe Highway, Palmers Folly, Perseverance Street, Ship Alley, Wellclose Square, Artichoke Street, Pennington Street, Angel Gardens, Betts Street, Princes Square, Bruswick Street, Neptune Street, Denmark Street, Well Street, and Cannon Street.
49 Anon, *Wonderful London: Its Lights and Shadows of Humour and Sadness* (London, Tinsley Bros, 1878), 338.
50 See Chapter 2.
51 See Chapter 7.
52 See Chapter 6.
53 Anon, *Wonderful London*, 337.
54 1891 Census. My thanks to researchers Eilis Phillips and Jessica Harper for their help in gleaning and analysing the Census material.
55 For example, see *East London Observer*, 10 October 1857.
56 Evidence indicates that sailors and their working-class neighbours socialised together. Indeed, newspaper reports show that they defended one another in confrontations with the police; see *East London Observer*, 17 April 1869.
57 1891 Census, Ratcliffe Highway; Hugill, *Sailortown*, 115.
58 Hugill, *Sailortown*, 115.
59 J. Brown, 'Charles Booth and labour colonies, 1889–1905', *Economic History Review*, 21(2), August 1968, 349–61; B. Beaven and J. Griffiths, 'Creating the exemplary citizen: The changing notion of citizenship in Britain, 1870–1939', *Contemporary British History*, 22(2), 2008, 203–25.
60 See Chapter 7 on male violence. For a discussion on fears about the degeneration of the 'Anglo-Saxon stock', see C.F.J. Masterman, *The Heart of the Empire: Discussion of the Problems of Modern City Life in England* (London, T.F. Unwin, 1901).
61 1861 Census.
62 See, for example, the transformation of Princes Square between 1861 and 1891; see B. Beaven, *Visions of Empire: Patriotism, Popular Culture, and the City, 1870–1939* (Manchester, Manchester University Press, 2012), Chapter 1.
63 *Morning Post*, 6 January 1899.
64 *East London Observer*, 31 August 1889.
65 See the Census for Wellclose Square. In 1861 number 31 was a large seaman's boarding house, and by 1891, the building had been converted into a tenement for labourers.
66 H. Jones, *East and West London: Being Notes of Common Life and Pastoral Work in Saint James's Westminster and in Saint George's-in-the-East* (London, Smith, Elder & Co., 1875), 283.
67 Mitchell, *Down in Limehouse*, 23.
68 Burton, '"As I wuz a-rolling down the Highway one morn"', 143.
69 G. Milne, *People, Place and Power on the Nineteenth Century Waterfront: Sailortown* (Basingstoke, Palgrave Macmillan, 2016), 226–7.

2

The imagined geography of Ratcliffe Highway

> *That high black wall could tell terrible scenes it has shut in from view. The houses of this dark by-way could tell tales more terrible still. But we can only wander through the long, narrow, winding way of wickedness to-day and imagine what the place was in its days of degradation.*
>
> A description of Ratcliffe Highway,
Pearson's Weekly, 24 January 1907

By the middle years of the nineteenth century, social explorers had concluded that Ratcliffe Highway was an extraordinary urban abyss that could not be easily classified alongside the 'classic urban slums' of Britain. To be sure, social explorers of the Highway followed common traits of slum reporting in creating a 'cultural performance' in their heroic descriptions of crossing into an unknown and dangerous district.[1] By their very nature, Victorian urban slums were districts devoid of commercial activity and populated by people at the margins of society. A sense of the 'idleness' of the district often pervaded classic slum literature, which emphasised how explorers were confronted by quiet, deserted thoroughfares and street-loafers by day, and mysterious criminals and dens of thieves by night.[2] However, Ratcliffe Highway did not easily fit the stereotype classic slum as its busy maritime micro-economy, local working population, and transient seafaring workforce manifested a rather gregarious and chaotic appearance during the night and day to the urban explorer.

This chapter will contextualise the early urban exploration of London's slumdom, before turning attention to how both novelists and journalists claimed that Ratcliffe Highway exhibited a malign and degenerate maritime culture that was ingrained in its geography, commerce, and people. Social explorers complained that all their senses, sight, smell, and hearing, were consistently offended as they made their way through the Highway and described the district as a throwback to a primitive and uncivilised age. This 'Othering' of people and place, however, did not go unnoticed by those who lived and worked on Ratcliffe Highway. The final section of the chapter will explore the responses of working-class people and the small business-class community who came to resent the popular representation of their district and the 'patronising' interventions of philanthropists. Indeed, their responses remind us that the dominant narrative of Ratcliffe Highway was not recognised by those who lived in the district, and their challenges provide us with a glimpse of a functioning working-class district that we will explore in later chapters.

The early Victorian slum

In mapping the urban environment, Victorian social explorers could not agree on what the term 'slum' actually meant, and consequently it was employed for a variety of social and political reasons.[3] There was also a fluidity when it came to mapping slum boundaries. While they would recall how they approached, crossed into, and immersed themselves in the depth of the slum, social explorers' geographies were often inconsistent. Some writers of Ratcliffe Highway confined their study to the main thoroughfare, while others who claimed to be on Ratcliffe Highway had wandered into neighbouring streets and areas such as Bluegate Fields. Part of this disparity was possibly due to the explorers' disorientation, but, more likely, for many writers, the inclusion of the neighbouring streets and districts made for more exciting and lurid stories. The sensational reporting of slums and the people who lived in them had become a staple form of journalism by the end of the nineteenth century.[4]

The absence of slum 'fixity' was certainly present in the writings of the first slum exposé of Victorian London. Georgian and Victorian social commentators began their early forays into modern urban slums in the general vicinity of St Giles in London during the late eighteenth century.[5] As the nineteenth century progressed, their investigations were given an added impetus and a wider scope with the 'condition of England crises' in the 1840s and later in the 1870s.[6] St Giles, or the 'Irish Rookery', was the archetypal urban slum, and it had become infamous for its dark byzantine mass of backstreets that were believed to facilitate vice, criminality, and disease. Contemporaries labelled St Giles as a 'whirlpool of moral ruin' and one of the foulest places in London.[7] It had been built on a medieval leper colony and was undoubtedly an area of inconceivable squalor that was on the brink of social and economic collapse. St Giles and its illicit reputation occupied centre stage in Thomas Beames's book *The Rookeries of London* (1852) as he likened the criminal fraternity to rooks, which unlike other birds made multiple nests in a colony.[8] To the social observer, St Giles was an impenetrable, dark labyrinth that, left to its own devices, would likely infect neighbouring communities with its moral degradation. For the commentators who penetrated St Giles, the only solution to improving the Rookery was its demolition, which was duly carried out in the 1850s.[9] Indeed, as Tom Crook has noted, St Giles haunted Beames as it was one of the last lingering physical manifestations of medieval squalor.[10]

While the St Giles Rookery was one of the first areas to receive scrutiny from journalists and social reformers, by the 1830s London's East End soon became the focal point of the press and slum explorer.[11] In 1850 Thomas Beames noted that the slum housing on Ratcliffe Highway was among 'the oldest in London' and were '*bonâ fide* Rookeries built for the inhabitants of the poorest classes two hundred and fifty years since'.[12] For Beames, Ratcliffe's early modern wooden constructions and its narrow streets were reminiscent of the worst parts of St Giles. He lamented that these 'courts and alleys remain in a condition little removed from their original form' for they had been spared by the Great Fire of London, or the 'wholesale purifier' as he termed it.[13] In most commentators' minds, Ratcliffe Highway was situated in the East End, though, as we shall see, its geography and maritime cultural connections excluded it from the dominant East End narratives. Indeed, to capture the full 'horrors' of Ratcliffe Highway, journalists, philanthropists, and social explorers would make specific journeys 'further east' to report on a very distinct, separate, and dangerous part of the metropolis.

As we have seen, Ratcliffe Highway's reputation as a perilous district began after the 1811 murders when seven people were brutally killed.[14] However, while the murders supplied the initial horror, the modern industrial city and its increasing impact on the docks and river further stoked these fears about the degeneration of the district. In recalling his frequent excursions around the dockland area, Charles Dickens described how modern industrialisation and urban squalor had not only contaminated the Thames environment but also the morality and decency of its communities. In one of his night-time wanderings with his policeman companion, Inspector Field, Dickens imagined the Thames as a malevolent force, 'creeping, black and silent', while at the same time 'hiding strange things in the mud', like suicides and 'accidentally drowned bodies'.[15] In another one of his night walks, Dickens placed the sinister qualities of the Thames at the centre of his description of Ratcliffe and Stepney and its people. The evening before his walk, he had viewed woodcuts of 'the famous Dance of Death', scenes which, for him, later evoked comparisons on his walk the following evening:

> The borders of Ratcliff and Stepney, eastward of London, and giving on the impure river, were the scene of this uncompromising dance of death, upon a drizzling November day. A squalid maze of streets, courts, and alleys of miserable houses let out in single rooms. A wilderness of dirt, rags and hunger. A mud-desert, chiefly inhabited by a tribe from whom employment has departed, or whom it comes but fitfully and rarely … they have come into existence and propagate their wretched race.[16]

Ratcliffe, then, was a separate and macabre district with the implication that the modern evils of industrialisation had polluted the Thames and unleashed poverty and want in the area. Moreover, there is more than a hint of Lamarckian theory in Dickens's writing since he implied that these desperate conditions had been instrumental in raising a 'race' of 'residuum' people. Indeed, his night walks seemed to have become an inspiration for passages in *Our Mutual Friend* as the riverside features as a dark, menacing space that is only visited by night. Two of the main characters, Mortimer Lightwood and Eugene Wrayburn, travel to the Ratcliffe area to inspect a body that was pulled out from the Thames. Lightwood and Wrayburn are lawyers and, like Dickens, are unacquainted with Ratcliffe and the riverside communities. In a scene similar to his own experience of the district, Dickens casts Ratcliffe as a hostile and unsavoury environment:

> The wheels rolled on, and rolled down by the monument and by the Tower, and by the Docks; down by Ratcliffe and Rotherhithe; down by where accumulated scum of humanity seemed to be washed from higher grounds, like so much moral sewage, and be pausing until its own weight forced it over the bank and sunk it in the river. In and out among vessels that seemed to have got ashore, and houses that seemed to have got afloat – among bow-sprits staring into windows, and windows staring into ships – the wheels rolled on, until they stopped in a dark corner.[17]

Once Mortimer Lightwood and Eugene Wrayburn reach Ratcliffe, they meet Gaffer, a dredgerman whose main occupation seems to consist of pulling bodies from the Thames, robbing them, and afterwards reporting the bodies to the authorities. This gruesome occupation was a consequence of modernity since dredgermen were formerly watermen who, with the introduction of steamboats, had been forced out of business.[18] These passages convey how the riverside unsettled Dickens. This was a disorienting physical space since the land and water appeared to have become indistinguishable and the forces of modernity had washed up a 'moral sewage' and the 'scum' of humanity on the banks of the river Thames. Ratcliffe Highway, then, had acquired a reputation for a dark Otherness well before the craze for slum journalism was fully underway.

The journey into Ratcliffe Highway

Alan Mayne's seminal work on 'the imagined slum' maps out some key characteristics that defined slum journalism in three different countries during the mid-nineteenth century. He notes that writers were engaged in a 'cultural performance' and that their narratives usually opened with descriptions of their first impressions of standing at the threshold of the slum borderlands. The author then moves on to their crossing into the slums, after which we reach the climax of the piece in which the intrepid explorer outlines the horrors of the territory itself.[19] Certainly, we can see similar literary devices used in the explorations of Ratcliffe Highway, and much is made about the explorer's experience in travelling east beyond the familiarity of central London. One *Daily Telegraph* 'special reporter' described how 'on leaving the silent city to go eastward at night, I have a feeling as though I had passed beyond the haunts of civilisation into some strange desert'. He added that 'nor is the idea hyperbolical; for that district lying along the Thames East of London Bridge is a country in itself'. Here in the 'wilderness' borderlands, there was a deathly silence where one could 'hear the echo of your own footsteps'.[20] For the writer, this symbolised the journey from civilisation to a heathen urban underworld. Indeed, Ratcliffe Highway was portrayed as an undiscovered and wild district beyond the comprehension of the social investigator's readership. *Household Words* speculated that 'nobody knows anything about Ratcliffe', and wondered if it had 'shared the fate of those lost countries recorded in the folk lore of nearly all primitive races overwhelmed by the waves, and now perhaps lying beneath the mud and ooze of the Thames?'[21] One journalist wrote: 'Ratcliffe Highway and Shadwell, a region, we believe, as utterly unknown to most Londoners – as a perfect terra incognita – as Iceland'.[22]

In a similar vein, James Ritchie, the Victorian travel writer, speculated that, for the uninitiated, Ratcliffe Highway had the appearance of a district 'cut off from the rest of the empire'.[23] Indeed, a common feature of these travelogues was that Ratcliffe was both a mystery to the average Londoner and a very different world. In his study of East London, Walter Besant was struck by the importance of the sea, which profoundly influenced the character of Ratcliffe Highway. He noted that the districts of Wapping and Shadwell were 'populated by sailors, belonged to sailors, and those who make their livelihood out of sailors'. He added that:

> Its riverside is cut up with docks; in and about among the houses and the streets around the docks rise forests of masts; there is no seaport in the country, not even Portsmouth, which is charged and laden with the atmosphere of ocean and the suggestion of things far off as this port of London and its riverside.[24]

Likewise, the author Cicely Fox Smith claimed that on approaching London's sailortown, you were crossing the borders into a 'queer amphibious country which lies as it were between land and sea' where the inhabitants and its atmosphere have the unmistakeable stamp of the sea.[25] She argued that on crossing the border, you were leaving the orthodox urban environment, for 'Sailor Town the world over is a realm apart. Under what ever flag it may happen to be – to whatever temporal sovereign it may owe its external allegiance – in spirit it is the Kingdom of Neptune'.[26] In the minds of social explorers, then, sailortown was a stateless entity, influenced by maritime traditions rather than national or local civic governance.

The maritime influence steered the narrator from the usual slum travelogue and into a 'different land' with its own people and unique customs and traditions. This fusion between urban and maritime living was noted by the eighteenth-century magistrate John Fielding, who noted of Wapping that 'a man would be apt to suspect himself in another country. Their [the sailors'] manner of living, speaking, acting, dressing and behaving are so peculiar to themselves'.[27] Another significant departure from the classic slum travelogue was Ratcliffe Highway's infamous reputation as a dangerous sailor saturnalia. The daytime slum explorers who entered the eerily quiet, shadowy, and dangerous rookery described a lethargic, slumbering population without purpose or hope who only came alive for the drunken night-time revelry.[28] In contrast, the explorer embarking on Ratcliffe Highway in the day or at night faced a busy, lit, noisy thoroughfare where they believed criminals, crimps, and prostitutes lay in wait to prey on the naïve and uninitiated. The *East London Observer* claimed that the Highway comprised 'drunkenness and noise – vice and blasphemy – robbery and obscenity by day – flaring gas lights – blue sulphuric acid – drunkenness and noise – vice and blasphemy – robbery and obscenity by night'.[29] Another social observer noted that 'at any time of day the Highway presents a spectacle which no visitor from the country should miss'.[30] Thus, apart from the flaring gas lights, there was little to separate the Highway's activities between night and day. A travel writer for the *Chambers's Journal* noted that 'even at high noon it is impossible for the most incurious observer to avoid noticing how the sailor is preyed upon by these wretched parasites as they share his pot of porter at the bars, or block his staggering tracks across the pavement'.[31]

It was the writer's task to introduce the reader to the characters they would meet, and guide them through the perils they may encounter should they foolhardily visit the 'Highway'. Often, these travel writers were accompanied by a local policeman who supplied insider intelligence on the worst places of the district but also provided a degree of protection.[32] It was a strategy later adopted by Charles Booth who invited divisional policemen to provide character assessments of the London streets they wandered through in his poverty survey in the late nineteenth century.[33] In enlisting help from the police, writers believed that they could capture the very worst parts of Ratcliffe Highway that were hidden from general observation. One writer boasted that 'I have started – always with the Inspector – to go round the cheap gaffs, squalid saloons, small music-halls, dancing-taverns, and concert rooms of Ratcliffe Highway and Whitechapel'. He added that he knew 'the abodes, haunts, ways, manners, foibles, tastes, and pleasures of the criminal classes; the lurking places of the professional mendicant, and the home of the swindling writer'.[34]

In crossing the boundary into Ratcliffe Highway, explorers described how their senses were assaulted by an exotic array of destabilising smells, sights, and sounds. On approaching the Highway, writers frequently noted that the area emitted a distinctive smell. Joseph Charles Parkinson, who was one of Dickens's journalists on the *Daily News*, wrote that 'the prevailing aroma is of tar, ropes, and salt fish, as if dried haddocks were being vended in the must hold of a superannuated ship'.[35] Similarly, another journalist described his first impressions of the district as a 'tarry, salt-smelling portion of the metropolis'.[36] On entering the Highway, social explorers were met with a vista of retailers selling distinctive marine clothing and equipment along with mysterious curios from far-flung places. The *Chambers's* journalist thought that 'almost all of the shops in the Highway smack somehow of the sea'. Moreover, the array of goods from all around the world, from 'ostrich-eggs converted into silver-rimmed drinking cups' to 'murderous looking knives', prompted the journalist to speculate as to the 'fates of those who brought them'. The curio-festooned shops added another layer of mystery to the Highway, as he whimsically added: 'if the weapons could tell of the hands through which they have passed, and foretell the hands which they are destined to pass, their dull steel might prove a goldmine to a sensational romancer'.[37]

Fox Smith also saw the 'junk-shop' curios as both magical and romantic as she described 'dried devil fishes that look so disconcertingly like bleached skulls in a dim light, lumps of coral plant ... white and rainbow coloured tropic shells, old jars as a jinn might lurk in and bottles of dusk-red Indian pottery'.[38] For Watts Phillips, the shops on Ratcliffe Highway exhibited a distinctly gothic character, and he described how he encountered a 'dingy, sinister-looking shop, at the corner of Ship-alley, bearing the name of the "British and Foreign Medicine Institution"' that was owned by a 'white-haired man, clad in a loose coloured dressing-gown' and went by the 'rather ominous title of Dr Graves'. Phillips described the shop's contents as a 'collection of horrors' such as waxed models of terrible diseases, 'bottled babbies [sic] in plenty; children with two heads ... a small serpent, taken from the body of a sailor; and here the skeleton of a small sailor, taken from the body of a serpent'.[39] The journalist Joseph Charles Parkinson similarly described the curious shops and array of goods that overhung the thoroughfare as he began his journey down the Highway.[40] He observed that Ratcliffe Highway was:

Where female apparel of the coarsest and gaudiest kind flaunts the doorways and is piled up in windows – where shiny water-proof coats hang flaccidly in shops open to the road, like seaweed thermometers steadfastly predicting rain, and long rows of tarpauling [sic] wide-peaked caps ranged like strings of Saturn-ringed cannon balls – where huge clasp knives, with holes in their common hafts are festooned with fancy pipes and metal Tabaco boxes.[41]

Likewise, one writer noted that on entering Ratcliffe Highway, the 'mixed population of the district is significantly indicated by the character of goods, which in a thousand commercial repositories, invite their selection'. After describing the marine clothing 'of every shape and colour', his attention was drawn to the dangerous and unsettling items on sale, and he noted 'revolvers, cutlasses, daggers and deadly weapons' on which, among other nick-nacks, 'Jack so often spends his hard-earned wages when he returns' from a voyage.[42]

Sailors also engaged in their 'own private ventures' and collected curios and animals on voyages to sell to retailers on Ratcliffe Highway. A reporter for *Household Words* interviewed one sailor whose captain had permitted the crew to bring as many parrots home as they liked. However, the birds created such 'an astonishing variety of discordant noises, that the men were, in self-defence, obliged to let some two or three hundred of them loose'. The journalist regretted to inform his readers that parrots who could swear were in great demand, and a bird that could 'rap out half-a-dozen round oaths in a breath will fetch you fifty shillings'.[43] The one shop that the explorers never failed to cite as they entered the Highway was Jamrach's animal emporium. Jamrach's shop and animal warehouse was a physical manifestation of London port's imperial maritime reach, and, on entering, it provided a passage into Britain's exotic overseas empire. The German entrepreneur Charles Jamrach commissioned ship captains to purchase exotic animals along with souvenirs to decorate his premises.[44] One writer, after passing through the first room full of Australian songbirds and 'Indian talking birds', entered a gallery full of a 'miscellaneous collection of curiosities' that included:

> a hideous heathen deity, all red paint and feathers, stands beside a figure of the Buddha; the symbol of savage fetishism beside that of philosophical contemplation. The walls are covered with South Sea Island weapons, portraits of Indian notabilities, and representatives of Nautch dances hung side by side with assegais from Zululand, nullas, canoe paddles and boomerangs, and shells of great beauty.[45]

In his one visit, the author viewed an astonishing array of captive animals for sale including bald vultures, a large puma, cheetahs, baboons, and a rhinoceros.

Having passed by the initial maritime shops and stores, the explorer was confronted with an array of public houses, singing saloons, and boarding houses that had contributed to Ratcliffe Highway's infamy. On encountering these venues, one writer could only see a scene of chaos, immorality, and danger:

> Up 'the Highway' I go myself, and find it in full swing; not that it is a merry, or a jolly, or a contented, or a generally thriving Highway by any means. It is a mad besotted, miserable, sullen, suspicious, quarrelsome, poverty-stricken, immoral, shambling Highway, for the most part – its voyages taking beacon-lights for harbours of refuge, and, when they are not pirates themselves, running into a flotilla of treacherous piratical junks lying hidden everywhere along the coasts, and some of which come boldly out to take their prey in tow under cover of a false-signal. Wherever sharks may be waiting for him, however, Jack is still in the same dull, half-besotted mood.[46]

This extraordinary description of the scenes on the Highway illustrates the writer's unsettling experience where, despite the open revelry, dangers remained hidden, and where both men and women brazenly behaved outside the norms of 'civilised-life'. Indeed, so exceptional were these scenes from ordinary Victorian street life that the writer emphasised the district's Otherness by recasting the scene in piratical and nautical terms. In this sense, the writer trod a familiar path in social exploration by compartmentalising Ratcliffe Highway and its residents from the rest of the metropolis. Thus, in this narrative the Highway's debased maritime culture was the malign influence that was degenerating its people and degrading the morality of the district.

The sense that Ratcliffe Highway harboured a debased and degenerate maritime culture was cultivated further by social explorers when they encountered groups of foreign sailors on the streets. In the age of social Darwinism, foreign sailors became both an exotic curiosity and a street menace. For example, in the 1890s Karl Baedeker published his London travellers' guidebook which provided visitors with directions and descriptions of the capital's historic landmarks. Among the famous monuments, theatres, and churches, Baedeker listed the 'notorious Ratcliffe Highway' and London docks where a 'motley crowd' with 'numerous dusky visages and foreign costumes impart a curious and picturesque air'.[47] James Ritchie observed:

> Up and down Ratcliffe-highway do the sailors of every country under heaven stroll – Greeks and Scythians, bond and free. Uncle Tom's numerous progeny are there – Lascars, Chinese, bold Britons, swarthy Italians, sharp Yankees, fair-haired Saxons, and adventurous Danes – men who worship a hundred gods, and men who worship none. They have ploughed the stormy main, they have known the perils of a treacherous sea and of a lee shore but there are worse perils, and those perils await them in Ratcliffe-highway.[48]

For Ritchie and other writers, this was a muddled, disordered, and 'floating population' who were not anchored in Christian morality. One reporter was disoriented by the large numbers of women of African origin openly wandering down the Highway. He complained that 'the dense population from the courts and alleys' that 'swarm into Ratcliffe Highway, is a very mixed and indiscriminate class'. He noted that they were chiefly female and there was 'an unusual proportion of people of colour'.[49] In these writers' minds, Ratcliffe Highway was an anarchic space in which foreign, heathen, and 'uncivilised' influences could flourish. Other writers coined Ratcliffe 'a regular Highway of nations' which set it apart from other great cities of the world. One *Household Words* journalist gazed upon the groups of sailors that made their way down Ratcliffe Highway and wrote: 'here is Sinbad the Sailor in his snowy turban, and there the forty thieves who hail from Singapore. Coolies troop about in queer part-coloured garments, with red caps, and white pilot jackets, with pointed Chinese shoes'. Much attention was paid to the various 'costumes' of the sailors and particularly the knives that they carried.[50] The *East London Observer* claimed that the 'Thames police records teem with highway stabbing cases that sicken humanity' as 'gin-mad' Malayans 'run amuck' with 'glittering' knives.[51]

This image of Ratcliffe Highway became firmly embedded in popular culture and the backdrop to Victorian slum novels such as Arthur Morrison's *The Hole in the Wall*, which was set in the 1850s. In the novel Ratcliffe Highway is described as both 'foul' and picturesque where 'everything and everybody was for, by, and of, the sailor ashore'. What struck Stephen Kemp (the main character) on his first encounter with the Highway was the plethora of knives on show and the colourful-costumed foreign sailors. In one shop he noted a row of large knives and daggers with the suggestive maxim 'Never draw me without cause, never sheathe me without honour.'[52] In the Highway itself were:

> Spaniards, swart, long-haired, bloodshot-looking fellows, whose entire shore outfit consisted commonly of a red shirt, blue trousers, anklejacks with the brown feet visible over them, a belt, a big knife, and a pair of large gold earrings. Big, yellow-haired, blue-eyed Swedes, who were full pink with sea and sun, and not brown or mahogany-coloured, like the rest; slight, wicked-looking Malays; lean, spitting Yankees, with stripes, and felt hats, and sing-song oaths; sometimes a Chinaman, petticoated, dignified, jeered at; a Lascar, a Greek, a Russian; and everywhere the English Jack, rolling of gait – sometimes from habit alone, sometimes for mixed reasons – hard, red-necked, waistcoatless, with his knife at his belt, like the rest.[53]

While the *London Daily News* was highly critical of Morrison's derogatory accounts of the East End in his novel *Child of the Jago*, it described *The Hole in the Wall* as 'more local history and topography, better suited to

Besant's "East London" than to the pages of fiction'.[54] Indeed, the sense that the Highway was an exotic fusion of mystery and colour, which was plagued by menacing foreign sailors, was conveyed by the press, social investigators, and novelists alike.

While writers described that danger was ever-present on the gas-lit street of Ratcliffe Highway, social explorers were keen to discover one of the many secluded side streets that adjoined the main thoroughfare. The hustle and bustle of a busy thoroughfare and glaring street lamps were absent in these side alleys, many of which had gained almost as much infamy for violence and vice as the Highway itself. Thus, narrow side streets such as Ship Alley, Wellclose Square, Old Gravel Lane, and Palmers Folly were mysterious locations that merited further discovery for the intrepid social investigator. For example, when walking through the Highway, the journalist F.W. Robinson noted: 'the streets debouching right and left of it are as dark and dense as ever', where 'murky figures' flit in and out of sight and 'even grim murder still stalks here'.[55] While writers described Ratcliffe Highway as a floating, chaotic, and unordered society, the dimly lit side streets drew very different responses from social investigators. Here, investigators believed that they had discovered a society that was underground, more organised, and significantly more sinister.

Thomas Archer wrote of being 'led through one long passage, so narrow that I can touch the houses on either side, and so dark that but for the click of a lock here and there, or a low whistle sounding from an open doorway, I should think the whole place deserted':

> It is the utter silence, and the impression of stealthy villainy which is conveyed by the sound of an occasional voice, the sudden shutting of a window, the disappearance of two or three shadowy figures in a passage, or round a dim corner, the sudden coming upon a ghostly group sitting before a door, and hushing their low talk as we go by.[56]

For Archer and other writers, this 'maze of foul courts' and alleys was where the organised 'criminal classes', who preyed upon the sailors, plotted and resided. The whole experience disconcerted Archer as the silence is only broken by sounds that he interprets as coordinated signals and messages from those living in the courts. The residents' fleeting appearances take on a spectral character and seem calculated to both unnerve explorers and also act as a form of surveillance on newcomers who had entered the neighbourhood. The sense that these side streets were mysterious and liminal was given further credence by those journalists keen to survey the notorious Palmers Folly (named Palmers Place on maps) and Perseverance Place since these courts were almost inaccessible from the main thoroughfare. Both courts were hemmed in by dense housing, an iron foundry, and commercial

The imagined geography of Ratcliffe Highway 51

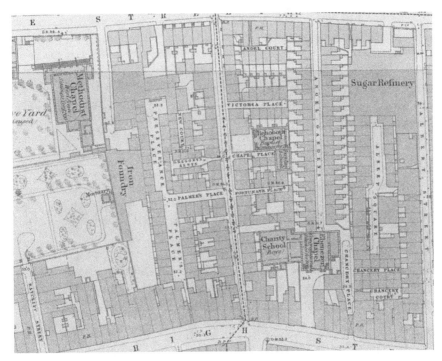

Figure 2.1 Palmers Folly/Place and Perseverance Place, c. 1870
(reproduced with the permission of the National Library of Scotland)

buildings and sat adjacent to Angel Gardens, another notorious street. The description of the enumeration district of the 1861 Census indicated that Palmers Folly and Perseverance Place (which ran on from Palmers Folly) were located on the south side of Ratcliffe Highway and between Chigwell Hill and the High Street (see Figure 2.1).

The difficulty of locating Palmers Folly and Perseverance Place on a map was matched by those who attempted to find the streets on foot. Parkinson noted that there was no signage but was told to go 'through an iron gate, and up a low-roofed tunnel leading from Ratcliffe Highway'. After passing through the tunnel, he found a place 'known as Palmer's Folly by every dweller in or periodical visitor to this section of the East'.[57] His first impressions after passing through the tunnel was that it was:

> A dreadful place. Shocking in the squalid vice making itself felt in the air you breathe, the sounds you hear, and the sights you see; doubly shocking from its reputation for deeds of lawless violence, for the shameless use to which its houses are put, and for the open unabashed wickedness of many of the dwellers within its gates.[58]

In stepping from the tunnel into the street, all his senses were offended by the shocking environment that confronted him. For Parkinson, this foreboding street was just a short walk from a major thoroughfare and yet at the same time dangerously isolated from civilisation. Journalists and social observers believed that the residents of Palmers Folly revelled in these shocking conditions as these were 'a people loving darkness rather than light' that enabled them to pursue their 'evil deeds'.[59] Like Archer, the experience unsettled Parkinson as he described how he tramped 'up the black gloom-stricken court, to see ill-omened figures flit about your path, and speculate upon the effect of the gate to your rear being suddenly shut and locked'.[60] Throughout his expedition through Palmers Folly, Parkinson was convinced that he was under surveillance and feared that he would not make it back on to the main thoroughfare. Afraid for his safety, he noted that in Palmers Folly, 'there is no honour amongst the people who make common war against society and the "Thou shalt want ere I want"' was 'the ruling principle of life'.[61] What both Archer and Parkinson had described were the furtive, dangerous, and organised underworlds that Dickens and Mayhew had imagined in their forays into East London.

The 'dark silence', which was only broken by whistles and hushed conversations, was the experience that most disconcerted social researchers in these narrow side streets from the Highway. However, Ratcliffe Highway presented a different soundscape that was equally notable in unsettling the intrepid reporter. In contrast to the classic slum *daytime* chronicler, who recorded silence and lethargy, their Ratcliffe Highway counterparts consistently recorded a cacophony as they passed into the Highway. One correspondent complained that as he entered the Highway, he was greeted with loud music and singing, drunken fiddlers, and marauding carts filled with 'screaming women and swearing sailors'. He protested that the pavement was obstructed for hours with 'drunken beasts in women's apparel, fighting foreign sailors and blaspheming obscene talking, lurches, idlers and thieves'.[62] To make matters worse, the social explorers were often unable to understand the conversations and loud oral exchanges that echoed through the Highway. Annie Besant, the socialist who was on an expedition to discover amusements in London's East End, observed that 'there is a strange out-of-the-world flavor [sic] in the Ratcliffe Highway district, so many foreign sailors, signs in so many languages, a general feeling of salt water and unaccustomed surroundings'.[63] Similarly, as he was passing through Ratcliffe Highway, Parkinson heard 'the tribes of Judah ... chaffering over their counters', noting that the district's 'language is ploygot, and when intelligible, strong – where each nationality has its house of call'.[64] A little further along, he passed a German dancing saloon 'where violins are giving out a very pronounced schottische' and 'strange ... gutturals in the speech' could be heard'.[65]

Visitors to the area noted that the local people had adopted a vernacular with a distinctive maritime identity that outsiders had difficulty in comprehending. One 'night-guide' book attempted to capture the dialogue of two women by conveying the conversation in their purported local dialect:

> she parades the starboard side of Ratcliffe Highway, occasionally bringing up at a lush crib to do the morning drain dodge, and hailing her pal on the opposite coast, with 'There you vos, then! How does it wag now? Did you doss for a square 'un last night? Good for a drain, in course?' And they blue a bob or so, get half malty, and she staggers to her ken to dress for the evening's promenade. It's then she comes out slap, and with a yellow fogle tied round her squeeze, and flashing a bandanna in her fam, she takes them by storm. She has her station near one of the flash houses, and as the loggers, alias tars, pass, she bounds on them at one spring, and hence achieved the name of 'Spring heel'd Jack.' They pronounce her to be a 'righteous square piece, and though a lushington, has a good heart; keeps a cozy crib, and does the dossment out and out.'[66]

The guide also provided its upper-class readers with a handy glossary of terms so that they could converse with the locals and navigate their way through the pubs and music venues of Ratcliffe Highway. While the genre of this writing did not take the serious tone of the philanthropists and religious missionaries, the passage confirms that visitors found the Highway to be an alien environment with its peculiar parlance. This disorientation increased as they journeyed past the maritime retail outlets and further into Ratcliffe Highway where the pubs, bars, and music venues were located. The echoes of the hustle and bustle of the busy shops gave way to the raucous sound of music and entertainment. What was particularly shocking for the bourgeois visitor was that this revelry was taking place during daylight hours. Thus, while the daytime slum was cast as a hopeless, aimless abyss, Ratcliffe Highway was seen to facilitate profligate behaviour and licentious debauchery. Parkinson observed that 'the music and dancing license known as the 25 George II is extensively taken' in the district.[67] He noted that many of the public houses had back rooms that facilitated 'fiddlers, pianoforte players, castanet clinkers, clog dancers, patter and other song singers, burlesque performers, and infant phenomenon, and ruddled elderly gymnasts'.[68]

Responses to slum tourism

The sensational writers who descended into Ratcliffe Highway from the 1850s continued to do so up until the fashion for slum tourism began to wane in the early twentieth century. H.M. Hyndman caustically noted that in the 1860s onwards, 'it became "the thing" to go down East ... My lady

Bountiful could be seen picking her way daintily through the unsavoury neighbourhoods of Limehouse, chance encounters of high-born personages were frequent in Ratcliffe Highway'. Hyndman claimed that when philanthropy 'became a bore ... our exquisites returned West with their carriages' and footmen.[69] However, during the late nineteenth century, with poverty very much on the political agenda, researchers, who were less concerned with sensational writing or missionary work, continued to observe the people of Ratcliffe Highway. However, significantly, they rarely challenged the sensational accounts of the Highway that had preceded them, and which had become the dominant narrative of the district. For example, Walter Besant, in his survey of East London of 1901, assumed many of the stereotypical accounts when introducing his readers to the Highway's history. He claimed that in the past, Ratcliffe Highway was a murderous place where 'Portugal Jack and Italy Jack and Lascar Jack have always been very handy with their knives'. He asserted that 'there lay men stark and dead after one of these affrays – the river would be their Churchyard'. He fully expected to encounter this lawlessness but was pleasantly surprised to find that he could walk down the street now 'without seeing a single fight, without being hustled or assaulted, without coming across a man too drunk to lift himself off the kerb'.[70] Without any explanation, Besant concluded that Ratcliffe Highway had undergone an important social change and that now it was a 'lively, cheerful street, with points which an artist might find picturesque; it is growing in respectability'.[71]

Similarly, in 1899, while surveying the district for Charles Booth, George Duckworth noted that on Ratcliffe Highway, the 'balmy days are over, many public houses, many beer shops, many lodging houses of a low class, many courts, and remnants of old wooded London, are its characteristics. The shops still redolent of the sea'.[72] Duckworth was describing a busy infrastructure of boarding houses, entertainment venues, and services for seafarers that was often at the core of sensational accounts of Ratcliffe Highway. Writing in the early twentieth century, Fox Smith drew on numerous sensational accounts and the language they deployed to describe Ratcliffe Highway in the late nineteenth century. She claimed that 'all the dregs and offscourings of male and female humanity swarmed in the foul and filth dens of the Highway, ready to prey on the lusts, the follies and the trustfulness of the sailor'.[73] The fact that not Duckworth, Besant, nor Fox Smith encountered murderous scenes as they strolled down the Highway may say more about the sensational reporters' imagination than it does about any significant social change in the district. Indeed, the sensational journalists' lurid claims about Ratcliffe Highway were openly challenged by philanthropists, clergymen, and working-class people who lived in the area.

The proposal to create a People's Palace in the East End and the fundraising campaign supporting the venture proved to be the catalyst for a concerted challenge to the dominant narrative that had cast Ratcliffe Highway as a degenerate abyss. The *East End Observer* was critical of Professor Huxley's attempts to elicit public donations at a Mansion House meeting on funding the enterprise in 1883. Huxley, who was leading the campaign for the institution, referred to his experience as a medical practitioner in the 'waterside districts of the East End'. He claimed that while he had experienced savagery and barbarianism in distant lands, nothing was more degraded and miserable than what he found in the East End. The newspaper challenged this perspective, arguing that this was a distortion of East End life that would 'have a bad effect' on the district and encourage the sensational journalist.[74] The following week, the newspaper's editor condemned 'the tendency, now common, to use the blackest of paint that can be used in the colouring of language in the current descriptions of East London'.[75]

Another writer in the *Saturday Review* also challenged the philanthropic campaigners' misguided perceptions of the East End. For example, while the author praised the People's Palace initiative, he took exception to further comments of Professor Huxley, that he would 'rather choose the life of a savage anywhere in the world than that of a man doomed to live in the East End'.[76] He agreed that 'no doubt there are few savages anywhere who have a worse time off than the poorest Londoner; but what has this dreadful fringe of helpless poverty to do with the People's Palace?' He maintained that Huxley was naïve if he thought that the People's Palace would reach the 'very poor'.[77] The writer argued that commentators like Huxley had been taken in by the 'sensational journalists' who had made 'the men and women who live by plundering sailors' their 'favourite quarry'. Journalists had ignored the industrious classes in the district for the 'worst bits, the raggedest [sic] children, the dampest and most dismal cellars'. He added: 'if, for instance, a pictorial paper thinks that the dreadful houses where the worst and lowest classes herd would make a good subject for illustration, a journalist and an artist are commissioned to visit the spots and do their best'.[78] Not only did critics cast doubt on the sensational journalists' and philanthropists' motivations for entering the district, their methods of research were also questioned. One correspondent of the *East London Observer* questioned whether a journalist who had written a sensational account of the East End in the *Daily Telegraph* had actually walked through the streets as he had claimed. The writer noted that the journalist stated that he had walked 'for miles' through the East End streets, and, through retracing the journalist's steps, the correspondent found that 'starting from Aldgate towards Stratford, I find that if one walked for "miles", firstly down

Leman-Street, through the Docks, he would be swimming in the Thames, a distance of, say one mile from the starting point – not "miles"'.[79]

Other researchers began to question whether missionaries and the police were distorting the East End and Ratcliffe Highway into a grotesque gothic caricature. Walsham How, the first modern suffragan bishop of London, was located on Ratcliffe Highway and had responsibility for the East End. Writing at the height of the Whitechapel murders, How rejected the idea that the atrocities were a natural outcome of a depraved area. He had witnessed a hard-working district and saved specific criticism for Mearns's *Bitter Cry of Outcast London* that, in his eyes, had contained large tracts of 'sensational and unfounded assertions'.[80] Having just arrived in Ratcliffe Highway, How was keen to understand and immerse himself in the area and so attended a talk by an American temperance orator named Mr Gough who had been working in the area. Gough implored How to take a tour of Ratcliffe Highway at night with him and his plain-clothed policeman friend. Gough explained on their last nocturnal exploration of the Highway that they had 'heard oaths and curses; we heard laughter, but no merriment in it; we heard music, but no tune in it; we heard the shuffling of poor women's feet coming to the public-house to seek for their drunken husbands – Murder! (this at the very top of his voice, making us all jump)'. The policeman added, in a rapid whisper, 'this happens every five minutes in these parts'. After reflecting on Gough's lecture and subsequent conversation, How began to suspect that the missionary was using his talks and tours as a vehicle for his own theatrical performance rather than as a means of discovering the lives of the poor.

Having declined Gough's offer of a guided tour, How turned for advice to Harry Jones, the well-known Rector of St George's in the East. Together, one Sunday afternoon, they strolled around Ratcliffe Highway visiting sailor homes, 'various street scenes', and lodging houses. How concluded that they were 'everywhere received in so friendly way that I already began to be very suspicious of Mr. Gough and his policeman in plain clothes'.

> Of course, Sunday afternoon is not the same as a week-day night; but I have been through Ratcliffe Highway at all sorts of hours since, and though I have met one or two noisy and quarrelsome Lascars there, yet I never met with the slightest incivility, or saw anything to shock me; and twice, when Mr Jones was ill, sailors have come up to me in Ratcliffe Highway, shaken my hand, and asked me if I could tell him how the Rector was.[81]

How was critical of social explorers who enlisted the help of sensational missionaries, journalists, or the police in their quest to understand the lives of the poor. Indeed, he was particularly critical of the tendency of sensational writers to imply that the 'hopelessly submerged' were 'typical of the whole district'.[82] There is little doubt that this distorted depiction of the East End led to an estrangement between philanthropists and missionaries that sometimes led to outright hostility.

The alienation of the sensational journalists and well-meaning philanthropists from the people of the East End was captured by a letter from a working-class man published in the *East London Observer* in 1884. He complained that 'we don't like being made a sort of show of, for fashionable parties to come and look at us if we was wild beasts in the zoological gardens. They seem to have discovered us all on a sudden [sic].' He added: 'they come to have a look at us just to see what our manners and customs is like, as a sort of entertainment, you may say'.[83] He was convinced that they entered into charity only 'to amuse themselves'. For this working man, sensational accounts of the East End had encouraged the 'slum tourist' and the pseudo-anthropologist who were keen to map out the strange rituals and culture of the East End. Moreover, the correspondent's interaction with a philanthropist further convinced him of their inability to understand the people or the district. He recounted an incident when he, his wife, and his daughters were approached by a woman philanthropist who had been working in the area:

> a young lady of a kind of perpendicular shape, with a untidy head of hair all flying about, she came up and she looks at us for a bit as if she thought of buying us for chimbley ornaments; and then she gives a sigh and she says 'And are you destitoot'? Destitoot! And I'd been flattering myself that I looked like a steady respectable man who knows how to keep his head above water, and his wife as well-dressed a little woman as you could wish to see, and carrying a babby what anybody could tell was made much of [sic].[84]

He went on to explain that he had a good artisan job, regularly paid into his club and union every week, owed no one any money, and that his eldest children all worked. He protested that it was 'irritating when gentlefolks insists in looking on you as if you was some poor creature incapable of looking after yourself'. He also explained that his conversation with the philanthropist had not gone well:

> I can tell you, to be talked to in that sort of way ain't calkilated to put us in a good temper. I am a quiet man myself, but my missis was a good deal raised, and I had some trouble getting her settled again. 'She meant it kind' I says, wishing to make the best of it. 'Yes, I daresay she did' says she; 'but she ought to have known better – hurting people's honest pride that keep themselves to themselves, and make their own way in the world by themselves, and don't want anybody's pity and don't want no patronage [sic].

This criticism of the journalists and philanthropists who descended into the East End reveals a fierce independence among working men and women in the district. Just as the social explorers often ridiculed the appearance of the poor they encountered, this working-class man mocked the hapless philanthropist for her accent, 'perpendicular' shape, and untidy hair. Furthermore, his wife was equally appalled at the woman's behaviour as the philanthropist had no understanding of working-class respectability or independence. Indeed, they were both shocked at the philanthropist's inability to distinguish between their own artisan appearance and those in absolute poverty. The working-class correspondent concluded that they advocated charitable causes, 'but don't let these benevolent people go think of us as "the masses", and mix us all up together in that aggravating way'.[85]

Conclusion

In short, this chapter has sought to explore the explorers of Ratcliffe Highway. It has investigated the fashion for slum tourism that led to the plethora of sensational accounts of the Highway and analysed the literary devices writers employed when retelling the journey to their readership. It is clear that while social explorers used many of the literary tropes familiar to East End slum tourists, Ratcliffe Highway researchers noted very different characteristics and experiences to the classic slum narrative. The Ratcliffe Highway district was unsettling for explorers as the maritime influences shaped the geography, landmarks, commerce, and street cultures that further alienated them from their bourgeois norms. As we have seen, this led explorers to identify a malign maritime culture as a principal cause for the infamous violence and moral depravity that was associated with the district. The transient nature of the sailor also made this maritime culture a dangerous one, since Ratcliffe Highway was characterised as accommodating 'hordes' of knife-wielding sailors, underlining the lawlessness of the area. Moreover, we have also seen how the explorers' assessments of Ratcliffe Highway clashed with the realities of popular culture. Thus, the sensational reporting, of course, did not operate in a vacuum of middle-class discourse. The dominant lurid narrative of Ratcliffe Highway was challenged by working-class residents, local religious leaders, and journalists alike. This chapter, then, has shone a light on the sensational reporting and identified why journalists and missionaries felt so unsettled when entering Ratcliffe Highway. While the analysis reveals how these narratives were constructed and the anxieties that underpinned them, it also represents a useful resource to investigate the nature of Ratcliffe further. Even though this chapter has unpacked explorers' assumptions and motivations, we can certainly identify a consensus among them that Ratcliffe Highway was imbued with an urban–maritime culture and a sense of Otherness. The following chapters will, at certain points, draw on this body of evidence, closely reading this material for the explorers' interaction with actors they met on their travels. Thus, while the explorers curated their narratives around a distaste for a primitive waterside culture, their subject's silences, pauses, behaviour, and responses will help us retrieve a more authentic experience of sailortown life in nineteenth-century Britain.[86]

Notes

1. A. Mayne, *The Imagined Slum: Newspaper Representation in Three Cities 1870–1914* (Leicester, Leicester University Press, 1993), 8.
2. See, for example, George R. Sims, *How the Poor Live and Horrible London* (London, Chatto & Windus, 1889), 4–5.
3. H.J. Dyos, 'The slums of Victorian London', in D. Cannadine and D. Reeder (eds), *Exploring the Urban Past: Essays in Urban History by H.J. Dyos* (Cambridge, Cambridge University Press, 1982), 32.
4. R. Crone, *Violent Victorians: Popular Entertainment in Nineteenth Century London* (Manchester, Manchester University Press, 2012), 262.
5. R. Kirkland, 'Reading the rookery: The social meaning of the Irish slum in nineteenth century London', *New Hibernia Review*, 16(1), 2012, 16–30, 16.
6. H. Shore, *London's Criminal Underworlds, c. 1720–c.1930: A Social and Cultural History* (Basingstoke, Palgrave Macmillan, 2015), 57.
7. *Morning Chronicle*, 14 January 1834, quoted in Kirkland, 'Reading the rookery', 16.
8. T. Beames, *The Rookeries of London: Past, Present and Prospective* (London, Thomas Boswell, 1850, 1970 edn), 2.
9. Kirkland, 'Reading the rookery', 17.
10. T. Crook, 'Accommodating the outcast: Common lodging houses and the limits of urban governance in Victorian and Edwardian England', *Urban History*, 35(3), 2008, 414–36, 423.
11. B. Beaven, *Visions of Empire: Patriotism, Popular Culture, and the City, 1870–1939* (Manchester, Manchester University Press, 2012), 43.
12. Beames, *The Rookeries of London*, 95.
13. Beames, *The Rookeries of London*, 95.
14. J. Flanders, *The Invention of Murder: How the Victorians Revelled in Death and Detection and Invented the Modern Crime* (London, Harper Press, 2011), Chapter 1.
15. C. Dickens, 'On duty with Inspector Field', *Household Words*, 64, 14 June 1851.
16. C. Dickens, *The Uncommercial Traveller* (London, Chapman & Hall, 1905), 268. Dickens's original essays were published in *All the Year Round* between 1860 and 1861.
17. C. Dickens, *Our Mutual Friend* (London, Penguin, 1998, original publication 1864–65), 65.

18 M. Cotsell, 'The uncommercial traveller on the commercial road: Dickens's East End', *Dickens Quarterly*, 3(3), September 1986, 115–22, 118.
19 Mayne, *The Imagined Slum*, Chapters 6, 7, and 8.
20 Printed in *East London Observer*, 1 January 1872.
21 'Sunday with the sailors', *Household Words*, 18 June 1881, 275.
22 'Some dark sides of our social life', *The Eclectic Review*, February 1865, 8, 199.
23 J. Ewing Ritchie, *The Night Side of London* (London, William Tweedle, 1857), 68.
24 W. Besant, *East London* (London, Chatto & Windus, 1901), 41.
25 C. Fox Smith, *Sailor Town Days* (London, Houghton Mifflin, 1923), 6.
26 Fox Smith, *Sailor Town Days*, 7.
27 Quoted in J. Marriott, *Beyond the Tower: A History of East London* (New Haven, CT: Yale University Press, 2011), 84.
28 Mayne, *The Imagined Slum*, 167–9.
29 *East London Observer*, 10 October 1857.
30 Anon, *Wonderful London: Its Lights and Shadows of Humour and Sadness* (London, Tinsley Bros, 1878), 338.
31 *Chambers's Journal of Popular Literature, Science and Arts*, 24 April 1879, 258.
32 'On duty with the inspector', *Temple Bar*, June 1881, 349.
33 See Booth's police notebooks, LSE, Charles Booth Archive, https://booth.lse.ac.uk/notebooks, accessed 9 April 2024.
34 'On duty with the inspector', *Temple Bar*, June 1881, 349.
35 *Daily News*, 31 August 1864.
36 *Household Words*, 6 December 1851, 254.
37 *Chambers's Journal*, 24 April 1879, 258.
38 Fox Smith, *Sailor Town Days*, 13.
39 W. Phillips, *The Wild Tribes of London* (London, Ward and Lock, 1855), 37.
40 My thanks to Jerry White who identified Parkinson as the anonymous writer in the *Daily News*.
41 *Daily News*, 31 August 1864.
42 *Daily News*, 31 August 1864.
43 'Jack Alive in London' *Household Words*, 6 December, 1851, 257. The standard rate for a parrot in 1851 was 30 or 40 shillings.
44 *Saturday Review*, 17 May 1879, 612; for a short biography of Charles Jamrach, see *The New Monthly*, July 1882, 573.
45 *Saturday Review*, 17 May 1879, 612.
46 'Some of the dark sides of our social life', *The Eclectic Review*, 8 February 1865, 199–200.
47 K. Baedeker, *London and Its Environs* (Leipsic, OH, Baedeker Publishing, 1902), 169.
48 Ewing Ritchie, *Night Side of London*, 73.
49 'A ramble below the bridge', *The Leisure Hour*, 21 September 1854, 597.
50 'Alongside the dockside', *All the Year Round*, 8 December 1883, 62.
51 *East London Observer*, 10 October 1857.
52 A. Morrison, *The Hole in the Wall* (London, Methuen, 1902), 100.

53 Morrison, *The Hole in the Wall*, 101.
54 *London Daily News*, 15 September 1902, 6.
55 F.W. Robinson, 'A night on the Highway', *Belgravia*, May 1879, 300.
56 'Some of the dark sides of our social life', *The Eclectic Review*, February 1865, 201.
57 *The Daily London News*, 1 September 1864.
58 *The Daily London News*, 1 September 1864.
59 *The Daily London News*, 1 September 1864.
60 *The Daily London News*, 1 September 1864.
61 *The Daily London News*, 1 September 1864.
62 *East London Observer*, 10 October 1857.
63 A. Besant, 'How London amuses itself in the East', *Our Corner*, August 1886, 115.
64 *Daily News*, 31 August 1864.
65 *Daily News*, 31 August 1864.
66 Anon, *The Swells Guide; Or a Peep through the Great Metropolis under the Dominion of Nox* (London, H. Smith, 1849), 27.
67 Legislators complained that the Act was now insufficient to control the conduct of the newly established singing saloons or music halls. See L. Levi (ed.), *Annals of British Legislation: Being a Brief Digest of the Parliamentary Blue Books* (London, Smith, Elder & Co., 1866), 394.
68 *Daily News*, 31 August 1864.
69 H.M. Hyndman, 'The revolution of today', Monthly Magazine of Scientific Socialism, January 1884, 17.
70 Besant, *East London*, 73.
71 Besant, *East London*, 73.
72 Charles Booth Archive, LSE, police notebooks B350, districts 7–11, 1898–99, 201, https://booth.lse.ac.uk/notebooks/b350#?c=0&m=0&s=0&cv=2&z=-111.2298%2C0%2C5953.4596%2C3541, accessed 25 March 2022.
73 Fox Smith, *Sailor Town Days*, 28.
74 *East End Observer*, 22 December 1883.
75 *East End Observer*, 29 December 1883.
76 'The East-End Peoples Palace', *Saturday Review*, December 1883, 794.
77 'The East-End Peoples Palace', 794.
78 'The East-End Peoples Palace', 794.
79 *East London Observer*, 2 October 1886.
80 W. Walsham, 'The East End', The Contemporary Review, December 1888, 793.
81 Walsham, 'The East End', 795.
82 Walsham, 'The East End', 797.
83 *East London Observer*, 6 September 1884.
84 *East London Observer*, 6 September 1884.
85 *East London Observer*, 6 September 1884.
86 J. Seed, 'Did the subaltern speak? Mayhew and the coster-girl', *Journal of Victorian Culture*, 19(4), 2014, 536–49, 536.

3

From Jolly Jack and Moll to proletarian Jack and Jill: The depictions of sailors and women in a nineteenth-century sailortown

> The 'bosom' of Father Thames at Wapping Old Stairs no longer finds anchored in its vicinity troops of ponderous samples of Britain's men-of-war and fast-sailing merchantmen. The hordes of the British sailor-man who made old Ratcliffe Highway merry throughout the live-long night are memories of the past, as also are the bevies of damsels of questionable repute who first feasted at Jack's expense.
>
> *East End News and London Shipping Chronicle*, 30 August 1904

The social investigators' exploration of Ratcliffe Highway's urban locality was, as we have seen, a set of recognisable tropes that retold the gothic horror of the East End's violence and grinding poverty. However, underpinning this familiar narrative was a sense of maritime 'Otherness' that signalled both the exotic and danger to the intrepid explorer. Indeed, Ratcliffe Highway's more 'eastern' geographical location, its reputation as a sailor saturnalia, and a persistent lament for a lost maritime culture set the district apart from the more orthodox East End social investigations. This chapter will open with how authors retold their experiences on the Highway in a formulaic style that drew on the notion of the eighteenth-century sailor as a national symbol. Journalists, such as James Greenwood, tapped into a growing maritime nostalgia for the 'traditional' characters of 'Jolly Jack Tar' and his companion 'Moll'. These forays into Ratcliffe Highway were curated to shock their readers with the revelation that Britain's once national symbol had become degenerate, decadent, and proletarian. It will be argued that an increased urbanisation and a growing industrialisation of the maritime trade, through steam and port mechanisation, had increased middle-class commentators' anxieties about a deterioration of social relations in the modern city. This anxiety had, in turn, informed their experiences and narratives of Ratcliffe Highway. However, these lurid accounts of the district did not go uncontested, and by the end of the nineteenth century, a small but growing band of philanthropists, traders, and working-class people began to openly reject Ratcliffe Highway's label as 'one of the most dangerous places in the world'.

The people of Ratcliffe Highway and a 'lost maritime world'

Ratcliffe Highway 'assaulted' the senses of the explorer, unsettling them as they walked along the thoroughfare. The further they penetrated the Highway, the more disturbed they became as they encountered the throngs of pleasure seekers, or those people living or working in the district. While Victorian explorers billed their journey as an 'expedition of discovery', most had preconceived ideas of what they would find on Ratcliffe Highway and its environs. The Ratcliffe Highway murders of 1811 had bestowed the district a brutal reputation, and social explorers were keen to capture the essence of this murderous reputation in their writing. Significantly, they were also keen to rationalise and explain *why* the Highway had slipped into a brutal anarchy and placed the people they encountered at the heart of their explanation. This section will explore the depictions of the sailors and women that appeared in the social investigators' narratives of Ratcliffe Highway and how they were portrayed as a dangerous departure from the traditional benign characters of 'Jolly Jack Tar and his companion Moll'.

Isaac Land's important study of the sailor in Britain has shown that their cultural representation underwent a significant transformation in the twenty-five years between 1750 and 1775.[1] From a figure of pillage and rape in the early eighteenth century, the sailor had come to represent the English qualities required to acquire and keep an empire. Land cites a humorous *Lecture on Hearts* in 1767 that included the line '"the heart of the British sailor" made of solid oak and having four chambers, respectively, courage, honesty, prodigal exuberance and love for "his Wapping landlady's daughter"'.[2] However, it was Charles Dibdin's songs that had the greatest and most enduring impact on the cultural representation of the sailor. From the 1770s, Dibdin rehabilitated the sailor and reinvented the sea song, casting the British tar as manly, honest, and patriotic.[3] Significantly, Dibdin projected the British tar as a 'lion in battle, afterward a lamb'.[4] Thus, the eighteenth-century sailor had a split personality since he was a loyal and fierce warrior at sea, while on land he was naïve and child-like. Dibdin's creation of a sailor who, though benign, was prone to gullibility and excess ashore found popularity as it was aligned with a Georgian toleration for licentious behaviour. Indeed, it was the presence of well-to-do libertines and flâneurs that, to a degree, legitimised sailortown hedonism and excesses. For example, the writer Pierce Egan fictionalised his experiences of 'slumming' in Georgian sailortown through his novel *Life in London*. His text provides an insight into how 'well connected socialites' integrated effortlessly from the affluent West End to the plebeian crowd in the East. Egan describes how his two heroes, Tom and Jerry, visit a sailor singing saloon in Wapping where 'every cove that put in his appearance was quite welcome; colour or country considered no obstacle'.[5] Moreover, as Land has argued, the sailor was both a fierce sea warrior and a benign Jolly Jack Tar ashore, a character that was 'frozen in time' at the Battle of Trafalgar. By the mid-nineteenth century, the martial qualities of the sailor had become bound with Britain's national identity and growing imperial successes.[6]

In visiting Ratcliffe Highway, social explorers claimed that they were in search of the traditional Dibdin-inspired patriotic sailor and his friends Moll and Poll. What they purported to discover was a far more disturbing and compelling story of a modern society destroying the social binds that produced an imagined patriotic and benign people of eighteenth-century Wapping and Ratcliffe. James Greenwood lamented that 'the nautical enthusiast who, in these degenerate days, set out on a pilgrimage' to pass a 'pleasant hour with the worthy descendants of the heroes and heroines immortalised by the late Mr. Dibdin, would probably find himself disappointed'. He continued: 'the modern Jack ashore is altogether a different being from that Jack of old ... the patron of fiddlers, and the very soul and essence of good humour and sprightliness'. While Greenwood had never claimed to have met any traditional sailors, he was certain that they were 'flip-swigging, hornpiping, free-handed noble old bragging sea dogs, brave as lions in battle, playful and blythe as kittens in their shore frolics'.[7] In a similar vein, an *East London Observer* journalist struck a nostalgic tone on the passing of the traditional Dibdin-like sailor. He noted that when sailors:

> made merry in England, tradition tells us of his gay doings in Wapping, where then the sound of the fiddle and shuffle of Jack's soles were never still. There are men yet living who can remember when Dibdin was merely chronicling admitted phases of maritime life in singing of the glories of Wapping Old Stairs and the Moll of Wapping – there are men who have years of life in them yet. Who can remember Wapping streets crowded with sailors and girls, and crimps and slop-shops, and when the public-houses there situate roared and blazed with custom.[8]

The *East London Observer* correspondent added: 'do sailors ever fry gold watches now, or make sandwiches of bank notes? Do they ever "shiver their timbers"? ... are mates continually "splicing the main-brace" and "bousing their jibs"? I am afraid not'. Such was the perceived honourable, skilled, and simple life of the traditional seafarer, the reporter saw a 'consistency of the character of a sailor and a Christian'.[9]

The *Reynolds Newspaper* continued to amplify this nostalgia when a correspondent wrote that 'the daily task of the seaman used to have a lot of poetry about it' for he was a man 'who pines for the rolling billows and the stormy winds ... hitches up his "britches"' and 'takes his rations of grog daily'.[10] Other social commentators, such as the merchant sailor Frank Bullen, described the traditional sailor as a 'great figure of romance' and claimed to remember how the bo'sun was the lynchpin of a sailing vessel.

> He is, of course, to the general, the *beau-ideal* of 'Jack Tar', a magnificent monster with a bull's voice, burned almost black by the tropical sun, with eagle eyes forth-looking from a thicket of beard ... brave as a man can be, he is terrible in his wrath, yet his heart is tender as a little child's, any tale of pity never fails to empty his pockets.[11]

Bullen's account closely resembled Dibdin's caricature of the eighteenth-century seaman, describing him both as a fearsome individual at sea and as 'just a big child' on land.[12] Dibdin's nostalgic portrayal of maritime life did not stop at the sailor but extended to 'his women', invariably named Moll and Poll. Dibdin's songs, such as 'Poll of Wapping Stairs', emphasised her gentle and passive femininity and her love and loyalty to her sailor. Just as they had with the sailor, commentators drew on Dibdin's powerful sentiments and looked back fondly to the stereotypical maritime women of the late eighteenth and early nineteenth centuries.

One observer warned his readers that nowadays they would search Ratcliffe Highway in vain for Molly and those kindly 'heroines immortalised by the late Dibdin's ballads'.[13] Greenwood's quest to find the 'Polly of Wapping Stairs' was just as fruitless as his search for Jolly Jack Tar. He wrote that 'in vain' he searched for Molly:

> Whose artless declaration of her virtue – spotless as those trousers which it was her proud privilege to wash – can no more be doubted, than the fact her love for Thomas was as warm and sweet as the grog she made, and presented to his lips at the very earliest opportunity after his landing from the ship that had so cruelly borne him away from her.[14]

Similarly, a theatre critic claimed to have remembered 'traditional Jack Tar' in the East End music halls who 'flocked to the boxes with Moll of Wapping Stairs, and with Susan from Deptford, and likewise Sal', who 'disported the most violent coloured silk handkerchiefs'.[15] Another correspondent of the *Reynolds Newspaper* mourned the vanishing Dibdin-esque sailor who was eagerly sought for by his companions 'Susan of Deptford and likewise by Sal'.[16] Writing in 1859, an investigative journalist assured his readers that twenty years ago on Ratcliffe Highway, 'Jack danced there and Jack drank there, and blowsey Molls and Meggs grew fat and flashy on Jack's hard-earned prize-money', and in lamenting their loss, the reporter bemoaned 'who can deny that the – well, the decadence has commenced?'[17] The last comment, on how Ratcliffe Highway had fallen into a damaging and new form of decadence, is quite telling. Their disappointment at not meeting Dibdin's fictional sailor-town creations was only matched by the horrors they did discover. The 'horrors' encountered on Ratcliffe Highway were largely the sailors, the women and men in the district whom the explorers had *observed* or *overheard*. Very few explorers interacted with their quarry, but they had nevertheless formulated firm conclusions on their morality and respectability. This assessment was largely based on the subject's physical and general appearance, the time and location of the observation, and their assumed vocation. The next section will explore how social observers explained the disappearance of Jolly Jack Tar, Moll, and Poll and speculated on how these imagined new sailors and women, by the mid-nineteenth century, had taken their place.

The cultural reconstruction of the sailors on Ratcliffe Highway: proletarian Jack

An increasingly urbanised and industrialised society was the modern force that so unsettled the social explorers of maritime London. It was thought that modernity had ushered in a different cast of characters in London's sailortown, all of whom were framed as an urbanised proletariat. Moreover, in their exploration of Ratcliffe Highway, social observers met a cross section of sailors, women, stevedores, 'crimps and bullies', and consistently saw in them a worrying moral and biological regression.[18] The loss of a Dibdin-esque socially stable world was vividly juxtaposed with the emergence and encroachment of an unpredictable proletariat. Most of these new types of sailors were described as morally and physically degenerate, but a small proportion of 'self-improving' and 'bookish' sailors were also causing concern due to their increasing independence and industrial militancy. For the bourgeois social investigators, the deterioration of social relations was moving at a seemingly faster pace, and even by the mid-nineteenth century, the old imagined Dibdin world seemed but a distant memory. Yet, as we have seen, it was at this point that the traditional Jack Tar had finally become the touchstone of patriotism and the national symbol of the British Empire.[19] Indeed, the demise of the very characters who were the plebeian backbone of the British Empire made their loss even more significant. With this cultural backdrop in mind, commentators set out to explain how an encroaching proletarianisation of Jack and his companions had eroded a once patriotic and benign Ratcliffe Highway community.

It was always going to be a hard task for the sailor to comfortably align with the new Victorian codes of morality that had taken ascendency by the mid-nineteenth century.[20] It was one thing for commentators to enshrine an imagined Georgian sailor as a symbol of the nation, but it was an altogether different matter to actually meet a modern Victorian sailor on Ratcliffe Highway. By the very nature of their transient work, sailors did not hold the qualities Victorians demanded of their fellow citizens. The sailor life was one far removed from the exemplary citizen who, it was imagined, had stable and regularised employment within a fixed locality and a stake in civic society.[21] Indeed, Henry Mayhew's monumental investigation into the labouring poor of London categorised workers' morality and standing in society through the stability of their occupation. Given this criterion for measuring morality, it is perhaps no surprise that Mayhew regarded sailors' spendthrift reputation as a characteristic that would lead them into destitution if left to their own devices on land.[22] Indeed, Mayhew viewed the urban and maritime worlds as entirely separate entities, and he regarded seamen ashore with great suspicion and liable to be 'professional beggars'. He claimed that 'a real sailor is seldom or never seen inland' and 'rarely brags of what he has seen, or done. In these respects and all other respects he is the exact opposite to the turnpike sailor [the professional beggar]'.[23]

George Sims also claimed to have regularly encountered the 'sham sailor' 'who generally hangs about the City on winter evenings' to beg for money or swindle young 'green clerks'.[24] For the nineteenth-century social scientist, the seafarer ashore transgressed significant bourgeois boundaries that defined and maintained 'good citizenship'; he was profligate, licentious, and nomadic. It was perhaps no surprise that to mingle with the metropolitan underclass, Jack London chose the disguise of an American sailor. London wanted to cut a tragic figure, 'stranded in a strange and terrible land', and, due to his exuberant living, was unable to keep either his money, clothes, or dignity. He wrote:

> We walked along, and when they grew bitter and cursed the land, I cursed with them, cursed as an American waif would curse, stranded in a strange and terrible land. And, as I tried to lead them to believe, and succeeded in making them believe, they took me for a 'seafaring man,' who had spent his money in riotous living, lost his clothes (no unusual occurrence with seafaring men ashore), and was temporarily broke while looking for a ship.[25]

Indeed, the modern sailor ashore was viewed by bourgeois commentators with a mixture of sympathy, curiosity, fear, and loathing.

According to commentators, the Dibdin sailor had fallen victim to a modernisation of the maritime industry which had augmented the introduction of steam, the employment of foreign sailors, and, significantly, a new workforce drawn from the slums of Britain's largest cities.[26] In 1903 Charles Booth captured these perceived changes in the sailors' skill set and status in society. In describing the changes in their occupation and traditions, Booth portrayed a declining English workforce who, at the same time, had benefited from parliamentary and philanthropic intervention to improve their material conditions and morality.[27] In short, the carefree jolly sailor, who was skilled in the art of sailing ships but subject to benign pleasures ashore, had been replaced by a proletarian Jack of the steam age who made use of the seaman rests and trades organisations that modern urban life afforded. In the age of steam, the sailing skills that had been passed down through generations of seafaring families were no longer relevant. Indeed, it was an observation shared by Bullen who noted that it was 'undoubtedly the advent of the steamship' that degraded the maritime profession, for all that was wanted in a steamer was a 'burly labourer who is able to steer'.[28] The highly skilled and much lauded 'ship's bo'sun' was much diminished in the steamship, and, according to Bullen, the classic Jack Tar character died with him.[29] Likewise, Booth declared that:

> the ordinary deck hands are little better than labourers. ... In place of the splicing, bracing, setting and general manipulation of ropes and sails and other work of navigation, they are now chiefly occupied in cleaning, scrubbing, scouring, holystoning, polishing and painting the different parts of the ship.[30]

Booth hints that, unlike the romanticised image of the sailing seafarer, this new breed of sailor was not drawn to an adventurous life on the high seas but instead was driven to mercantile shipping due to personal misfortune. He observed that the steam seamen 'are generally of a rather lower class than sailors, and often take to the sea because they have failed to obtain work, or because disreputable habits have brought them into disgrace, at home'.[31] Booth was not alone; one social observer contrasted the sailing seafarers' high spirits of the early nineteenth century with the modern sailor's 'dullness and spiritless nature' who 'indulged in foul mockeries of recreation'.[32]

According to *Reynolds Newspaper*, the modern sailor 'has had all the poetry knocked out of him'. The correspondent pointed to the changing working conditions on the steamship in which the 'rollicking sailor' who 'reefed the sails in a gale of wind' had been replaced with 'a half-naked man who shovels coals into a raging furnace thirty feet below deck'. He added:

> There is no poetry in his life; he is merely a shifter of fuel, doing the work which might be better done by machinery. If he be not a man who has a particular partiality to fire his life is one of dire monotony, with ever-present reverberations of the mighty engines tearing at the screws, while the heat oppresses and roasts him. And there is always the terror and risk of a life which may be snuffed out any day at any moment. If he is not a fireman he has to spend his time working cranes ... and 'doing time' in some way or other.[33]

These steam sailors of the late nineteenth century, then, were essentially an undesirable stratum of the working class, a classification that made these seafarers a more dangerous and streetwise social group than their sailing forebears. Among Victorian commentators of both the merchant and naval services, it was generally agreed that the stoker on the steamship was the lowest role occupied by the worst class of men. Christopher McKee has noted that the contemporary perception of stokers was that they were 'big, strong, illiterate, dumb guys; all brawn and no brain recruited to do the ship's heavy lifting in torrid, coal and soiled engine spaces'.[34] Subsequent commentators such as B.W. Beresford adopted the stoker Victorian stereotype, describing him as of simple character with an 'ape-like' appearance.[35]

The steam sailor and stoker (or fireman) seemed to embody the encroachment of an industrialised society into the maritime profession during the second half of the nineteenth century. Bullen described the thought of becoming a stoker as 'terrifying' and defined the job as more akin to factory work or coal mining than to traditional seafaring. He noted that the stoker descends into the bowels of the ship to face the boiler that 'claims him as its slave for four hours'. He is surrounded by 'strange-looking taps and gauges and tubes, with the use of which he must be familiar'.[36] For the trimmer, who was tasked in supplying the stoker with coal, conditions resembled a coal face. Bullen pronounced the Trimmer's job 'so terrible that he should receive the sympathy of every kindly man and woman he serves'.[37] For the Trimmer,

> his labour knows no respite as he struggles to keep the fireman's needs supplied. And there is no ventilator pouring down fresh air into the bunker. In darkness, only punctured by the dim light of a safety-lamp, in an atmosphere composed of exhalations from the coal and a modicum of dust-laden air, liable at any moment to be overwhelmed by the down-rushing masses of coal as the ship's motion displaces it, the grimy, sweat-soaked man works on.[38]

Such a description of the modern sailor's work clearly aligned him with the industrial proletariat. Indeed, it was a comparison made explicitly by the *Reynolds Newspaper*, a publication that commanded a large working-class readership. The correspondent, who was campaigning for better conditions, argued that 'a man who goes to sea or a man who goes into the bowels of the earth day after day, and who is liable to be killed or maimed at any moment ought to be the best paid man amongst all workmen'.[39]

In the eyes of social commentators, the streets of Ratcliffe Highway thronged with a different type of sailor, one who was less noble, honest, and more engaged with the urban world. In essence, the modern sailor was streetwise, and the child-like portrayals of traditional seafarers were replaced by narratives that embraced a quasi-social class dimension. However, further changes to the shipping industry seemed to compound the theory that sailortown's traditional English Jack Tar was in decline. By the mid-nineteenth century, commentators declared that most English ships recruited foreign sailors at the expense of 'the old Tar' who 'may be occasionally observed, seeming like visions of the past'.[40] One reporter noted that:

> The great resort of sailors in London is now almost exclusively occupied by foreigners, who keep boarding houses, public houses, and houses of a still worse nature, where the allurement is offered, and every means employed to obtain Jack's cash and copper.[41]

The *Reynolds Newspaper* observed that the 'British sailor is gradually retiring and the foreign sailor coming forward'. The newspaper added: 'why is this? It is a monstrous question for the great maritime nation in the world and must not lightly be passed over'.[42] Similarly, throughout Bullen's account of the merchant shipping service, he returned to the question of the foreign seafarer who now seemed to dominate English-owned ships. While Bullen could appreciate why foreigners with traditional maritime skills had replaced the declining sailing Jack Tar, he failed to understand why unskilled foreign sailors were replacing British crew on English steamships. He could only suggest that the unskilled British working class 'are getting more and more loth to work at all' while the foreign sailor will 'work till they sink from exhaustion' and 'swarm into every opening that presents itself'.[43]

The fear that foreign sailors were replacing British seamen was taken on by the seamen trade unions towards the end of the nineteenth century and the early twentieth century. The labour press and unions offered their explanations for the shipping companies' preference for foreign sailors that was often cast in overtly patriotic, racist, and social Darwinist terms. *The Seaman*, a mouthpiece for seamen's organised labour, accused the shipowners of preferring cheap Chinese seafarers at the expense of the English and warned that this policy would have dire consequences for the empire. The newspaper added: 'but what avail is it to England that she celebrates the jubilee of the Indian Mutiny while she handed over to the Continental foreigner and the Asiatic? The British mercantile marine is dependent on them!'[44] The National Amalgamated Sailors' and Firemen's Union (NASFU) had established a campaign against foreign labour from when it was founded in 1887.[45] NASFU's leader, Havelock Wilson, led a series of strikes from the 1880s, principally challenging the Shipping Federation over their employment of Chinese labour. Havelock cast the debate in racial terms and drew on social Darwinism as evidence of the Britishers' superior moral and physical strength.[46] Havelock claimed that captains had reported that Chinese sailors were 'constantly fighting amongst themselves using knives' and that 'they were very poor sailors' and 'caused a great deal of trouble with opium and drink in Chinese ports'.[47]

In another account, Havelock quoted one captain who alleged that the Chinese were 'lazy, dirty and insolent, and gave way to drink much more than the much-maligned Britisher. In my opinion, if the white man got half the consideration that the yellow heathens do, there would not be so much talk about trouble on British ships'.[48] Havelock maintained that it was the Shipping Federation's patriotic duty to employ English sailors, and the British Empire depended on it:

> Great Britain's Empire was won for her by the daring of her seamen. When once Great Britain loses its sea power it will become a decadent nation and the Empire will crumble to dust. If the Chinaman is to supplant the Britisher in his national vocation, how will it be possible to maintain our supremacy on the sea?[49]

Thus, social observers and trade unions were aligned in the view that the decline of the traditional English sailor seriously undermined the nation's maritime identity and ultimately its sea power. In short, it was a sure sign of a decadent society that would inevitably lead to the collapse of the British Empire.

As the nineteenth century advanced, the reimagining of the Ratcliffe Highway sailor was negatively framed with ever more certainty along social class and racial lines. In a modern urban and industrial landscape, Jolly Jack Tar, the backbone of the British Empire, was losing out to the unskilled proletarian worker and the 'inferior' foreign sailor. The Highway's apparent slide into decadence led commentators and social surveyors to recommend philanthropic and state intervention to aid the English sailor, who continued to remain a symbol of the nation. Help for the English sailor was still understood in terms of saving him from himself. While Dibdin's sailor was a 'lion in battle' and a 'lamb' on land, the modern sailor lacked heroism at sea and was debauched and sometimes dangerous on land.[50] Even Charles Booth, who cast himself as a man of social science, fell prey to the stereotypes of the eighteenth- and nineteenth-century sailor. Of the old sailing seafarer, Booth noted that 'his free and open disposition, appeal strongly to the sentimental side of human nature, and consequently "poor Jack" is a people's idol'.[51] Booth was content to draw from popular stereotypes of Jack Tar, suggesting that he was 'childlike in his guileless simplicity' and that his 'helplessness' was taken advantage of while ashore by '"land sharks" – crimps and loose women'. These seafarers of sail who enveloped Wapping High Street when ashore in the eighteenth and early nineteenth centuries were sailors who were shunned by 'callous legislators' because the seafarer 'rarely has a vote to give'.[52]

Writing in 1903, it seemed clear to Booth that the sailors of sailing vessels belonged to a different age, an age in which seamen were honest but gullible, and skilled in their trade but profligate with their earnings. This seafarer was a master of the sea but was prey to the vices of urban society ashore. It is perhaps no surprise, given his advocacy for state intervention, that Booth emphasised the importance of parliamentary legislation in addressing the hardships of merchant seamen. The Merchant Shipping Act of 1894 consolidated earlier maritime legislation stretching back to 1836 that meant, according to Booth, 'few genuine grievances remain unaddressed'.[53] Booth also noted that London was well served with philanthropic institutions specialising in seamen's welfare, and they had 'to some extent supplanted the old boarding houses, many of which were dens of iniquity'.[54] Such moral and material progress had, however, evolved alongside a more disturbing development in the seafaring profession. Booth's portrayal of the seafarer's character tapped into a popular nostalgia of the traditional sailor that had begun with the transition of steam in the mid-nineteenth century. Booth's assessment of the sailor's flawed character required state intervention and philanthropy as, in his eyes, sailors were too profligate and irresponsible while ashore to shape their own lives.

As we have seen, this was a widely shared opinion among commentators, and it often came as a surprise to them when sailors behaved more independently than the stereotypical Jack ashore. By the third quarter of the nineteenth century, a sizeable number of sailors began pursuing self-improvement activities, and rejecting 'Jacks" traditional 'spree ashore'.[55] Complaining of the demise of the eighteenth-century sailor, one correspondent complained that 'what with Institutes and Sailor Homes, and Teetotal ships, and gentlemanly captains, and intelligent mates, and floating libraries, Jack grows more exacting in his requirements and more refined in his tastes'. He added that 'his singing-room must rival the music palaces of Marseilles and Genoa'.[56] Indeed, commentators found it difficult to explain the rise of the 'intellectual sailor' which ran counter to the dominant narrative of the depraved modern sailor ashore. One theatre critic captured this contradiction when reviewing how sailors were portrayed on stage. He noted that:

> Either Jack is low, brutal, ignorant, degraded, sordid, indulging in pleasures compared to which even the miserable amusement of real nautical melo drama is elevating and refining, or he is a smart dapper fellow dressing in shore togs and reading the Times, and studying Norie and patronising sailors' institutes.[57]

The social commentators' unease at the sailors' reported shift to intellectualism can be explained by the growing industrial unrest among seamen from the middle of the nineteenth century.[58] Bullen had concluded that British sailors had adopted a proletarian union militancy and blamed their demise on their industrial action, claiming that 'if a shipmaster happens to have had much trouble with the crew of his own countrymen',[59] he will look to foreigners next time. Reporting on a seamen's strike in the 1850s, one reporter wondered 'what would become of us, if even our very sailors were obliged to become agitators[?]'. This intellectual type of modern sailor was an altogether different persona ashore; no longer 'like a lamb', nor morally degenerate, but agitating against authority. He was surly, independent, moody, and 'wandered up and down with hands in pockets, eyes bent downwards'.[60] Another journalist compared old 'Jolly Jack Tar' who was fun, straightforward, 'generous and open handed' with his modern counterparts '*solemn* Jack Tar or *sordid* Jack Tar', adding that now 'sailors are like other labourers'.[61]

For these commentators, given the classic proletariat working conditions that steam sailors and stokers toiled in, it was no surprise that they adopted urban forms of industrial protest. Unlike their seafaring forebears, the steam sailor was perceived to have possessed a modern political dimension grounded within urban industrial contexts. In 1869 one reporter noted that the modern sailor complains about his pay and has 'followed the example of his brother workmen on shore and struck. He has paraded the streets of seaports with bands and music, and the triumphant British flag borne aloft'.[62] Striking sailors received much press attention in 1881 when a national strike over pay was sparked after shipowners refused sailors' demands for a 'fair day's pay'. Significantly, sailors appeared to have forged informal strike committees that predated the official trade unions such as NASFU, which was founded six years later. These informal committees took a radically different approach to Havelock's jingoistic policy of campaigning for the employment of solely British sailors at the expense of what he deemed physically and morally inferior foreigners.

In 1881 a strike committee was convened that met daily at the Royal Crown public house on Ratcliffe Highway, which seemed to command considerable support from the sailor and wider population. The committee had also initiated a successful subscription list where the general public could pledge funds to aid the striking sailors, helping over fifty applicants within a couple of days of its launch.[63] Inviting its readership to pledge funds, the *London Evening Standard* reported that the strike promised to be of 'considerable magnitude' among the sailors of Ratcliffe and Shadwell. The reporter noted that 'almost every seafaring man to be met with in the streets in the locality is decorated with the blue ribband denoting him as one of the men on strike'. The report further observed that most of the shop windows were plastered with posters demanding a 'fair day's pay for a fair day's work'.[64] Indeed, the local community seems to have supported this industrial action with the boarding house masters being described as particularly sympathetic to the seamen's cause.[65] The committee organisers appeared to have instituted a more inclusive approach to their campaign, as the *London Evening Standard* explained:

> The procession, which was orderly, started yesterday morning from the Royal Crown, and comprised about one hundred and fifty British seamen, about the same of number of Germans, Swedes, and Norwegians, and a score of coloured men. All of these wore the blue ribband, and perambulated Mercer-Street, Cable Street, King David's Lane, High-Street, Shadwell (as far as Regent's Canal), Commercial-road, Burdett-road, Stepney-green, Whitechapel, Algate, the Minories, and Tower-hill.[66]

The strike lasted only a few weeks as the shipowners agreed to the sailors' demands and raised wages.[67]

The fear was that these modern 'bookish' sailors were organising themselves, showing visible strength through the thoroughfares of London, and independently raising funds for their cause. Furthermore, with support emanating from the pubs, lodging houses, and the broader local community, sailortown had become a political arena that had galvanised support for the sailors' wage demands and conditions of employment. This turn of events alarmed the shipowners as this industrial militancy had been adopted by a cross section of seafarers and had been successful. For the social observers, the proletarian sailor came to represent a confused cocktail of anxieties about modern society. In some instances he was purported to exhibit the worst physical and moral traits of the degenerate urban slum dweller, while on other occasions he was denounced as evolving into an organised militant worker. Either way, he had cast off his benign maritime traditions and identity and now had more in common with his urban proletarian counterparts. This was the proletarian sailor, a man of urban identity who took to the streets rather than the sea to wield influence in an increasingly mass democratic society. These anxieties about encroaching modernity in the Victorian city and the confused evaluation of the sailor's character were also clearly present when social commentators extended their analysis to the portrayal of women on Ratcliffe Highway.

The cultural reconstruction of the women on Ratcliffe Highway: the 'petticoated biped predators'

Chris Willis in her study on slum journalism and contemporary Victorian fiction has argued that working-class slum women were perceived 'as a figure of pathos and a threat, a virtuous victim and a vicious virago'.[68]

Indeed, these confused depictions were even more pronounced on Ratcliffe Highway as women were traditionally more publicly visible in sailortowns. Furthermore, as we have seen, women who were sailor companions had been romanticised by the likes of Dibdin in the late eighteenth and early nineteenth centuries. While Dibdin and subsequent commentators implied that 'Moll, Poll, and Susan' were prostitutes, they were cast as wholly feminine, romantic, and devoted to 'their' sailor. Significantly, in nostalgic commentaries about Moll and Poll's conduct, they were only visible on the streets and in the public houses when they were *accompanying* Jack. In essence, they were largely benign and silent characters of Ratcliffe Highway, and only audible when singing a dreamy ballad for Jack while he was away at sea.

While Moll did not meet the standards of the 'deserving poor' woman, she did share some of her qualities as she retained an element of attractiveness and was cast as Jack's homemaker.[69] Even when the harsh realities of prostitution were addressed by contemporaries, the tragic fallen woman who, due to the shame of her depravity, took her own life was romanticised through poems such as Thomas Hood's 'The Bridge of Sighs'. Hood based his poem on a bridge in Old Gravel Lane, just off Ratcliffe Highway, which was coined the 'Bridge of Sighs', as it was a well-known location where women ended their lives by jumping into the Thames. Hood's poem, which was published in 1844, tells the story of a pregnant, unmarried woman who ends her life by throwing herself off the bridge. The image he describes is one of lost innocence, and while in her death, the Thames washes away her sins.

> Make no deep scrutiny
> Into her mutiny
> Rash and undutiful:
> Past all dishonour,
> Death has left on her
> Only the beautiful.[70]

In this romanticised image of the prostitute, despite entering a life of sin, her beauty and femininity had remained intact, and her pitiful end was a result of the wrong moral path having been taken. This imagery of the fallen woman was reinforced by William James Grant who, in the mid-1850s, painted *The Bridge of Sighs*, the title taken from Hood's poem. This grim painting depicted two men carrying a young woman's body from the Thames dressed in a white dress and a colourful shawl. The painting included a stanza from the poem: 'Take her tenderly, Lift her with care, Fashion'd so slenderly, Young and so fair'.[71] This sentimentalised interpretation of the early-to-mid-nineteenth century prostitute was adopted by members of the

Pre-Raphaelite Brotherhood, Rossetti and Hunt, who were keen to explore the darker side of Victorian society.[72]

To the social investigator, the modern woman of Ratcliffe Highway was a coarse imitation of her romanticised predecessors. She was far more visible on the streets and sailors were her quarry, and certainly not to the liking of the commentators. One anonymous writer mused that:

> As a rule, the savages in question are of the she kind. There are, of course, males of the community, but in this instance the natural order of things appears to be reversed. Ordinarily, as regards predatory creatures, it is the male who tracks and brings down the game to share it with the she; but amongst the savages of Ratcliffe Highway it is the female who hunts.[73]

The male observer consistently noted that, unlike their imagined forerunners, these women were loud and usually encountered in all-female groups both inside public houses and on the public thoroughfares. Journalists' descriptions of the physical appearance of the groups of women who congregated on Ratcliffe Highway were in stark contrast to the sympathetic depictions of 'lusty Moll and Poll'. A commentator for the *Chambers's Journal* wrote:

> Oh, such hideous sirens! – flaunting about bare-headed, in dirty hideous white muslin and greasy, cheap blue silk with originally ugly faces horribly seamed with small pox, and disfigured by vice; eyes freshly black from last night's blow, or circled with the stale rainbow of an ancient bruise.[74]

Similarly, the Reverend Edward Thomas, an East End missionary, wrote that young women were 'brazen-faced' and 'vicious to a painful degree', while the oldest included the 'inured harridan of the streets, coarse, and cunning, with countenance as low as vice could make it, and as hard in sin as flint'.[75]

On entering a Ratcliffe Highway pub in the 1870s, James Greenwood described the women he met as 'brutal, blear-eyed, savage-looking, from fifteen to fifty and over, all with a thirst for gin as ferocious as that of a tiger for blood'.[76] Unlike their earlier counterparts, these 'black-eyed Susans' had no affection for their sailors and methodically fleeced them of their money. The modern prostitute, then, was cast as 'bestial', sexually assertive, and streetwise. Greenwood described these women as 'a heartless, cold-blooded set of ogres' who were 'haunting' Ratcliffe Highway

> and lying in wait like beasts of prey for spoony modern Jack ashore, to hocus and pillage him. They are a peculiar breed of females, I believe, that they have lairs in Tiger Bay, and Black Church-Lane, and Palmer's Folly, and other awful places continuous to the Docks. They appear different from the vilest creatures of any other part of London, and they act differently. The grit of vice seems to have scoured their nature bare of all that is womanly, while it gives the keenest edge to cunning and rapacity.[77]

He added that these 'petticoated biped' predators were a dangerous species and the product of the urban abyss.[78] Indeed, correspondents frequently complained that on Ratcliffe Highway, respectable people were plagued by the 'audacity and obscenities of the hordes of prostitutes who congregated in the street'.[79] According to Greenwood, these women were predatory, and he claimed that as he walked through the streets that branched off Ratcliffe Highway:

> It was not quite late enough for the tigresses to make themselves sleek and trim, preparatory to doing on their customary prowl through their familiar hunting ground; and there they sat, lolled, or squatted at their doors, bleareyed and touzle-haired from last night's debauch.[80]

Likewise, Frank Bullen claimed that 'along the shores of our great ports wallowed villainous creatures, ruthless as the dragons of the elder slime, their evil eyes ever a watch for the sailor'.[81] The Ratcliffe Highway women's sexuality was projected not only as a danger to the sailor but also presented as a threat to respectable people and the 'innocent male *flaneur*' chronicler.[82] For these commentators, the brutal condition of the modern city was reversing Darwin's theory of evolution and fostering a degenerate female proletariat that had all the hallmarks of a primaeval and savage race.[83]

Not only had Ratcliffe women become physically degenerate and 'petticoated biped predators' but, in the eyes of social commentators, the police, and magistrates, they had taken on masculine forms. One journalist claimed that sailors were targeted by prostitutes, night and day; 'even at high-noon it is impossible for the most incurious observer to avoid noticing how the sailor is preyed upon by those wretched parasites as they share his pot of porters at the bars, or block his staggering tracks across the pavement'.[84] Greenwood claimed that on entering a pub, he witnessed the women 'demand more gin or rum with the air of a Whitechapel fighting man in female disguise and spill it down their capacious gullets without so much as a bare "thanky"'.[85] The appearance in the press of women embodying masculine traits was particularly evident when they committed violence against men. Ratcliffe Highway, like other large urban areas, was subject to the garrotting panics of the 1860s. However, unlike orthodox accounts of garrotting, female garrotters were purported to prowl Ratcliffe Highway and prey upon unsuspecting sailors.

In one garrotting incident in 1862, Catherine Harrington was charged with the assault and robbery of seaman Morris Hurbur. As the sailor left the United States public house down a narrow alley, a passing policeman

> saw the prisoner, another prostitute, and a man following the sailor. He suspected them and followed. He heard money fall, and when he came up with the party the prisoner had her arm round the neck of the sailor, while the

others were riffling his pockets. The other two saw him approaching, and ran away. He seized the prisoner, and took from her 3s.[86]

Undoubtedly, throughout the attack, Harrington was the violent perpetrator who attacked and restrained Hurbur while her accomplices robbed him. This, of course, deeply unsettled Victorian gender roles and led to uncomfortable moments for the sailor in the court case. For a sailor to be overpowered, garrotted, and robbed by a woman was a clear slight on his masculinity, and throughout the proceedings Hurbur repeatedly informed the court that 'if he had an instrument in his hand he would have killed all three'. Harrington was no stranger to crime and had been convicted on five occasions and been in custody twenty times. In this instance, she was sentenced for six months with hard labour. The only description of Harrington in court was that she was 'a strong and masculine woman'.[87] Harrington was the antithesis of the eighteenth-century feminised 'Moll and Poll' and instead was perceived to have a menacing, masculine presence with the strength and aggression to match. Magistrates, the police, the press, and social investigators shared a common narrative and language about the women who appeared before them in the Thames police court and the streets of sailortown. While Jack had been a casualty of maritime industrialisation, women were symbols of urban decay.[88] They were inevitably defined as physically degenerate, masculine, morally corrupt, dirty, and slovenly at home. These women were also cast as predatory, decadent, living beyond their means, and exploiting a naïve Jack for his hard-earned money.

Communal responses to working-class stereotypes

These representations of working-class people and the areas in which they resided were not a discourse limited to the social commentators and their bourgeois readership. These often social Darwinist accounts of the physical and moral degeneration of the people of Ratcliffe Highway were devoured by the popular sensational press. Newspapers such as the *Reynolds Newspaper* and the *East London Observer* would have been commonplace in working-class homes and public houses in the district. Indeed, there is some evidence that working people were well aware of their depictions in the popular press and the impact that these would have on their general reputation but also, importantly, for how these representations could sway magistrates in courts of law. As we shall see in Chapter 7, the 1830s innovation of the district police court began the gradual process of incorporating working-class people into a formal justice system.[89] It was also a public stage on which the actors could further their cause and a forum where sensational journalists could make a living. Acutely aware that sensational media reports on Ratcliffe Highway could damage their chances of escaping a fine or imprisonment, defendants attempted to impress upon the magistrates their respectability. One reporter complained that the Thames police court was subject to almost 'daily scenes of noise and disorder' owing to 'the daily assemblage of loose women' from the district. He added that some of the defendants 'carried children in their arms for the purposes of exciting sympathy'. However, it was also a performance that Mr Paget, the magistrate, was well accustomed to as he imposed severe sentences of two months' imprisonment on the women with the threat of increasing the term of confinement should they reoffend.[90]

In a response to the concern that the lurid reputation of a particular working-class community would undermine justice, the neighbourhood would sometimes raise subscriptions to appoint lawyers who were intimately known within the district and had previously represented its people. Thomas Wright, the working-class writer, discovered this form of grass-root crowd funding while exploring the working-class communities on the Thames in the 1870s. A local woman, going by the name of 'Sugar Bags', as she worked in a sugar refinery, was accused of murdering 'Fly Palmer', a well-known criminal and police informer. The dispute arose after Sugar Bags had accused Palmer of informing on her husband who had subsequently been imprisoned for a wharf robbery. After Palmer struck Sugar Bags, a fight broke out, ending with the man being fatally stabbed.[91]

Wright had been wandering through the district when he chanced upon meeting 'Shiny Smith', who Wright described as a 'horsey looking gentleman'. The gentleman, known as 'Shiny Smith' as he always 'cut a shine', wore a 'suit of light grey tweed' which was 'tight fitting and sportingly cut', with a colourful scarf, fancy buttons, glittering boots, and a 'curly brimmed hat, stuck on the side of his head'.[92] Wright's first impressions of Smith were that he was a 'Swell-mobsman', but in discussions with the local missionary he was informed that he was 'a regular scribe and irregular lawyer to the doubtful and dangerous classes hereabouts'.[93] Smith appeared to operate in the twilight world of journalism and legal representation and had clearly forged a substantial level of trust in the district. Indeed, the Swell-mobsman attire ensured his appearance was not out of character for the neighbourhood, which further established local confidence in him.[94] Wright also noted that Smith had the ability to mix local dialect and slang with flowery speeches, which were useful skills when communicating with defendants and magistrates in the courts. Smith explained to Wright that learning Shakespeare is 'part of my business', as 'the rank and file of such quarters as this are greatly taken by the "flowery". As long as it's given with a flourish'.[95]

Wright met Smith while he was organising a subscription for Sugar Bags so she could be represented in court. While Wright was familiar with the circulation of subscription lists for funerals in poor neighbourhoods, he had not encountered the idea of using them to defend people in court.[96] Furthermore, when Wright exclaimed surprise that local people would help a murderess, Smith spoke with 'the utmost vehemence and with a sternness of expression'.

> Yes, the woman who murdered Fly Palmer, if you like to put it that way. The Woman whose hands are stained with the life-blood of a fellow creature – who, knowing only that of her, the world will be inclined to regard as a 'female fiend', 'a human tiger' or any other penny-a-liner christened monster; a thing to shudder at and shrink from – perhaps strangle … Still that is how Sugar-Bags *would* appear to outsiders if she went before them undefended; and my object is to see that she does not stand friendless in her hour of need.[97]

Smith's explanation for initiating a subscription vividly conveys the concerns that working people held regarding their depiction in the media. They were clearly alert to the 'penny-a-liner' journalists whose intention was to sensationalise their reporting and paint a grotesque picture of the district and its people. Wright also discovered that the subscription was largely a success and attracted contributions from the poorest sections of the populous. In reviewing the subscription list, Wright noted that written boldly across the top was:

> THE SUGAR BAGS DEFENCE FUND
> NEIGHBOURS, ATTENTION!
> To Be or Not to Be? That Is The Question.
> Shall poor Sugar-bags go undefended?
> Remember! Many Can Help One.
> *The smallest Donation Thankfully received.*[98]

Underneath the heading, there was a large number of signatures, though 'most of them in one handwriting, but attested by the crosses of individuals – as Crockery Jack, a shilling; Big Kate, sixpence; Donkey Smith, a shilling; Dry Land Lawson, sixpence, [and] Mother Badger, a shilling'.[99] In his subscription campaign, Smith had emphasised the importance of collective support – it's a case of 'help one another boys', as he explained to Wright. The initiative was largely a success as sufficient funds were raised for Sugar Bags to be represented and her crime was reduced to manslaughter and punished by a short-term prison sentence.[100]

By the late nineteenth century, criticism of how both journalists and religious missionaries were representing the people in the East End was aired in the local press. Indeed, in 1883 the publication of the sensationalist pamphlet *The Bitter Cry of Outcast London* by Andrew Mearns only heightened the feeling among the working class that they were being 'libelled' by outsiders for their own financial gain. One correspondent, who described himself as 'an old resident of the East of London', complained that the *Bitter Cry* cast those who lived in the East End as 'on the broad road to destruction', whereas, in fact, most of the exaggerated claims 'exist only in the imagination of those fervid writers'. He concluded by pleading that 'abler pens will stop this disparagement of a poor, struggling, yet independent district'.[101]

In 1886 another correspondent noted how residents of the East End were often portrayed as 'people without hope' and that writers described 'thin, white, haggard faces glance furtively at any strangers within the precincts of their neighbourhood'. As we have seen, the poor in the district were cast as strange exotic peoples residing in the extremities of the east, which prompted the writer to quip that he 'didn't think we "Oriental Cockneys" were half so interesting in our horrible conditions'.[102] In a mocking fashion, he went on to explain why outsiders saw them as an alien population:

> We are without hope as, being an uneducated body, such a fine word would not be found in our vocabulary. Our faces are white and haggard through being a species of earthmen, and living beneath the surface. We glance furtively at the strangers, as being thieves, rogues, and vagabonds, & ourselves, we suspect everything and everyone to be of our own standard of merit.[103]

The correspondent was particularly critical of the missionaries who descended upon the East End and attempted to raise funds for their religious colonies. They were 'clerical slanderers' who 'sacrifice truth at the shrine of falsehood, misrepresenting, and so forth, and obtain the lucre which, as ministers of God's Word, are supposed to despise – but do not'.[104]

A more formal body emerged a year later that sought to defend the East End from slanderous assaults on its people and business. The 'East London Defence Alliance' was formed in 1886 'for the purpose of refuting and counteracting the injurious effects of the false statements repeatedly made regarding the East End of London'.[105] The Alliance comprised local business leaders and stall holders, and while the *East London Observer* actively supported the group, they did not make significant inroads into changing the damaging and sensational narratives about the neighbourhood. Indeed, two years later, the East End was engulfed in the Whitechapel murders, and the district's lurid reputation was set for future generations.[106]

Conclusion

When visitors explored London's Ratcliffe Highway, they never failed to note its sense of 'Otherness' from the rest of the city. Their accounts invariably looked seaward to explain the maritime traditions that were inscribed in the working, living, and leisure patterns of the district. For example, Fox Smith noted of Ratcliffe Highway in the early twentieth century that 'you might always know when you have entered the borders of that queer amphibious country which lies as it were between land and sea, even were there no visible signs of actual ships to inform you of it'.[107] It was in these districts of English and foreign transient sailors, boarding houses, and 'low' entertainment venues that 'unconventional' gender roles flourished. However, to fully appreciate Victorian representations of sailortown, we also need to understand their anxieties towards urban modernity that informed their gas-lit wanderings. Through examining the texts of a range of social commentators during the nineteenth century, this chapter has argued that a common narrative emerged which recast the sailor from benign jolly sailor to proletarian Jack and the feminine Moll to the masculine predatory prostitute. Likewise, the portrayal of sailortown was transformed from a socially heterogeneous playground to a place of danger and depravity. In some respects, the writers were echoing the urban anxieties found in other industrial cities. However, sailortown's liminal urban space and relative isolation from civic and religious influence gave Ratcliffe Highway a notoriety that both excited and appalled social commentators.

Notes

1 I. Land, *War, Nationalism and the British Sailor, 1750–1850* (Basingstoke, Palgrave Macmillan, 2009), 21.
2 Land, *War, Nationalism and the British Sailor*, 90.
3 Land, *War, Nationalism and the British Sailor*, 89.
4 Land, *War, Nationalism and the British Sailor*, 78.
5 P. Egan, *Tom & Jerry: Life in London; Or the Day and Night Scenes* (London, John Camden Hotten, 1820, 1868 edn), 320.
6 Land, *War, Nationalism and the British Sailor*, 158.
7 J. Greenwood, *In Strange Company: Being the Experiences of a Roving Correspondent* (London, Henry S. King and Co., 1873), 188.
8 *East London Observer*, 6 August 1859.
9 *East London Observer*, 6 August 1859.
10 *Reynolds Newspaper*, 21 November 1897.
11 F.T. Bullen, *The Men of the Merchant Service* (London, Murray, 1900), 151.
12 Bullen, *The Men of the Merchant Service*, 154, 257.
13 *Daily Telegraph and Courier*, 16 October 1871.
14 Greenwood, *In Strange Company*, 188.
15 *East End Observer*, 17 August 1861.
16 *Reynolds Newspaper*, 21 November 1897.
17 *East London Observer*, 6 August 1859.

18 G. Ginn, 'Answering the "bitter cry": Urban description and social reform in the late Victorian East End', *The London Journal*, 31(2), November 2006, 179–200, 184.
19 Land, *War, Nationalism and the British Sailor*, 158.
20 For the rise of Victorian ideas about 'civilisation', see J. Carter Wood, *Violence and Crime in Nineteenth Century England: The Shadow of Our Refinement* (London, Routledge, 2004).
21 B. Beaven and J. Griffiths, 'Creating the exemplary citizen: The changing notion of citizenship in Britain 1870–1939', *Contemporary British History*, 22(2), 2008, 203–25.
22 H. Mayhew, *London Labour and the London Poor*, Vol IV (London, Griffin, Bohn & Co., 1862), 417.
23 Mayhew, *London Labour*, 417.
24 G.R. Sims, *Living London*, Vol 3 (London, Cassell and Co., 1902), 155.
25 J. London, *The People of the Abyss* (New York, Grosset & Dunlap, 1903), 77.
26 Bullen, *The Men of the Merchant Service*, 154, 257.
27 C. Booth, *Life and Labour of the People of London*, Vol VII (London, Macmillan, 1896), 359.
28 Bullen, *The Men of the Merchant Service*, 277.
29 Bullen, *The Men of the Merchant Service*, 154, 257.
30 Booth, *Life and Labour of the People of London*, 361.
31 Booth, *Life and Labour of the People of London*, 362.
32 *East London Observer*, 13 August 1859.
33 *Reynolds Newspaper*, 21 November 1897.
34 C. McKee, *Sober Men and True: Sailor Lives in the Royal Navy 1900–1945* (London, Harvard University Press, 2002), 103.
35 Quoted in T. Chamberlain, 'Stokers – the lowest of the low? A social history of Royal Navy stokers, 1850–1950' (unpublished PhD thesis, University of Exeter, 2013), 71.
36 Bullen, *The Men of the Merchant Service*, 317–18.
37 Bullen, *The Men of the Merchant Service*, 323.
38 Bullen, *The Men of the Merchant Service*, 324.
39 *Reynolds Newspaper*, 21 November 1897.
40 *East London Observer*, 24 April 1869.
41 *East London Observer*, 24 April 1869.
42 *Reynolds Newspaper*, 21 November 1897.
43 Bullen, *The Men of the Merchant Service*, 278.
44 *The Seaman*, No. 4, Vol 1, February 1908, 3.
45 J. Eaton and C. Gill, *The Trade Union Directory* (London, Pluto Press, 1981), 50–4.
46 See Modern Record Centre (MRC), University of Warwick, MSS.175/3/14/1–2, 1913. National Union of Seamen Archive: 'The Chinese invasion of Great Britain'. The document sets out the physical and moral flaws in Chinese sailors and claims they are cheaper to employ as they do not require as much food and supplies.

47 'The Chinese invasion of Great Britain', 3.
48 'The Chinese invasion of Great Britain', 15.
49 'The Chinese invasion of Great Britain', 4.
50 Land, *War, Nationalism and the British Sailor*, 90.
51 Booth, *Life and Labour of the People of London*, 359.
52 Booth, *Life and Labour of the People of London*, 359.
53 Booth, *Life and Labour of the People of London*, 359.
54 Booth, *Life and Labour of the People of London*, 360.
55 The drive towards working-class self-improvement was widespread during this period; see B. Beaven, *Leisure, Citizenship and Working-Class Men, 1850–1945* (Manchester, Manchester University Press, 2005), 66–72.
56 *East London Observer*, 6 August 1859.
57 *East London Observer*, 17 August 1861.
58 See, for example, *Household Words*, 5 April 1851, 36; *Morning Post*, 6 January 1899.
59 Bullen, *The Men of the Merchant Service*, 278.
60 *Household Words*, 5 April 1851, 36.
61 *Good Words*, December 1873, 246.
62 *East London Observer*, 24 April 1869.
63 *London Evening Standard*, 12 August 1881.
64 *London Evening Standard*, 12 August 1881.
65 *East London Observer*, 13 August 1881.
66 *London Evening Standard*, 12 August 1881.
67 *Pall Mall Gazette*, 18 August 1881.
68 Willis, C. 'From voyeurism to feminism: Victorian and Edwardian London's streetfighting slum viragoes', *Victorian Review*, 29(1), 2003, 70–86.
69 A. Mayne, *The Imagined Slum: Newspaper Representation in Three Cities 1870–1914* (Leicester, Leicester University Press, 1993), 191.
70 T. Hood, 'The Bridge of Sighs', in A. Quiller-Couch (ed.), *The Oxford Book of English Verse: 1250–1900* (Oxford, Clarendon Press, 1900, 1912 edn), poem 654, 759.
71 The Mass Gallery, William James Grant, 'The Bridge of Sighs', www.maasgallery.co.uk/component/joomgallery/british-pictures-2014/48-william-james-grant-1829-1866-1011, accessed 2 March 2022.
72 Alternatively, Watts Phillips described the Bridge as a 'dismal' place with 'inky' and 'sluggish waters'. See W. Phillips, *The Wild Tribes of London* (London, Ward and Lock, 1855), 22. For a broader perspective on Victorian art and suicide, see B.E. Maidment, *Reading Popular Prints, 1790–1870* (Manchester, Manchester University Press, 1996), Chapter 5.
73 Anon, *Wonderful London: Its Lights and Shadows of Humour and Sadness* (London, Tinsley Bros, 1878), 336.
74 *Chambers's Journal*, 24 April 1869, 258.
75 E.W. Thomas, *Twenty-Five Years' Labour among the Friendless and Fallen* (London, Shaw & Co., 1879), 36.
76 *Daily Telegraph and Courier*, 16 October 1871; Greenwood, *In Strange Company*.

77 *Daily Telegraph and Courier*, 16 October 1871.
78 *Daily Telegraph and Courier*, 16 October 1871.
79 *The Globe*, 18 May 1855.
80 Greenwood, *In Strange Company*, 230.
81 F. Bullen, *The Palace of Poor Jack* (London, James Nesbit and Co., 1900), 17.
82 Willis, 'From voyeurism to feminism', 80.
83 For other commentators who shared similar views, see B. Beaven, *Visions of Empire: Patriotism, Popular Culture and the City, 1870–1939* (Manchester, Manchester University Press, 2012), 44–5.
84 *Chambers's Journal*, 24 April 1869, 258.
85 Greenwood, *In Strange Company*, 189.
86 *East London Observer*, 20 December 1862.
87 *East London Observer*, 20 December 1862.
88 Mayne, *The Imagined Slum*, 191.
89 J. Davis, 'A poor man's system of justice: The London police courts in the second half of the nineteenth century', *Historical Journal*, 27(2), June 1984, 309–35
90 *The Sun*, 7 May 1867.
91 T. Wright, *The Great Army of London Poor: Sketches of Life and Character in a Thames-Side District* (London, Charles H. Kelly, 1875, 1890 edn), 76.
92 Wright, *The Great Army of London Poor*, 69.
93 Wright, *The Great Army of London Poor*, 76.
94 A Swell-mobsman was a description of a well-dressed swindler and thief. See P. Quennell (ed.), *H. Mayhew and Others: The London Underworld in the Victorian Period* (New York, Dover Publications, 2012), 204.
95 Wright, *The Great Army of London Poor*, 71. The tactical deployment of Shakespeare in working-class language, writing, and politics was employed widely. See A. Murphy, 'The rise of the working class Shakespeare reader', in P. Bickley and J. Stephens (eds), *Shakespeare, Education and Pedagogy: Representations, Interactions and Adaptations* (London, Routledge, 2023), 23–31; K. Prince, 'Shakespeare in the early working-class press', in A. Krishnamurthy (ed.), *The Working-Class Intellectual in Eighteenth and Nineteenth-Century Britain* (Farnham, Ashgate, 2009), 129–42.
96 Wright, *The Great Army of London Poor*, 73.
97 Wright, *The Great Army of London Poor*, 72 (Wright's italics).
98 Wright, *The Great Army of London Poor*, 83.
99 Wright, *The Great Army of London Poor*, 69.
100 Wright, *The Great Army of London Poor*, 85.
101 *East End Observer*, 28 February 1885.
102 *East London Observer*, 2 October 1886.
103 *East London Observer*, 2 October 1886.
104 *East London Observer*, 2 October 1886.
105 *East London Observer*, 20 November 1886.
106 Ginn, 'Answering the "bitter cry"', 189.
107 C. Fox Smith, *Sailor Town Days* (London, Houghton Mifflin, 1923), 6.

4

Leisure in a sailortown

Satan is daily exerting his influence in Ratcliffe Highway.

The Lord Bishop of London, British Parliamentary Papers,
On the Means of Devine Worship in Populous Districts, 1858, 518

From the mid-nineteenth century, Ratcliffe Highway had become infamous as a sailors' international playground. Sometimes dubbed the 'sailor bacchanalia', it was a thoroughfare brimming with public houses, singing saloons, and dance rooms that entertained all those who crossed the threshold, with the proviso that they leave 'knives and pistols at the door'.[1] Indeed, contemporaries and historians have often emphasised the dangers that awaited sailors as they entered London's sailortown. Along with the decadent pleasures on offer, Ratcliffe Highway was portrayed as harbouring a dark criminal underworld that systematically preyed upon unsuspecting sailors who had overindulged. The leisure the sailor consumed has been somewhat overshadowed by writers who have cast the Ratcliffe Highway pub, singing saloon, and the thoroughfare itself as sites of violent robbery, kidnap, or even murder. This chapter will argue that leisure institutions provided important contact zones that fostered an urban–maritime culture that enabled seafarers of differing subaltern ethnicities to engage and negotiate their way through sailortown. Thus, they were more than spaces where sailors simply became ensnared with prostitutes, bullies, and crimps, as they were also sites where subaltern cultures were appropriated, reproduced, and synthesised.

As we have seen, the 'horrors' of the East End were sensationally exposed by journalists from the mid-nineteenth century. Writers such as George Sims and Andrew Mearns both exaggerated their observations and were often vague about the precise geographical locations that informed their narratives. The whole of the East End was written off as a sink of iniquity, a slander that drew the wroth of the *East London Observer*, which complained that 'it has become fashion to regard the East End as a barbaric waste, filled with crime, destitution and ignorance'.[2] However, while 'crime, destitution and ignorance' formed part of the narrative of Ratcliffe Highway, social observers of this district particularly focused on the depravity and danger of sailor leisure. These accounts were especially prominent in religious missionary pamphlets, and several organisations had successfully 'colonised' former public houses and music halls that had formerly been 'notorious dens of iniquity'.[3] Missionaries contended that indulgences in depraved leisure activities and violent crime were two sides of the same coin on Ratcliffe Highway. It was a narrative that was hardwired into the popular culture of the Highway, well into the twentieth century. For example, as late as the 1940s, the religious missionary newspaper the *East End Star* made wild claims that the Old Mahogany Bar 'had been built in a way that made violent robbery easy'. On entering the former music hall, the author alleged that there was 'a trap in the hall floor down to a sinister dungeon. Here among the barrels many a doped seaman or unsuspecting toff must have been laid while his limp body was stripped to the skin'. A less fevered imagination may have interpreted this structure as a standard pub trap door that gave access to the beer cellar, but the more lurid explanation fitted the newspaper's series of sensational articles on 'uncovering sailortown'.[4]

These missionaries portrayed sailors as naïve victims of professional criminal gangs who would lie in wait for them as they stepped ashore in sailortown. For example, Charles Lowder, an East End missionary, claimed that English sailors hailed from simple villages, were pure and innocent when they set out, and were naïve of the urban landscape. On returning to shore, however, 'they are seized upon by harpies, liers in the wait of blood, who rob them of all their hard-earned gains, and worse than rob them, spiritually murder them'.[5] Indeed, once aboard their ship, their profession dictated that sailors were separated from modern urban life. The Reverend Thomas Beames declared that 'sailors are proverbially ignorant of the world; they live for years together at sea; and having few opportunities of getting ashore, they never go inland'. He believed this isolation led them to being 'fleeced' by the crimps and 'harpies' of sailortown.[6] Similarly, one observer noted that 'poor Jack is thought fair game by most of the prowlers in Ratcliffe Highway', while James Ritchie stated that 'Jack is prone to grog and dancing' and is met at every turn by 'wild-eyed women' who are 'all equally resolved on victimising poor Jack'.[7] Perhaps, though, Charles Dickens's *Household Words* captured the social observers' belief that sailors' leisure pursuits and urban naivety exposed their vulnerability ashore:

> It is my personal opinion that Jack is robbed – that he is seduced into extravagance, hoodwinked into spendthrift and dissolute habits ... he is robbed by tavern keepers, the crimps, and the boarding masters. He is robbed by his associates, robbed in business, robbed in amusement. 'Jack' is fair game to everyone.[8]

'Jack's amusements' were of particular interest to both journalists and philanthropists as lurid tales of drinking and vice proved good copy for the sensational press, while philanthropists saw rational recreation and teetotalism as tools to reform the most offensive elements of working-class culture.[9] However, recently, historians have argued that Victorian criticism of working-class leisure was more nuanced than previously thought. Geoff Ginn has shown that some social observers and philanthropists rejected these popular lurid stories of depraved leisure and began constructing a different narrative that played down the sensational elements of East End leisure. Thus, Samuel Barnett and Walter Besant attempted to foster social reconciliation between the people, the traders of the East End, and social reformers by emphasising the 'dullness and monotony' of people's lives rather than its depravity (see Figure 4.1). As Ginn convincingly argues, this also provided the opportunity for both men to claim that the working class could be culturally elevated through benevolent schemes such as the People's Palace.[10] Similar

Figure 4.1 Ratcliffe Highway, early 1900s (the sense that Ratcliffe Highway was now 'dull' was captured in this photograph and accompanying caption: 'notorious early in the last century, owing to a series of murders and to various acts of lawlessness committed by Jack ashore: but now the street is chiefly remarkable for the shops and dealers in wild beasts, birds, etc.')
(author's own collection)

well-meaning social explorers on Ratcliffe Highway judged sailor leisure as less depraved and dangerous, and rather more monotonous and insipid.

The Reverend Harry Jones, who had great sympathy with the people of Ratcliffe Highway, implied that the 'dreary' environment of the Highway drove people into uninspiring amusements. He claimed it was difficult to 'escape from the monotony of the grimness which broods over the miles upon miles of dull straight streets'. This 'dull' environment was matched by a 'monotonous toil, relieved by slovenly idleness and drink'.[11] Similarly, the journalist Joseph Parkinson noted that in venturing down Ratcliffe Highway for several hours, 'we had ample opportunities of estimating the entertainments provided for Jack [and] we failed to find a single oasis in the barren desert of unattractive dullness'.[12]

According to Victorian contemporary criticism of sailors' leisure, the seafarer was either a spendthrift whose predilections led him to destitution and depravity or his amusements lacked intellectual stimulation and were ultimately 'dull' and monotonous. Both analyses regarded 'poor Jack' as a helpless, child-like actor who required external supervision through stricter entertainment and licensing laws or philanthropic mediation via rational recreation schemes.[13] However, such a binary analysis poses problems for the historian attempting to assess the character of sailor leisure. With so few sources available, historians inevitably turn to the eyewitness accounts of bourgeois chroniclers who were engaging with an alien culture and environment. The men and women who were part of this subaltern culture also recognised the intrusion into their leisure and adapted their behaviour accordingly. For example, during the 1880s, George Sims recalled that he received a distinctly frosty reception from locals both in sailor leisure venues and outside in the surrounding streets. On visiting the East London Music Hall on Ratcliffe Highway, Sims noted that:

> all the vast audience was purely local. Our advent, through our attire was a special get-up for the occasion, attracted instant attention, and the cry of 'Hottentots' went round. 'Hottentots' is the playful way in this district of designating a stranger, that is to say, a stranger from the West.[14]

The view that there was a stranger from the west within their midst, then, was clearly formed based on class identity. Sims's dress and behaviour signalled to the audience that he was an outsider, unfamiliar with the informal protocols of the working-class music hall. On another occasion, Sims stumbled across 'al fresco gambling' where some 'hundreds of lads' were watching a game of cards 'presided over by a villainous-looking Jew'. On his approach, he witnessed a series of scouts signalling to the men to cease playing, and, as Sims came closer, the crowd 'dispersed as if by magic, and the gentleman with the board produced from his pocket a quantity of cough drops and flung them upon the board, bawling aloud "Six a penny!"' After this incident, Sims reported that as he and his associates left the scene, they were followed and watched for over a hundred yards by some of the gambling participants.[15]

In stepping into this alien world, the sensational journalist and philanthropic social reformer would often see danger and criminality around every corner. Undoubtedly, between 1850 and 1900, cases in the Thames police courts and the Old Bailey reveal that sailors were robbed, violently assaulted, and even murdered. However, as Chapter 7 argues, serious violent crime on Ratcliffe Highway was seldom committed. Nevertheless, according to social explorers, the leisure spaces were at the fulcrum of low-level criminality and accommodated 'dens' where thieves would meet and were places where crimes were committed. This narrative also aligns with the 'poor Jack' stereotype, where the public house provided cover for a criminal fraternity to prey upon the naïve seaman. This was certainly the view of Admiral Hope, who gave evidence to the *Select Committee on Public Houses* in 1853. Admiral Hope was the Chairman of the Board of Directors of the Sailors' Home on Ratcliffe Highway and had unsuccessfully petitioned the authorities to prevent the licensing of new public houses in the vicinity of the Sailors' Home. Admiral Hope stated that the public houses had considerably increased after the establishment of the Sailors' Home and they were being run in a disorderly manner, and that 'loose characters' had taken possession of the streets. Furthermore, he added that 'there are rooms for dancing, in short all the attractions enticing sailors out of the Sailors' Home, and the consequence is that they are plundered'.[16] When the Committee asked him for evidence of 'riot, noise and fighting', Admiral Hope admitted he had not entered any of the pubs or dancing rooms but maintained that the people in the streets were in a state of intoxication.[17] Not satisfied with this response, the Committee pressed Admiral Hope further:

> [Committee] And you have real evidence of the fact, that some persons belonging to the Sailor's Home have been enticed into the public-houses, made drunk, and plundered? [Hope] – I cannot say that we could put our hands on the men, because they are gone. The Home is a house of passage; they are only with us for a short space of time ... I have no complaint of a certain man who has been plundered.[18]

Having never entered the public houses or dancing rooms or identified one plundered sailor, Hope offered little evidence to support his claims. The Committee next called James Steed, who was the Superintendent of the H Division in the Metropolitan Police. Asked whether there was disorder in the streets around the Sailors' Home, Steed replied that while there was a great number of sailors and girls congregating there, 'they were perfectly orderly' and so he had no power to remove them. He was then questioned on the riotous and disorderly conduct within public houses. Steed revealed that within the half a mile radius of the Ratcliffe Highway district, there were over 500 public houses or beer shops and only one landlord in the last year had been summoned for having riotous and disorderly persons in his house, and he was cautioned with a fine as it was his first offence. He also stated that of these 500 pubs, only thirty-five patrons had been convicted for creating a disturbance or wilful damage over the last six months. Within the vicinity of the Sailors' Home, Steed reported that there had been no convictions for disorderly behaviour over the same period.[19] He was unsurprised at the numerous public houses in the district as the 'neighbourhood is supported entirely by sailors and the girls; the houses have existed there, and they have been allowed to go on this way for years'.[20] Finally, the Committee questioned Steed about whether the public houses and dancing rooms were places of danger in which sailors were plundered and ill-used. Steed firmly believed that most robberies took place in sailor lodging houses rather than pubs, though the Committee continued to push him further:

> [Committee] you have never heard any report in the neighbourhood of people plundered in certain houses? [Steed] – Certainly not; some of those dancing rooms, as far as they are concerned, are conducted well; there are some well conducted men holding those licences, who are in the room themselves, and will not allow the least impropriety to be carried on. I have visited them, and I know it. [Committee] You do not know anything bad of this kind against any other sort of houses? [Steed] – No.[21]

Steed's experience of engaging with sailors' leisure venues in the district did not accord with Admiral Hope's contention that the public houses had a dangerous impact upon sailors' welfare. Throughout the next two decades, anxieties about sailors' entertainment continued to be aired in the sensational press; there was, however, little evidence that criminality in music halls or dancing rooms was increasing. In 1866 Richard Reason, a London police officer, and Sir Richard Mayne, the Chief Commissioner of the Metropolitan Police, were questioned by the *Select Committee on Theatrical Licences and Regulations*. Significantly, both witnesses reached similar conclusions to Steed's assessments of sailor behaviour made ten years previously. Reason stated that Ratcliffe Highway's public houses and dancing rooms did not cause the police any problems, while the sailors' favoured music halls were of a respectable character.[22] Mayne, in his overall assessment of the clientele and leisure venues of Ratcliffe Highway, reported that:

> The women there are, perhaps without exception, women of the town, but their behaviour is perfectly decorous. I have been struck, too, in those houses

where foreign sailors and foreign women are found, by noticing that their conduct is much better than that of our own women, and much more decorous externally both with regard dress and manner.[23]

The 1850s and 1860s represented the height of bourgeois anxiety about popular leisure patterns, drinking, and prostitution in Britain.[24] Given London's sailortown reputation, Ratcliffe Highway ought to have been awash with plundered sailors, and riotous and disorderly behaviour. However, the police evidence indicates that sailors' leisure venues did not cause any more problems for the authorities than working-class amusements in other parts of the metropolis. The belief that 'Satan was daily exerting his influence in Ratcliffe Highway' and exploiting naïve 'poor Jack' seems wide of the mark.[25] Most sailors were well equipped to navigate their way unharmed through the hundreds of public houses and dancing rooms on Ratcliffe Highway.

Despite the problems associated with the sensational accounts of how Jack was exploited by a criminal fraternity, they have remained powerful in shaping the history of the seafarer's leisure experience. For example, Graeme Milne has recently argued that in exploring sailors' leisure ashore, 'the seafarer's wages sat at the heart of his entanglement with sailortown, and the waterfront streets were the front line in the battle to separate a seaman from his lump sum in cash'.[26] Thus, in this interpretation, sailors experienced an 'entanglement' with leisure that, by the mid-nineteenth century, had become a 'battle' between sailors and those supplying leisure in sailortown. Milne's research is particularly influenced by Stan Hugill's invaluable history-cum-memoir on international sailortown. Hugill was one of the few seafarers to record his memories of the last vestiges of the age of sail in the twentieth century.[27] However, for seafaring in the nineteenth and early twentieth centuries, Hugill draws extensively from Fox Smith and other writers who tend to stereotype the dangers that would enmesh sailors as they stepped ashore.[28] This rather conflictual view of how sailors engaged with leisure ashore tends to assume many of the stereotypical characteristics found in the social observers' accounts of 'poor Jack'. It leaves little room for sailors to deploy a cultural capital that was accumulated in both their urban working-class experiences and their international seafaring lives. It is argued here that this cultural capital enabled sailors to negotiate their leisure encounters within the urban landscape far more successfully than the contemporary social observers and recent historiography would have us believe. The next section will investigate the character and nature of sailor leisure and explore how the maritime nature of sailor amusement provided key reference points that enabled an international sailortown to flourish.

Pleasure seeking in sailortown: the most popular institutions

At the height of its infamy between the 1850s and the 1860s, Ratcliffe Highway's busy thoroughfare of public houses, dancing rooms, beer shops, and brothels, interspersed with shops, housing, and sailor boarding houses, made for a striking leisurescape. Sailors could also wander off down the many side streets of the Highway to be greeted by a plethora of entertainment that, according to observers, became 'lower' in decency the further into the murky 'labyrinth' they roamed. The district was dominated by a handful of larger public houses such as the Rose and Crown, the Jolly Sailor, the Prussian Eagle, the Hoop and Grapes, and Paddy's Goose. These public houses had large so-called green rooms for dancing and entertainment. The larger establishments held dancing and entertainment licences and were recognised as the most popular venues on Ratcliffe Highway. The Reverend Edward Thomas explained that the singing or dance halls were 'erected for the most part in the rear of flaming gin-palaces' and that Ratcliffe Highway was 'thickly studded with these resorts'.[29] Patrons would enter a saloon bar and make their way to the 'green room' annex, which usually comprised a long, well-lit chamber with a stage at the back and tables scattered around the room where the audience would eat and drink. Opposite the stage stood a bar, which normally was 'replete with every kind of drink'.[30] There was no entrance fee, though performers would mingle among the audience with a hat asking for contributions after their act.[31] They resembled the traditional singing saloons of the 1840s and 1850s, but rather than evolve into the more formalised music halls, these institutions continued to offer a hybrid of drinking and entertainment through to the late nineteenth century.

A key reason for the longevity of the 'green room' was that the district's two formal music halls endured a rather intermittent existence, closing down and reopening and eventually going out of business by the turn of the twentieth century. They also did not occupy a central position in the Highway as they were both situated on streets leading from the thoroughfare. Moreover, the green room annex proved a very flexible venue as it could host music hall-like artistic performances, comedy, or music, or alternatively the tables were cleared to create a dancing room. As Annie Besant noted in 1886, the nearest music hall to Ratcliffe Highway at the time was in Whitechapel, and, consequently, 'the public house concert or dance is the highest form of art available' for those living in the Ratcliffe district.[32] However, St George's in the East's two music halls focused their businesses on attracting sailors. The East London Music Hall was situated opposite New Gravel Lane, while the Old Wilton's Music Hall was in Grace Alley, which was located between Ratcliffe Highway and Cable Street. The music halls charged an entrance fee and had a more theatre-like construction as, for example, Wilton's Music Hall proprietor had built 'a special gallery for sailors and their women'.[33] Nevertheless, it was not unknown for smaller public houses without the appropriate licences, such as the Prince Regent, to entertain sailors in a similar manner.[34] Unless there was riotous behaviour, the police often turned a blind eye to these breaches of licensing laws. Mayne, the Chief Commissioner of the Metropolitan Police, reported that:

> many of those places, especially in the sailors' part of town, they dance, and I am not aware of any evil arising from that; the women are not very correctly dressed, but I think it would be over-squeamish, looking at the class of persons who frequent those places, to find fault with them.[35]

The entertainment in these smaller venues was noted by Annie Besant who observed that when a ship comes in, 'the concerts will be started in the public-houses', and they would be advertised by 'a card in the window'. These concerts were held at the back or over public houses and appeared to be 'free-and-easys', where a 'chairman presides, and generally has two or three friends ready to "oblige with a song"'. Thus, while the larger public houses with separate 'green rooms' were the most well-known establishments, the smaller venues would often stage more flexible entertainment that could quickly respond to an influx of sailors ashore.[36] It was this agility that the traditional music hall was not able to consistently compete with and it explains the longevity of the green rooms and the singing saloons on Ratcliffe Highway.

Venturing inside: maritime material culture in leisure venues

Those visiting Ratcliffe Highway's public houses and singing and dancing saloons for the first time were struck by the maritime influence that was both characterised by the entertainment and embedded into the material culture that adorned the entertainment venues. Reverend Edward Thomas noted that in the East End of London in the neighbourhood of the docks, the public houses 'are arranged to suit the peculiarities of their frequenters, namely, sailors, harlots, and crimps'.[37] Even journalists and philanthropists who were accustomed to the regular East End amusements remarked how they had unexpectedly stepped into a maritime-immersed world of entertainment. The Reverend Thomas Beames, no stranger to the 'darker' side of London life, noted that many of the pubs and dancing saloons were decorated to entice seafarers. He noticed that one dram shop had a mural of 'sailors dancing the horn-pipes – sailors carousing with their sweethearts; a sailor with a huge punchbowl ... crammed with guineas and labelled "prize money", which he was supposed have brought home to his "Molly"'.[38] In one dancing room, Beames described 'the walls of which are decorated with nautical scenes very fairly painted: in one compartment is a shipwreck in another, a vessel on her beam ends; in another, a vessel in full sail – perhaps a man of war'.[39] Thomas noted that most of the entertainment venues had seafaring signs and once inside, they were 'brilliantly decorated' with ships and shipping.[40] Watts Phillips, who had toured most of the larger public houses on Ratcliffe Highway, noted that the décor depicted similar maritime themes. Examples included 'the Parting', where the young lady weeps on the shore waving 'a good sized tablecloth' to a distant ship, or the 'Return Home', where she welcomes her sailor who has returned with a 'money-bag of a dimension that would make even the heart of a successful gold digger grow sick with envy'. He noted that the 'Ship on Fire' and 'The Storm', where a lonely sailor clings for his life to mast in the sea, were endlessly reproduced on the walls of Ratcliffe Highway taverns. Other popular murals, though less numerous, adopted a naval theme and included the Nile, Trafalgar, and Copenhagen.[41] The majority of the murals that adorned these public houses, then, appealed to a sailor's sentimentality and reminded him and his loved ones of the dangers he faced at sea. However, the recurring image of the 'return', depicted prominently in public houses, spelled out the potential rewards a sea voyage could offer and was an unsubtle prompt to sailors of where they could spend their money.

Significantly, even towards the late nineteenth century, entrepreneurs of public houses or music halls did not adopt imperial names; nor did they adopt an aggressive imperial agenda in their décor, which was so common in other urban areas.[42] Crucially, in the world's largest merchant port, entertainment venues adopted a maritime identity that was universally known throughout different cultures and nations. It was a cultural identity that would provide a frame of reference for sailors and those who worked in ports and, unlike imperial imagery, would cross nations, boundaries, and cultures. For entrepreneurs who were keen on attracting a regular and wide custom base, it was commercially astute to underplay the British Empire. Indeed, some foreign sailors found Ratcliffe Highway a place of liberty compared to their life at home. In the 1850s, one sailor of colour told the journalist Phillips 'of his love of England and hatred of New York' as there was no racial segregation in the leisure venues of Ratcliffe Highway.[43] Certainly, during the late eighteenth century to the first half of the nineteenth century, the Wapping and Ratcliffe Highway dancing rooms were populated with both men and women of colour. In his semi-biographical novel published in the 1820s, Pierce Egan wrote that in Ratcliffe Highway pubs 'all was *happiness* – everybody free and easy, and freedom of expression allowed to the very echo'. He described his fellow dancers as a 'motley' group of 'lascars, blacks, jack tars, coal heavers, dustmen, women of colour, old and young, and a sprinkling of the remnants of once fine girls' who were 'all *jigging* together'.[44]

However, ports were nodes of significant cultural exchange, and there is evidence that American racial segregation, along with the growing influence of social Darwinism in British society, began impacting the leisure institutions on the Highway.[45] In 1859 one journalist expressed his surprise that one pub on Ratcliffe Highway was '"used" exclusively by "coloured people"' as 'no white man will enter it'.[46] The reporter concluded that when sailors from all nationalities undertook work on an American ship, they became 'imbued with the national prejudice to an ineradicable degree'. Thus, while these racially exclusive public houses remained the minority on the Highway, racism within some quarters of the sailor population was becoming more pronounced as the nineteenth century progressed.

Clearly, maritime images and themes that adorned the public houses and green rooms on Ratcliffe Highway proved to be an appealing environment for the international sailor population. A key attraction for sailors within these institutions was the dance rooms that were annexed to the sides of the large public houses.[47] On entering Ratcliffe Highway from the direction of the tower, the first dance room a sailor would encounter was the Rose and Crown, which stood opposite Ship Alley. This public house in the 1870s and 1880s had a reputation for 'vigorous dancing', performed by women in a type of 'cancan' costume. Although it was known locally as the 'Spanish House', due to its Spanish landlord Pedro Femenia, the pub was an eclectic mix of cultures and people.[48] One visitor noted that although the lady dancers adopted the continental practice of smoking paper cigarettes while they waltzed, 'they were unmistakably Ratcliffe Highway birth and breed'. The public house had acquired a reputation for staging entertainment that was 'a little bit spicey' and was a place where women, who wore 'low-necked dresses' and 'short skirts', sought sailors to meet.[49]

However, in 1896 Femenia took exception to the claim by two Methodist preachers that the Rose and Crown housed criminal gangs who systematically robbed and assaulted sailors, an accusation that led to a prolonged court case. After losing his licence, Femenia sued the Reverends Peter Thompson and John Howard for libel. The ensuing court case shone a light on the Rose and Crown's patrons and a flavour of the entertainment that was on offer. The range of witnesses called suggests that this public house was popular with sailors but also the local men and women in the area. Witnesses included one foreign and two English sailors, and four labouring men, three of which worked in the docks. Sarah Turner and Mary Kerr, former prostitutes, both confirmed that it was a well-known place where 'us girls used to go to the Rose and Crown to find sailors'. The women themselves, they noted, were mainly English, Scottish, Dutch, and German.[50] In defending the public house's reputation, Mr Candy QC observed that women in the neighbourhood 'were prepared temporarily to attach themselves to sailors while ashore and be kept by the sailors as long as they had any money to spend on them'.[51] Indeed, in giving evidence, Pedro Femenio questioned: 'how could he ask whether the women who frequented his house were prostitutes? Could he have asked them whether they were single? It would have been a most rude question. Nobody in the neighbourhood except "these people", the defendants, had objected to his house'.[52] Thus, the relationships that were fostered between women and sailors blurred the line between sex work and friendship, which complicated the policing of soliciting and morality in these venues.[53] The second accusation, that the public house was a den of violent thieves and crimps, was perhaps even more damaging for the publican. However, despite claims by some of the witnesses that they were robbed in the public house, the allegation that the Rose and Crown was home to a brutal criminal gang seems less certain. Joseph Marrott, a retired police inspector, reported that he 'had never heard a single complaint against the house, and many of the witnesses spoke of the orderly conduct of the house'.[54] Such was the uncertainty regarding the alleged criminality, the jury was unable to come to a verdict after two years, and each side paid their own costs.[55]

Perhaps the most striking feature about the Rose and Crown, or the 'Spanish House', was that its patrons were a truly international crowd with foreign sailors mixing with English sailors and working men and women in the district. Indeed, the cosmopolitan character of the clientele, staff, and entertainment of the Highway's major public houses and dance rooms in the district was consistently noted by social observers. F.W. Robinson, the journalist, chronicled a night-time journey that he and his associates took down Ratcliffe Highway in the 1870s. He visited all the significant entertainment venues and regularly noted the international nature of the pleasure seekers that filled the pubs and dancing rooms. On entering the Jolly Sailor's dance room, he observed an orchestra playing and sailors and women dancing polkas and waltzes 'in a purely extempore fashion'. He noted that the waiters were acting as the masters of ceremonies and that, though it was noisy, it was perfectly orderly. He recalled that 'excited folk of all the nations … came up and shook hands as though they had known us all our lives'.[56] However, the reputation of Ratcliffe Highway had led Robinson to believe that 'grim murder' stalked the district, and it was with some trepidation that he entered the Prussian Eagle in Wellclose Square, which had a fearsome standing among the social explorers and reformers.

The Prussian Eagle was perhaps the institution that was known to be very popular with foreign sailors. Indeed, the alien language, the 'exotic' clothing of the sailors and women, and the 'strange' dancing may have accounted for why the venue was often the most unsettling to the bourgeois social explorers. Sure enough, as Robinson entered the Prussian Eagle, he recalled the warnings not to patronise the pub and was struck by the 'greater number of foreign sailors, and sailors and women of a lower class'. He claimed that there was more drunkenness, blasphemy, 'and general viciousness' there, though he did acknowledge that this may have been due to the later hour. Nevertheless, he continued to describe the clientele as a 'heterogeneous half-mad class' of people who were dangerous and quarrelsome, and yet, throughout his visit, he did not encounter any threatening behaviour or violence.[57] In a similar vein, a social explorer writing under the title of 'gaslight wanderings' began to fear for his life after entering the Prussian Eagle, reading the placard demanding that patrons leave their weapons at the bar. He described a German brass band at one end of a narrow room with tables and seats aligning the walls but was shocked at the array of nations assembled:

> There were French, Spanish, Italian, German, and Dutch seamen; there were Greeks from the Aegean Sea; there were Malays, Lascars, and even the 'heathen Chinese' disguised in European costume, with his pigtail rolled up in a navy cap. There were mariners in fezes and serge capotes; there were Mediterranean dandies, girt with broad crimson scarves, and with massive gold earrings glistening as they twirled about. No wonder it had been found necessary to collect the knives and pistols from the hot-blooded cosmopolitan crowd. A blow is soon given, and with weapons at hand, who can tell where a quarrel might end?[58]

The mixing of European sailors and English women with Malays, Lascars, and the 'heathen Chinese' offended the Victorian sense of orderliness, morality, and decency. On witnessing these scenes, social explorers would immediately render the venue dangerous, both in a physical and moral sense. However, like Robinson, this anonymous explorer could find no cases of actual disorderliness. He admitted that 'while we were present, everything was conducted in the most orderly manner, though the animated impassioned talk in a dozen different languages led one to imagine that a breach of the peace was imminent at any moment'.[59] The subaltern protocols of finding a dancing partner and the 'mysterious' form of dancing also seemed to breach all respectable conventions. Annie Besant noted that within the dance room itself, women were not the wall flowers that society expected. She observed that 'introductions at a Ratcliffe Highway ball are not necessary; the lady selects her partner, pulls him into the middle of the floor, and off they go'.[60] Robinson, Besant, and the anonymous explorer were all surprised at how the sailors and women knew the intricate dances and were disciplined in their dance manoeuvres. The anonymous explorer estimated that there were over 100 dancers and 'each couple made three or four sharp turns, and then came to a pause with a smart stamp and heads thrown back defiantly. Catching the time to a nicety, they would repeat the movement'.[61] Robinson noted that when the music started, 'the majority of the company would be gyrating swiftly and gracefully, some of the foreigners indulging in the most extraordinary *pas seuls* and fancy steps'. These rather complex dances required practice and some prior knowledge, a fact all too painfully borne out when William Smith, an English seaman, stumbled into the Prussian Eagle in 1871. Smith, who on entering the dance room was 'three sheets to the wind', became 'confounded with the mystery and evolutions of the Sahgieder dance … [which] capsized the dancers', and the tables. Smith was eventually escorted from the premises for abusing the staff.[62]

However, such episodes of disruption appear to be rare as Robinson stated that on his visit, the patrons' conduct within the Prussian Eagle was orderly, not in small part due to a woman who seemed to manage the establishment. He noted that: 'One good-looking Irishwoman, very shabbily attired, and with a rough, unkempt head of hair growing all kinds of ways and suspiciously gritty in appearance, seemed to be the ruling spirit of the place, and to be on speaking terms and cheek-slapping terms with the whole community.'[63] He continued to describe her as 'a bold-faced, dark-eyed woman, with the ready wit of her country at her fingers' ends', and she sat with her valuable Maltese dog called Marconi, 'indulging on a running commentary of chaff upon all and everything that came beneath her notice'. As Robinson and his associates left the Prussian Eagle, the woman followed them at some distance down Ship Alley, 'evidently suspicious of our movements or anxious to see in which way our destination lay.'[64] Thus, despite the Prussian Eagle's reputation as an anarchic and violent public house, social explorers failed to find any lawlessness and, conversely, found that it was being run in an orderly fashion by a matriarchal Irish woman. Moreover, like the other institutions on Ratcliffe Highway, they discovered that despite the public house's association with one nationality, the customers were a 'mix of nations'. Indeed, this was the abiding memory of the anonymous explorer who wrote that to step inside the Prussian Eagle 'is absolutely as though one had been transferred, magically, to a casino in the neighbourhood of the docks of Marseilles or Genoa, or to the halls of "Tutti Nazioni" (all nations) on the Marina of Messina'.[65]

These public houses were more important as ethnically diverse plebian contact zones rather than as venues of violence and robbery. The social explorers' surprise that such a heterogeneous group of over 100 men and women were dancing in sync to a range of cosmopolitan music reinforces the notion that these were spaces where an international maritime culture was negotiated, duplicated, and appropriated. While dancing was a popular amusement for sailors ashore, the public houses and music halls also provided a variety of entertainment quite specific to the district.

Audience, performers, and maritime entertainment

Along with dancing, music hall-style acts were staged at the principal public houses on Ratcliffe Highway. The composition of the audience and the type of entertainment on offer particularly interested social explorers as they were keen to assess the moral character of the district. In the 1850s Watts Phillips noted that the audience in the East London Music Hall comprised mainly sailors and women of different generations:

> The men are principally sailors, young and old; boys with the down scarce showing on their chins, yet loud in oath and big with swaggering talk, drinking fierce liquors with women whose vice-hardened faces show strangely beside their own. Able seamen, fine, jolly-looking tars, smoking and drinking too; but deaf to the noise around, they listen intently to the songs. Old men – ancient mariners – with grizzled heads, and whiskers streaked with frost, who smoke lazily and drink deeply.[66]

He also noted there were plenty of sailors of colour who were 'laughing and chattering the loudest in the room'. There seems to have been as many women in the room as sailors, who Phillips categorised as prostitutes mainly due to their visiting a music hall unchaperoned. His opinion was confirmed when he struck up a conversation with a woman who declared that she herself was a prostitute, and that the venue was a good place for business.[67] However, for his research on prostitution in the late 1850s, William Acton visited Ratcliffe Highway entertainment venues and formed a more nuanced opinion on the different characters of women he observed. He noted that in the main auditorium were men, wives, and daughters, while:

> in and out of the passages and bar were passing crowds of well-dressed women, according to East End fashions; some were prostitutes, but many were married women, according to the belief of my informants. This was a curious amalgamation – this elbowing of vice and virtue – constituted a very striking feature, and was to me a novel one.[68]

He speculated that this fluid social mixing was brought about through the 'modern plan' of the public house that incorporated the green room annex to allow a 'mechanic' to watch entertainment with his wife and daughters. However, according to Acton, the darker side of this new structure enabled prostitutes to mix freely with respectable women and 'flaunt' their enjoyment of vice as they were not 'burdened' with domestic ties or children.[69] Acton noted that the green rooms attracted a significant number of women from different backgrounds and cast doubt on the assumption that these venues were primarily masculine spaces. It appears that women often outnumbered the sailors and broke all bourgeois protocols by behaving conspicuously within the public sphere.

As we have seen, some women were licensees for these institutions, while the large crowds of women who gathered in pubs or music halls exhibited a robust and belligerent culture. In the course of his research, Thomas visited several green rooms and found that women outnumbered men on every visit. He noted that the women were 'remarkably well clothed' and prominent and wore 'gowns very low in the neck, and equally limited in length' with fancy shoes and slippers. He disapprovingly noted that there was not 'a bonnet or headdress of any kind' in sight.[70] Women social explorers tended to agree that the women's 'garish' attire ensured that they were the most visible and flamboyant patrons of both the dance and entertainment rooms. For example, while sailors 'spruced themselves up' with 'flashy rings' and 'brand-new silver watch chains', they did not change from their seafaring clothes.[71] In contrast, Annie Besant recalled that the women wore white flounced skirts, velvet jackets, and large feathered hats. She commented that the 'brilliancy of the ladies' dresses was appalling' and she was astonished to see so much finery amid the 'rough crowd and dirt'.[72] Their prominence was not restricted to their clothing but also extended to their conduct within the entertainment venue as the Master of Ceremonies regularly complained about their conduct during performances in the green rooms:

> In all things prominence seemed to rest with the females: they talked and laughed, and called across the room to their acquaintances in spite of singing or conversation; and even the loud and customary raps of a hammer held by an officious master of ceremonies, who combined business with pleasure by smoking a cigar and drinking beer, while vainly attempting to regulate the proceedings, did not result in keeping many of them in order. As the entertainment continued, the audience increased in noisy demonstrativeness, the women laughed and shouted the louder, and the band grew more boisterous still.[73]

In Thomas's account, women were the most prominent sex in venues, as the organisers found them difficult to manage, and they were actively leading the performers into more 'boisterous' entertainment. The clientele of the green rooms and music halls on Ratcliffe Highway, then, were a generational mix of sailors and women who were of differing ethnicities. These entertainment spaces shocked social explorers as they contravened bourgeois Victorian moral codes that deemed that women ought not to behave so conspicuously in public and frowned upon women socialising with men of different ethnicities. Given these assumptions, it is no surprise that the male social explorers often sweepingly categorised the women they watched in these institutions as prostitutes.

Phillips's recollection of his visit to the East End Music Hall noted a strong maritime dimension in the entertainment that was a mixture of sentimental songs and comedy. Dibdin's maritime songs, which had been popular over seventy-five years earlier, were still regularly sung in venues across Ratcliffe Highway. Phillips recalled the first act was Rosina Douglas, a young woman who sang a sentimental ballad that caught Jack's attention as 'they go to the sailor's heart'. He noted that 'the girl sings with feeling, and, for place, well; the rough natures of the men seem softened beneath the charm of her voice, and at the conclusion of her song, a perfect hurricane of applause ensues'.[74] Douglas was followed by a 'prima donna' who sang another sentimental ballad, a comic, a hornpipe dance, and, finally, Douglas returned with another Dibdin song. In total, three out of the five acts had a nautical theme.[75]

Wilton's Music Hall during the 1850s had a similar diet of entertainment that combined sentimental songs with comedy that had nautical themes, including the comic character sailor who performed an eccentric hornpipe dance, which he executed to the 'great delight' of the audience.[76] Some twenty years later, Thomas discovered that this nautically themed entertainment in the green rooms he visited was still going strong. He noted that in one venue, 'it was curious to observe how studiously the sea element was represented throughout the whole of the arrangements; nor was it less conspicuous in the songs and choruses'.[77] Indeed, Thomas's observations provide an insight as to why Ratcliffe Highway venues continued to stage nautically themed entertainment and hint that it was demanded by the lively clientele. He wrote that:

> After a while the first *artiste* (rather a melancholy looking man), apparently of the Jewish persuasion, mounted the platform and sang a somewhat elaborate and lengthy song, having for its burden, 'The ship coming home' and which was continually taken up in the chorus by the company. The interest was centred in the audience, and to it attention was chiefly given.[78]

Similarly, Phillips discovered that such was the familiarity between performer and audience that popular singers were rewarded with pots of beer by patrons. After Madame Bettina Sulvyne, described as a 'prima donna singer', performed a sentimental song to much acclaim, the audience showed their admiration. He noted that 'a hand stretched across the foot-lights – the goblet is received – she raises high the polished pewter, bows gracefully over its glittering surface, and then her face is lost in the foam of its contents'.[79] The intimacy of the venues also allowed appreciative audiences to shower performers with coins while on stage, though less successful acts were pelted with missiles.[80] Annie Besant was told by one performer on Ratcliffe Highway that 'it is wise to be sure that you can hit the taste of your auditors; otherwise you may be hit yourself with a pewter pot, or other sign of disapproval'.[81] On rare occasions, however, the proximity between performers and the audience could also lead to violence and disorder. In one extreme case, Peter Melloy, a comic entertainer, was charged with manslaughter after the death of Thomas Bunn. Bunn, a local English sailor, had returned ashore and had spent the day drinking heavily and getting into disputes with fellow drinkers. He had entered Wilton's Music Hall in a state of intoxication and took exception to Melloy's sentimental ballad 'God bless the honest working man', shouting 'shut up' from the front row. Melloy threw his hat at Bunn but he continued to heckle, at which point the singer jumped from the stage and struck him several times. Melloy then returned to the stage to finish his act. Bunn died a few hours later from what appears to have been a brain haemorrhage. The jury strongly recommended mercy as the blows were given under great provocation, and Melloy was found guilty of manslaughter and confined for two weeks.[82]

While it was extremely unusual for performers to physically engage with the audience, the case shows that music hall or green room audiences were not passive bodies and that encores or heckles could either prolong or shorten acts. Both the audience and the performers were consistently shaping and co-producing the nature and character of the entertainment. Given the intimate structure of these halls, it is perhaps no surprise that visitors to Ratcliffe Highway consistently remarked on the unique and specifically nautical character of the entertainment on offer. Like the very extravagant nautical décor that characterised the venues, maritime themes appear to have pervaded the entertainment of Ratcliffe Highway and provided a cultural marker for both international seafarers and the women of Ratcliffe Highway. The melodrama of the sailor leaving and returning ashore was a trope that continued to find popularity with audiences throughout the nineteenth century. Indeed, the audiences in these venues used the intimacy of these spaces to voice their preferences. Social observer testimonies suggest that the audiences of Ratcliffe Highway engaged with the performers, through 'hissing and cheering' or even missile throwing.[83] The green rooms created an intimate environment, and the close proximity between performer and audience allowed the clientele to shape the entertainment programme, a dynamic that was present in singing saloons of the 1840s and 1850s in Britain.[84] However, unlike in most urban areas of Britain, the intimate structure of the halls allowed this relationship between the acts and the crowd to continue and may explain the predominance of nautical entertainment in this district.

In addition to the pubs, green rooms, and music halls, Ratcliffe Highway also accommodated a popular resident circus. Situated on the outskirts of Ratcliffe Highway, the Royal Circus was housed in a dilapidated, barn-like construction that, by the 1850s, had seen better days. Phillips described a vast whitewashed building with a smoke-blackened ceiling from which 'large cobwebs hang waving slowly in the foul air'. Surrounding the ring were tier upon tier of crudely fashioned benches that became obscured by the 'masses of people who swarm over them'. Phillips and his companions sat on a tier above these benches and critically surveyed the audience. Phillips had concluded that the circus's cheap entrance fee and its ramshackle environment would attract only the lowest characters, and unsurprisingly he depicted a 'sea of villainous faces' with 'scarcely a redeeming point'. According to Phillips, there was a range of ages in both sexes, though there were more women than men, who, he claimed, all exhibited the 'stamp' of 'vice'. Sailors from different nations, he noted, made up most of the male audience, with a strong contingent of African seafarers. Indeed, apart from 'the many children' on the crowded benches, the audience profile appeared to mirror that of the green rooms and music halls.[85]

Circus entertainment during this period often mixed comics and singers with equestrian performances, and the Ratcliffe Circus was no exception.[86] However, like much of the entertainment on offer on the Highway, the circus also included a strong maritime theme. The resident star attraction at the Ratcliffe Circus was Master Halfonso, who dressed 'in sailor's jacket and trowsers that once were white, is leisurely dancing a hornpipe upon the back of a feeble-minded horse, who is as leisurely proceeding round the circle, amidst the admiring plaudits of an audience, numerous if not select'.[87] Phillips estimated that there were over 1,000 people in the audience, and while he was dismissive of the entertainment, this unusual equestrian–nautical fusion seemed to impress the patrons. Halfonso was followed by a prima donna-style singer and a comic, and while Phillips did not allude to the content of these performances, in selecting similar types of acts to the green rooms and music halls, it would follow that there is a strong chance that a nautical element would have featured.

If the green rooms and music halls were certainly the most prominent and garish forms of entertainment on offer on Ratcliffe Highway, the Royal Circus probably represented the cheapest commercial entertainment in the district. However, for those people in the working-class and sailor communities who could not afford the prices of these venues, there was a plethora of informal street entertainment on offer. Social observers consistently noted that in the evening, the Highway was often populated by performers, sailors, and women dancing impromptu in the streets. During the 1850s in Britain, the law enforcers placed greater scrutiny on subaltern street activity as it transgressed many bourgeois civic codes of decency and respectability that were rising in prominence.[88] In 1858 one newspaper correspondent wrote that street disorder had created a 'great moral awakening' and commentators had complained that their 'quiet homes have been invaded by the vocal and instrumental music of travelling trades and professions, and at night by tavern broils, and noisy uproar of the free-and-easy'. That the respectable person is 'jostled' by the rabble and forced to listen to the 'babel of profane tongues in our streets and Highways'.[89] Indeed, in the evenings, Ratcliffe Highway itself became the location for the poorest to amuse themselves.

George Sims surmised that while the green rooms, music halls, and penny gaffs were the principal places of entertainment for the people of the slums, there were even cheaper ways of accessing amusement. He noticed that 'the streets themselves offer to many a variety of entertainments for which there is no charge'. While he added that a fight might attract 'hundreds', there were more artistic performances on offer, such as the boy who played popular tunes down the spout of a coffee pot, which was 'largely patronised'.[90] The grinding poverty of the district did not prevent people from engaging with popular music, even if they were unable to access the dancing rooms. Besant described two women, who had been barred from entering a dance room as they were improperly dressed, dancing 'gaily' outside to the beat of the music.[91] In Ritchie's account of London, he found that the popular songs of the music hall were being replicated on Ratcliffe Highway for free to an appreciative crowd. He recalled encountering an 'old woman' who was singing to a crowd on the street the song 'Saucy Sailor Boy', a popular melodramatic tale about a sailor returning to a lost love.[92] Thus, these street performances often mirrored the character of the entertainment found in the green rooms or music halls and allowed even the poorest in the district to engage with popular culture.

However, bourgeois social explorers were often uncomfortable with subaltern street life and were keen to draw parallels with 'primitive societies'. For example, Annie Besant wrote about Ratcliffe Highway: 'surely in few civilised cities can women be seen in the state of semi-nudity'.[93] On the same tour, her companion claimed that 'two women, for a wager, raced each other around Wellclose Square stark naked and not ashamed while, on another occasion, three men and women were dancing in their window naked in full view of the public'. These descriptions of working-class street nudity were common in sailortown social investigations as it placed their subaltern subjects closer to their colonial counterparts, implicitly paralleling their own research with the glamorised African expeditions.[94]

Conclusion

The violent reputation of the Highway had led social investigators to believe that on entering infamous pubs and music halls, they would witness robbery, assault, and worse. The Ratcliffe Highway pub was often conveyed in the sensational press as a venue for dangerous knife-wielding foreign sailors, prostitutes, crimps, and thieves. However, the social explorers disappointed their readers, as on almost every occasion, they found the venues fairly orderly and even 'respectable' at times.⁹⁵ This corresponds with the evidence heard at Parliament's select committees on public houses and theatrical places of entertainment as the police in the district testified that there were very few incidents of disorderliness. However, the social investigators' accounts do illustrate how Ratcliffe Highway's leisurescape was markedly different to the rest of the metropolis. Almost all the surviving first-hand accounts of the district describe a waterfront community that patronised institutions that had a maritime influence inscribed into their material culture and entertainment. Indeed, the emphasis on all things maritime was an important attraction and a cultural marker for the heterogeneous mix of sailors and women from different nations, and local working-class people who frequented these venues.

Moreover, the genuine cosmopolitan nature of these venues meant that they were more important as ethnically diverse plebian contact zones rather than places of conflict and violence. The social explorers' discovery of 'exotic' dancing, clothing, and the variety of languages they overheard points to a space in which sailors, women, and working-class people in the district were nuanced in their negotiation through the cultural traditions and rituals that were exhibited on Ratcliffe Highway. Furthermore, the behaviour and conduct of this heterogeneous audience at the staged entertainment events also reveals that it was rooted in a wider working-class culture found in urban Britain. The criticisms that music hall entertainment was 'dull' and 'passive' could not have been further from the truth, as social explorers inadvertently recorded many incidents of the audience actively shaping the entertainment programme through encores, hissing, or even missile throwing. Moreover, nor was this combative crowd a bastion of sailor masculinity, as many writers have assumed, but was instead a predominantly female audience who were as unruly as their male counterparts. Thus, the people of Ratcliffe Highway enjoyed themselves in a leisurescape that evolved from the strong sense of an urban–maritime identity found in the district and a wider working-class leisure culture in Britain.

Notes

1 *Metropolitan*, 14 September 1872.
2 Quoted in G. Ginn, 'Answering the "bitter cry": Urban description and social reform in the late Victorian East End', *The London Journal*, 31(2), November 2006, 179–200, 186.
3 *East End Star*, June 1928.
4 *East End Star*, March 1944.
5 M. Trench, *Charles Lowder: A Biography* (London, Kegan Paul, Trench & Co., 1882), 108.

6 T. Beames, *The Rookeries of London: Past, Present and Prospective* (London, Thomas Boswell, 1850, 1970 edn), 100.
7 *Chambers's Journal of Popular Literature, Science and Art*, 24 April, 1869, 258; J.E. Ritchie, *The Nightside of London* (London, William Tweedie, 1857), 74.
8 *Household Words*, 6 December 1851, 258.
9 B. Beaven, *Leisure, Citizenship and Working-Class Men in Britain, 1850–1945* (Manchester, Manchester University Press, 2005), Chapter 1.
10 Ginn, 'Answering the "bitter cry"', 183.
11 H. Jones, *East and West London: Being Notes of Common Life and Pastoral Work in Saint James's Westminster and in Saint George's-in-the-East* (London, Smith, Elder & Co., 1875), 290, 274.
12 *Daily News*, 31 August 1864.
13 For attempts to implement rational recreation in seaman homes, see Chapter 5.
14 G. Sims, *How the Poor Live and Horrible London* (London: Chatto & Windus, 1889), 84.
15 Sims, *How the Poor Live*, 84.
16 British Parliamentary Papers (hereafter BPP), *Select Committee on Public Houses* 1853, 493.
17 BPP, *Select Committee on Public Houses*, 493.
18 BPP, *Select Committee on Public Houses*, 494.
19 BPP, *Select Committee on Public Houses*, 495–6.
20 BPP, *Select Committee on Public Houses*, 498.
21 BPP, *Select Committee on Public Houses*, 499.
22 BPP, *Select Committee on Theatrical Licences and Regulations* 1866, 274–5.
23 BPP, *Select Committee on Theatrical Licences and Regulations*, 44.
24 Beaven, *Leisure, Citizenship and Working-Class Men in Britain*, Chapter 1.
25 BPP, *On the Means of Devine Worship in Populous Districts* 1858, 518.
26 G. Milne, *People, Place and Power on the Nineteenth Century Waterfront: Sailortown* (Basingstoke, Palgrave Macmillan, 2016), 72.
27 See V. Burton on how this period reimagined a toxic and masculine sailortown: '"As I wuz a-rolling down the Highway one morn"': Fictions of the 19th century English sailortown', in B. Klein (ed.), *Fictions of the Sea: Critical Perspectives on the Ocean in British Literature and Culture* (Oxford, Routledge, 2002).
28 S. Hugill, *Sailortown* (London, Routledge and Kegan Paul, 1967), xviii.
29 E.W. Thomas, *Twenty-Five Years' Labour among the Friendless and Fallen* (London, Shaw & Co., 1879), 95.
30 Thomas, *Twenty-Five Years' Labour*, 36.
31 Journalists give consistent accounts of the structure of the green rooms; for example, see J. Greenwood, *In Strange Company: Being the Experiences of a Roving Correspondent* (London, Henry S. King and Co., 1873), 90; W. Phillips, *The Wild Tribes of London* (London, Ward and Lock, 1855), 23.
32 A. Besant, 'How London amuses itself', *Our Corner*, August 1886, 116.
33 Hugill, *Sailortown*, 118.
34 *East London Observer*, 4 January 1879.
35 BPP, *Select Committee on Theatrical Licences and Regulations*, 42.

36 Besant, 'How London amuses itself', 115.
37 Thomas, *Twenty-Five Years' Labour*, 95.
38 Beames, *The Rookeries of London*, 21.
39 Beames, *The Rookeries of London*, 97.
40 Thomas, *Twenty-Five Years' Labour*, 39, 36.
41 Phillips, *The Wild Tribes of London*, 25.
42 B. Beaven, *Visions of Empire: Patriotism, Popular Culture and the City, 1870–1939* (Manchester, Manchester University Press, 2012), Chapter 7.
43 Phillips, *The Wild Tribes of London*, 29.
44 P. Egan, *Tom & Jerry: Life in London; Or the Day and Night Scenes* (London, John Camden Hotten, 1820, 1869 edn), 321.
45 Within the British Empire, race became significantly important; see D. Arnold, 'Race, place and bodily difference in early nineteenth-century India', *Historical Research*, 77(196), 2004, 141–288. For an example of how the 'race debate' was not compartmentalised to either a centre or periphery discourse, see C. Heere, '"That racial chasm that yawns eternally in our midst": The British Empire and the politics of Asian migration, 1900–14', *Historical Research*, 90(249), 2017, 591–612.
46 *East London Observer*, 13 August 1859.
47 BPP, *Select Committee on Theatrical Licences*, 274.
48 *Reynolds Newspaper*, 16 February 1896.
49 F.W. Robinson, 'A night on the Highway', Belgravia, May 1879, 311.
50 *Reynolds Newspaper*, 16 February 1896.
51 *East End Star*, June 1928.
52 *East End Star*, June 1928.
53 For the sailor and the sex worker relationship, see Chapter 6.
54 *Reynolds Newspaper*, 16 February 1896.
55 *East End Star*, June 1928.
56 Robinson, 'A night on the Highway', 304.
57 Robinson, 'A night on the Highway', 308.
58 *The Metropolitan*, 14 September 1872.
59 The *Metropolitan*, 14 September 1872.
60 Besant, 'How London amuses itself', 115.
61 *Metropolitan*, 14 September 1872.
62 *The Illustrated Police News*, 4 March 1871.
63 Robinson, 'A night on the Highway', 309.
64 Robinson, 'A night on the Highway', 310.
65 *Metropolitan*, 14 September 1872.
66 Phillips, *The Wild Tribes of London*, 28.
67 Phillips, *The Wild Tribes of London*, 28.
68 W. Acton, *Prostitution, Considered in Its Moral, Social, and Sanitary Aspects in London and Other Large Cities and Garrison Towns* (London, John Churchill and Sons, 1857, 1870 edn), 22.
69 Acton, *Prostitution*, 22.
70 Thomas, *Twenty-Five Years' Labour*, 37–8.

71 Greenwood, *In Strange Company*, 190.
72 Besant, 'How London amuses itself', 115.
73 Thomas, *Twenty-Five Years' Labour*, 38.
74 Phillips, *The Wild Tribes of London*, 27.
75 Phillips, *The Wild Tribes of London*, 27–8. See also Ritchie, *The Nightside of London*, 73.
76 *East London Observer*, 12 June 1858.
77 Thomas, *Twenty-Five Years' Labour*, 40.
78 Thomas, *Twenty-Five Years' Labour*, 36.
79 Phillips, *The Wild Tribes of London*, 28.
80 Besant, 'How London amuses itself', 110.
81 Besant, 'How London amuses itself', 115.
82 *Old Bailey Proceedings Online* (www.oldbaileyonline.org, version 6.0, 3 June 2022), 14 December 1863, trial of Peter Melloy (t18631214-133); see also *Morning Post*, 27 November 1863.
83 Besant, 'How London amuses itself', 110.
84 Beaven, *Leisure, Citizenship and Working-Class Men in Britain*, 51.
85 Phillips, *The Wild Tribes of London*, 38–9.
86 For an analysis of the early circus, see M. Kwint, 'The circus and nature in late Georgian England', in P. Tait and K. Lavers (eds), *The Routledge Circus Study Reader* (Oxford, Routledge, 2016), 331–48.
87 Phillips, *The Wild Tribes of London*, 36.
88 R. Crone, *Violent Victorians: Popular Entertainment in Nineteenth Century London* (Manchester, Manchester University Press, 2012), 60.
89 *East London Observer*, 8 May 1858.
90 Sims, *How the Poor Live*, 84–5.
91 Besant, 'How London amuses itself', 116.
92 Ritchie, *The Night Side of London*, 72.
93 Besant, 'How London amuses itself', 116.
94 For example, J. Clayton, *Father Dolling: A Memoir* (London, Wells Gardner, Darton and Co., 1902), 23; B. Beaven and M. Seiter, 'Regulating sin in the city: The moral geographies of naval port towns in Britain and Germany, c.1860–1914', *Britain and the World*, 13(1), 2020, 27–46.
95 Phillips, *The Wild Tribes of London*, 27–8.

5

The inner world of the seafaring boarding house

The road is badly lit, and the big, black wall has a menacing, sinister effect. On such a road might occur acts of violence and horror. At the corner of it you will see through the dock gates the tall masts of ships, towering dimly. Near by is Pennyfields. A short, narrow, tortuous street ... A louring, ugly street. A clammy, evil atmosphere is upon it. Draggled women move and flit through it. It is lined on both sides with sailors' boarding-houses. Here, in this sinister London stew, live men who fight the waves and winds and storms.

Evening News, 7 November 1900

In 1862 Robert Rawlinson, the sanitary engineer and inspector, described districts with concentrations of common lodging houses as 'volcanic regions', where the earth trembles beneath the feet of the dwellers and where a 'sudden outbreak might at any time take place, and overwhelm all in ruin'.[1] Rawlinson's vivid analogy of the common lodging house presented it as a place of volatileness and danger that was liable to erupt at any moment on to the civilised streets of Victorian England. Similarly, in 1855 Captain Hay, the Commissioner of the Metropolitan Police in London, reported that 'the common lodging-houses are sources of streams of mendicants to all parts of the country; they are a refuge for them, and in many cases are in fact most infamous brothels'.[2] Typical common lodging houses were perceived as chaotic institutions where transient men and women shared dirty, cramped, and insanitary living areas and were spaces in which drunkenness, sexual impropriety, decadence, and even incest would flourish. In short, common lodging houses were perceived as institutions that had somehow escaped Victorian moral scrutiny and were a throwback to a more barbarous and uncivilised age. The unsettling character of common lodging houses was felt even more acutely on Ratcliffe Highway as the district was populated by numerous 'sailor boarding houses', which were perceived as common lodging houses in all but name. Sailor boarding houses were included within the government legislation that covered common lodging houses and were a constant source of interest for journalists and commentators on the moral failings of the district. Indeed, the 'low' boarding house was inevitably perceived in the popular imagination as a significant pillar in the criminal underworld, as it was run by crimps and prostitutes who sought to exploit, rob, and occasionally murder the naïve sailor ashore.

This chapter will offer an alternative perspective to the dominant assumption that lodging houses were part of an urban criminal network and instead argue that boarding houses provided considerable cultural benefits for sailors and gave them a degree of agency while ashore. It will be argued here that sailor boarding houses were one of the key institutions in sailortown that facilitated this urban–maritime culture and should be distinguished from the more orthodox common lodging houses. However, there was an important exception to this international maritime culture as, by the end of the nineteenth century, South and East Asian sailors appeared to have been excluded from seamen's lodging houses on Ratcliffe Highway. These sailors either established their own lodging houses further east in Limehouse or were offered beds in sailor homes by religious or philanthropic bodies with the expectation that they would be 're-patriated' at the earliest opportunity. It appears that a racist stereotype of the Chinese and Indian sailor that influenced the social relations of the crew at sea was replicated in lodging house culture ashore. Consequently, Chinese seafarers in particular rarely shared boarding houses with sailors of other nationalities.[3]

Finally, the chapter will turn to investigate the establishment of philanthropic sailor homes, institutions that were seen as the antidote to the 'criminal' boarding house. Alston Kennerley's work examined sailor welfare in the nineteenth and twentieth centuries and noted that there were few histories of seamen's missions, and those that exist were written by practising pastors. He added that these histories are not 'tempered sufficiently with discussions of the wider historical social context' and 'awkward negative issues' such as the self-interest of the clergy themselves.[4] The sailor homes were established in response to the 'low boarding house' and lauded by many contemporaries for reforming sailors' behaviour. However, it will be argued that the most successful sailor homes actually appropriated many of the characteristics of the seaman's boarding house and generally could not compete with their popularity.

Common lodging houses in London, legislation, and law enforcement

The 1851 Common Lodging Houses Act gave local authorities the power to supervise public health within these transient institutions. The cities with a significant number of lodging houses were, perhaps unsurprisingly, port cities, with over 15,000 lodging per night in Glasgow and 878 common lodging houses recorded in Liverpool during the 1890s.⁵ It was estimated in 1853 that there were around 3,300 common lodging house keepers in London, with many blurring the line between private residences and commercial boarding houses. Indeed, the 1861 Census reveals that sailors were lodging with heads of the households who did not describe themselves as lodging house keepers. For example, James Brown, a head of household in Palmers Folly, described himself as a carpenter but presided over a house that contained eight lodgers including seamen, dressmakers, and servants.⁶ The Census returns of Ratcliffe Highway and the surrounding streets also align with the assumption that these were small institutions as there was an average of six boarders per lodging house in 1861.⁷ The state's increasing interest in auditing and regulating lodging houses would explain the decline in the number of lodging houses as the century progressed. By the mid-1880s, the Metropolitan Police reported that there were about 1,100 lodging houses in London, a figure that dropped to approximately 1,000 in 1906.

In London, it was the Metropolitan Police who were responsible for regulating common lodging houses until 1894 when this task was passed to the London County Council (LCC).⁸ In 1903 the LCC took the rare step of annually licensing common lodging homes and differentiating between the standard lodging home and the seaman's lodging house. The LCC's decision to record the seaman's lodging house separately allows us an insight into the structure of London's provision of lodging houses at the end of the nineteenth century. It was reported in 1908 that, excluding philanthropic sailor homes, there were seventy-four seaman's lodging houses in London that were located in St George's in the East and Limehouse. Saint George's in the East was the location of 38 per cent of London's seaman's lodging houses while the developing Limehouse district contained 48 per cent due to its close proximity to the new docks opening further east.⁹ These two adjoining maritime-influenced districts were not entirely masculine strongholds as some historians have suggested as many as 37 per cent of the seaman's lodging houses were kept by women.¹⁰

Another important feature of seamen's lodging homes was their international character. In 1903, of the sixty-one lodging houses where the boarding house keepers' nationalities were identified, 69 per cent were from overseas. The biggest development from the mid-nineteenth-century seaman's lodging house culture was the increase in private lodging houses for Chinese sailors that began to group in the Limehouse district. While there were no Chinese boarding houses in Saint George's in the East, of the thirty-eight seaman's lodging houses in Limehouse, fifteen or 39 per cent were managed by Chinese keepers. Finally, in contrast to the large sailor homes that catered to upward of 350 guests, seaman's lodging houses were usually small, intimate places where there were on average nine lodgers per institution.¹¹ At the start of the twentieth century, the LCC carried out inspections on lodging houses and issued formal warnings to those that had failed to maintain standards. A failure to comply with the LCC demands would result in the refusal to grant a licence. On the whole, most lodging houses complied with the recommendations outlined in the formal warnings, and this good working relationship between the LCC and lodging houses avoided formal court hearings. However, the lodging house keepers who were persistent offenders or had failed LCC licence renewal conditions did end up in court. Surviving records from 1908 indicate that the court proceedings taken out on lodging house keepers fell into two main categories: a failure to maintain cleanliness (47 per cent) and the failure to register as a lodging house (53 per cent). Interestingly, despite their reputation for criminality, and in particular theft and prostitution, these offences did not appear in any court proceedings in 1908.[12] However, as Crook has pointed out, the legislation's ambiguous definition of a lodging house and the desire to maintain the lodger's privacy ensured that it was difficult to convict lodging house keepers of keeping a disorderly house.[13]

Victorian critiques of the sailor boarding house

While the regulation of common lodging houses during the nineteenth century did not result in mass prosecutions, in Victorian popular discourse, sailor boarding houses were inevitably associated with the infamous 'crimp' and the crimp economy. The term crimp referred to a brokering role sometimes related to cargo but more commonly used in the recruitment of sailors. As so often with the classic 'middleman', crimps gained a low and untrustworthy status in the eyes of the press and the public. They were sometimes referred to as landsharks or parasites and were perceived to trade in human commodities and, in some extreme cases, compared with slave traders.[14] This reputation arose from the tradition of crimps gaining commission for the recruitment of sailors to ships through their ready supply of seafarers in the boarding house networks. In addition, crimps, or their 'runners', would board ships and hand out cards for their boarding house and outfitters, and offer sailors drinks as an enticement to stay at their premises. Boarding house crimps also gained a reputation for charging extortionate rates for rooms and loans to sailors who, having been plied with drink, accepted the terms on offer on their arrival.[15] As early as the 1820s, religious missionaries were producing pamphlets warning readers of the 'snares awaiting the young and unsuspecting seaman approaching the shores of a large sea-port' as crimps would entice their victims and entrap them 'in such labyrinth of misery and vice that his health of body and peace of mind are assailed'.[16]

Milne has noted that the crimp was surrounded in mythology and by the end of the nineteenth century had almost become a maritime legend. Stories ranged from conning a commission from a captain for an unresponsive drunken sailor who, once they set sail, was found to have been dead when they boarded him, to 'skinning' or robbing sailors at their boarding houses. With little or no evidence to cite, the Edwardian press revelled in stories of how the Ratcliffe Highway crimp and their boarding houses were at the centres of criminal networks that sought to 'traffic' sailors to unscrupulous sea captains. These fictional accounts were amplified by Hugill some fifty years later when he claimed gullible sailors were routinely doped in boarding houses, dropped through waiting trapdoors, and transported on to waiting ships.[17] As Milne has shown, while the dead-sailor scam was almost certainly fictitious, and the doping of sailors uncommon, cases of crimps 'skinning' sailors in boarding houses did occasionally arise in police courts both in Britain and overseas.[18]

In 1850 the Old Bailey heard how the sailor Frederick Thomas had been violently assaulted and robbed of his money and clothes by three men and three women. Thomas had met Eliza Wilson on Ratcliffe Highway and went with her to bed in a lodging house in Whitechapel. He was awoken in the early hours of the morning and became suspicious when several men and women entered the room. He explained that:

> I then got up to go away altogether, and the three girls put the sheet round my head, tied it round my neck, and began handling my throat, and the men got to the foot of the bed, unbuttoned my trowsers, and pulled them off – they got their hands up at the foot of the bed, and pulled off my stockings and waistcoat – my jacket was off – before I could get the sheet off my head they all went down-stairs, and I was left in the room by myself – I laid there till morning – I had had three shillings and one sixpence in my trowsers – in the morning, about eight o'clock, or between eight and nine, Walker and Elliott came to me and told me I was to leave the room and go away: I did so – I had nothing on then but my shirt and my inner trowsers.[19]

The crime was adjudged to have been coordinated and premeditated and was not taken lightly by the judge and jury. Despite the press describing the six defendants as 'a notorious gang of thieves and prostitutes infesting Whitechapel', the women served the more severe sentences.[20] While all six defendants were found guilty and condemned to transportation for seven years, the three men's sentences were commuted to fairly short prison sentences. The young women Sarah Clement (twenty-three), Eliza Wilson (nineteen), and Selina Langley (eighteen) were perceived by the judge as the most dangerous and calculating of the 'skinning' gang and were all transported to Van Diemen's Land, Australia, between 1850 and 1851. The Victorian police and courts viewed 'skinning' as a particularly repugnant crime as it was often initiated by women who 'lured' unsuspecting sailors into criminal lodging houses. Thus, the woman breaks every feminine moral code as she not only embarks on prostitution but engages in violence and theft. The male protagonists were merely seen as opportunists and were therefore served with a lesser sentence. In his investigation into sailor boarding houses, Henry Mayhew interviewed several people who were 'well acquainted with the subject' and concluded that the crimp and the sailor boarding house were the fulcrum of a criminal network that targeted the unsuspecting sailor. One informant claimed:

> the men who keep the worst class of lodging-houses for sailors are often the lumpers – men who are employed by the stevedores to stow cargo of a ship. They are not fully employed, and, having idle time, look out for lodgers … The keepers of these low houses are generally of the lower order of the Irish. They hang about the docks, infesting the bridges as the ships come home from a voyage.[21]

Another interviewee declared that 'the worst sort of boarding-masters are Irish, and foreigners … more than 50 take occasional boarders – two or three; but they are generally the worst of all', adding that they only charged two shillings a day.[22] It appears that sailors could stay in larger boarding houses but also as temporary lodgers in working-class homes as it was a useful source of income for stevedores and dockyard workers who were engaged in casual or seasonal occupations.[23]

Other sailor boarding houses doubled as brothels but to outward appearances looked respectable.[24] In 1851 John Hatch, a merchant sailor, was robbed of his belongings in what he thought was a standard sailor boarding house. When the magistrate asked why he had entered 'such a disgraceful place', he replied: 'I thought it was a respectable house. There was a good deal of very nice furniture in it, and it was very clean, but it turned out to be a brothel'.[25] Indeed, during the 1850s, it was not uncommon for magistrates to puzzle over whether keepers of these hybrid lodging houses and brothels could be convicted under the Common Lodging Houses Act. Kirby, a police sergeant based in Shadwell, claimed that having entered Mary Buckley's premises, he discovered prostitutes in bed with sailors in the same room. Buckley charged 1s 6d a night for the women, who then made their own arrangements with the sailors. The magistrate complained that the wrong charge had been brought against Buckley and the case was dropped until the police indicted her with owning a common brothel.[26] Only three years earlier, Buckley described herself as a 'laundress' and was head of a small household that comprised three children and a lodger. Her youngest child was not yet one, so it would be safe to assume that her partner had either left or died before the Census. At some point she moved from 38 Angel

Gardens a short distance to 8 Bluegate Fields to become a boarding house keeper. Despite her many convictions for brothel keeping, she continued to live with her two daughters and enlarged her business so that in 1861, she had moved to nearby 4 Victoria Street and rented rooms to four women. The Census enumerator did not allocate any of the four women with a profession. The only other person present on the night of the Census was an Irish seaman, which indicates that Buckley continued to do business with the seafaring community.[27]

Mayhew and his informants categorised these smaller and informal boarding houses as the worst type as they sat outside of common lodging house legislation and, in their view, were run by foreigners, prostitutes, and untrustworthy characters. The women-run boarding houses also transgressed bourgeois rules on sexual relations and decency by openly engaging in prostitution and fostering relationships under the sham of a 'marriage'. The sailor lodging houses were also located in what Mayhew and later Booth determined as the uncivilised and brutal areas of the waterside districts of London such as Shadwell, Wapping, St George's, and East Smithfield. Here, 'the courts are unpaved' and 'a sensible seaman might be frightened at the look of them'.[28] It was in the courts off Ratcliffe Highway, such as Palmers Folly and Wellclose Square, where stories about crimps orchestrating the drugging, robbery, assault, and murder of their sailor lodgers were most associated. However, when Mayhew enquired about the cases of sailors being drugged and robbed in these low boarding houses, he was unable to identify any actual cases. One man informed him that 'I never heard of men being hocussed [drugged] in these places. The girls are not of that class'.[29] Likewise, Mayhew was forced to acknowledge that the 'skinning' of seafarers in boarding houses, where crimps and women would steal the sailor's money and the clothes they were wearing, was not a regular occurrence. Mayhew wrote: 'I was told by an experienced person that seamen are not robbed in this manner so frequently as they used to be – or so frequently, perhaps, as people generally imagine'.[30]

This perspective is given credence by an analysis of the Old Bailey papers between 1850 and 1900. Using the Old Bailey online database, a search for the key terms of 'boarding house' and 'any crime' was undertaken and accrued 105 results. Once cases that did not take place in a boarding house were eliminated, only fifteen trials remained. Of the fifteen cases, only eight successful convictions involved sailors and seven of these were on Ratcliffe Highway. Furthermore, while theft accounted for two thirds of the boarding house crimes, almost a third of the defendants were prosecuted for defrauding the boarding house keeper. Thus, while the legendary 'crimp' continued to dominate discussion of boarding houses in the press, the Old Bailey proceedings suggest their behaviour had long ceased to be a significant problem. The Old Bailey, of course, only presided over serious cases, and boarding houses no doubt suffered from lower-level criminal activity that the Thames police courts would have dealt with. While the incomplete records of the Thames police courts hamper our investigation of the petty crime that undoubtedly occurred in sailor boarding houses, it would be safe to assume that the lawless and murderous stories that surrounded these institutions were somewhat exaggerated.

The sailor boarding house: social networks, contact zones, and maritime material culture

The Victorian press, authorities, and social observers associated the sailor boarding house with crime and the underworld throughout the nineteenth century. Indeed, given their reputation, it is a wonder why sailors continued to prefer these sailor boarding houses over common lodging houses and, to some extent, even the sailor homes that became more prominent in the latter half of the nineteenth century. Both the contemporary and historiographical accounts of the criminality of boarding houses have led us to miss how the character and operation of these lodgings attracted vast numbers of sailors. In advancing Crook's argument further, it can be seen that sailor boarding houses were 'Othered' and had cultivated rules and rituals peculiar to these institutions that defied the norms of even common lodging houses.[31] First and foremost, sailor boarding houses made for important contact zones for sailors who were ashore in the port for the first time or for those meeting up with existing friendship networks. One religious missionary recalled that on Ratcliffe Highway, 'sailor's boarding-houses thickly abound in all directions', where 'beds could be had at common lodging house prices' and that 'all closely resemble each other' for they were fairly small in size.[32] The boarding house keepers, more often than not, were either ex-sailors or wives of former seafarers. For newly arrived sailors ashore, the boarding house keeper was, therefore, a wealth of information on the immediate locality and also on the maritime employment prospects in the port.

The established boarding house keepers were also important and trusted members of the onshore maritime community, a quality often forgotten in narratives that focus on the crimp's exploitation of the sailor that dominates boarding house histories. For example, William Brown, a sailor from the Isle of Man, was saved from a prison sentence after he was convicted of assault. Mrs Turner, his boarding house keeper, testified for the defence and stated that she had always found him 'a very civil, well conducted and inoffensive young man'.[33] This trust between lodger and boarding house keeper, which in this case had evolved over five years, often worked for both parties. When John Frost, a sailor boarding house keeper, was charged with receiving stolen property in 1883, his landlord and three sailors, from differing national backgrounds, testified to his 'excellent character', which was accepted by the Old Bailey court. Axel Reiss declared that:

> I am a seaman ... I have seen Mr. Frost since 1878 – for the last three years I have used his boarding-house when on shore – I have met a number of other sailors there – I have left some of my property in his custody; some is there now – I have known sailors leave property with him while they went to sea – Charley Steinaveldt is one, he is on a voyage now – my things have always been kept safely for me – Frost has not advanced money on them – I have seen watches and rings and Alberts belonging to sailors in his possession.[34]

As a foreign sailor, Reiss found Frost's lodgings a safe and secure base from which he could stow his property, without having to advance money on his valuables, before setting out on another voyage. In addition, his testimony gives an insight into how boarding houses were an important contact zone as he and the other sailor witnesses stated that they always returned to Frost's establishment as it was a relatively secure environment that was networked into the latest shipping and maritime intelligence for the area.

In some cases, the tradition of sailors returning to the same boarding houses after a voyage led them to develop more intimate relationships with the boarding house keepers, often referring to each other as 'husband' and 'wife'. Indeed, these women could have several 'husbands' at once. The peculiar sailor boarding house culture, which was even more unorthodox than the common lodging house traditions, proved beneficial to sailors and women. One German woman explained to Mayhew in 1851:

> I have been in England nearly six years. When I came over I could not speak a word of your language, but I associated with my own countrymen. Now I talk the English well, as well as any, and I go with the British sailor. I am here tonight in this house of dancing with a sailor English, and I have known him two week. His ship is in docks, and will not sail for one month from this time I am now speaking. I knew him before, one years ago and a half. He always lives with me when he come on shore. He is nice man and give me all his money when he land always. I take all his money while he with me, and not spend it quick as some of your English women do. If I not to take care, he would spend all in one week. Sailor boy always spend money like rain water.[35]

In this narrative, the sailor boarding house enabled both the sailor and the woman to establish a level of financial security and short-term companionship. Indeed, as Booth noted, sailors' wives 'have a very hard life. Do all sorts of rough work for a living and many have to go on the streets'.[36] However, for the authorities, the relationships between some boarding house women and sailors led to confusion and doubt as to whether these women were boarding house or brothel keepers as 'they importune none but sailors'.[37]

The boarding house system also allowed sailors to carve out a degree of autonomy as trusted lodging house keepers would conceal sailors who wanted to end unreasonable employment contracts and negotiate new ones. Desertion from a ship was one of the few options open to exploited sailors, and the secretive network of lodging houses and the goodwill of their keepers were central to fostering a measure of sailor agency while ashore. In 1853 the *Daily News* reported that 'both English and foreign lodging-house keepers in the port of London were in the practice of encouraging foreign seamen to desert their vessels and harbouring and secreting them in their houses until an opportunity offered to ship them in British vessels'.[38] Similarly, in 1851 Mr Coleman, the Register-General of Seamen, reported that desertion of foreign sailors in London had become a serious problem. He noted that the boarding house system was intrinsically linked to the desertion process and claimed that:

> In the yard of one of these houses I knew of a place which was fitted up for the reception of the foreign seamen in such a manner as to escape notice of those who were not more than ordinary observers. In these dens were deserters concealed until the vessels they belonged to sailed.[39]

This boarding house culture was replicated in sailortowns around the world and enabled sailors to escape unfavourable contracts or exploitative captains in any port they had docked. *Lloyds Weekly* claimed that in New York, there were many places for British sailor 'confinement', while in Quebec, if a sailor deserted a ship, 'there was a street two miles long containing numerous houses where they were concealed, and captains of ships could not enter that street to search for their men without being well armed'. The newspaper claimed that New York authorities were 'anxious to suppress this odious practice'.[40]

However, in Britain, attempts to prosecute lodging house keepers for encouraging seamen to desert and conceal them within their premises were largely unsuccessful. For example, John Seymour, a Greek lodging house keeper, was accused of encouraging Gabrielle Viscovich, an Italian sailor, to desert his ship in 1853. Seymour, who had anglicised his name, ran a large boarding house in Wellclose Square and successfully argued that he had no knowledge that Viscovich had deserted his ship. Indeed, Viscovich supported Seymour's stance, claiming that the boarding house keeper had not persuaded him to desert the ship, which was fully his own decision due to a disagreement with the captain. The case reveals that prosecutors had difficulty in convicting lodging house keepers as their relationship with sailors was mutually supportive.[41] The close relationship between lodging house keepers and deserting sailors continued into the late nineteenth century. It was reported that a boarding house in Limehouse had 'tempted' sailors to desert:

> On Saturday last the police made a raid on a 'boarding house' in Limehouse and arrested a number of Chinese and Lascar seamen, part of the crew of the steamship *North*, who, after receiving their advance notes, had been tempted by the boarding house keeper to desert. Two were engaged in opium smoking, and the rest were dragged from beneath beds and from other hiding places, and marched out of the house in the face of a crowd of countrymen, who at one time threatened a rescue, and sent off by rail to rejoin their ship at Glasgow.[42]

Significantly, crowds had gathered outside the boarding house in an attempt to prevent the sailors from rejoining the ship, furthering the sense that boarding houses were deemed safe houses within the sailortown community and a bulwark against the civic and shipping authorities.

Not only did seamen's boarding houses provide a network of secretive spaces for concealment, but they were also an important place of contact for sailors of differing nationalities. As we have seen, the majority of boarding houses were run by foreign former seafarers who often displayed flags outside their premises denoting their nationality. Richard Rowe noted the 'little painted ensigns' on the exteriors of lodging houses and the texts in windows indicating the languages spoken.[43] Similarly, Mayhew reported that Ship Alley, close to Ratcliffe Highway, was 'full of foreign lodging-houses'. He added:

> You see written on a blind an inscription that denotes the nationality of the keeper and the character of the establishment; for instance Hollandsche lodgement, is sufficient to show a Dutchman that his own language is spoken, and that he may have a bed if he chooses.[44]

The Victorian social observers seemed to approve of foreign sailor boarding houses arranged according to nationality as it appealed to their sense of racial exclusivity and order. However, the national flags and insignia that adorned boarding houses, though highly visible to the social observers from the street, provide a misleading impression of how these institutions actually operated. An analysis of the 1861 Census for the Ratcliffe Highway district reveals that sailor boarding houses generally attracted patrons of mixed nationalities, despite flags and insignia that represented a specific country. For example, John Seymour's boarding house in Wellclose Square had six Greeks, four Southern Europeans, five Germans, two Austrians, and two sailors from the United Kingdom lodging at his premises. Likewise, Turkish, English, and Finnish sailors were staying at Charles Cowley's boarding house on the High Street. Of the twenty-five boarding houses identified in the 1861 Census for this district, only four small institutions were patronised exclusively by English sailors, a surprisingly small number given that 45 per cent of all the sailors detected residing in this district were English-born.[45]

The mixing of nationalities in boarding houses and the international maritime culture that it fostered appears to have been an attraction for seafarers. Thomas Beames reported in 1850 that a 'foreigner'-run boarding house he visited was a resort for French, Italian, German, Spanish, Portuguese, and Greek sailors. Here they met in a common room and kitchen where there were 'several men here sitting or lounging about, some drinking; the landlord and his wife were attending on them, and they were conversing in various languages'.[46] Likewise, one religious missionary entered a boarding house and remembered:

> a small apartment, which might be called the parlour or common room, about half a dozen men were whiling away the morning in what sailors would call real cosy style ... the inmates, representing various nationalities, were quite at their ease: one bronzed and weather beaten veteran lay the length of the sofa, without heeding our intrusion.

The visitor noted that this set-up was 'virtually repeated' in the other boarding houses and that in less than half an hour, they had met with Germans, Swedes, Danes, Finns, Austrians, Italians, Dutch, and English.[47] Boarding houses, then, were social settings that facilitated relaxation, drinking, and conversation. Indeed, they were spaces that enabled cultural transference and were not generally organised on national or cultural exclusivity. However, while sailor boarding houses reflected the heterogeneous nature of seafarers ashore in London, the keepers would often decorate and furnish their institutions to distinguish them from common lodging houses.

This maritime material culture was transnational and adorned the exteriors and interiors of sailor boarding houses. This décor sidestepped language barriers and was clearly designed to attract sailor patrons rather than the orthodox boarding house lodger. Beames noted that in the boarding house he visited, there was 'a small common room, garnished with prints on nautical subjects; a very fine macaw (for sailors love parrots like children) was flapping his wings at one end'. He then advanced to the first floor where he discovered the sailors' dormitories where 'the rooms were fitted up, like the cabins of steamers, with tiers; so that there were an upper and lower range of beds or rather berths'.[48] Another contemporary visitor observed that all of the boarding houses had 'the same kind of little rooms, decorated with pictures and ornaments likely to suit the sailor taste'.[49] Likewise, Hugill claimed that some boarding houses 'had rooms built in imitation of a ship's fo'c'sle, to make Jack feel at home'.[50] On his visits to boarding houses in the district, Mayhew also noted the maritime décor that dominated their interiors. In one boarding house, he noted that shells 'were in every room' and 'some were specimens of exquisite beauty, while others were remarkable for their size, or delicacy, richness and iridescence of their colours'. Alongside the shells were large masses of coral and maritime 'curiosities of all kinds' including whalebone on which had been carved drawings of seamen's lives. Nor was this boarding house an aberration, as Mayhew reported that 'the other houses more or less presented the same characteristics; shells and other sea curiosities, were the chief ornaments, with live parrots and cockatoos, some of them noisy enough'.[51] Thus, for boarding house keepers, appealing to a transnational and multi-lingual seafaring population, there were distinctly practical reasons for the display of ornamental signs, maritime imagery, and curiosity about the exterior and interior of their premises.[52]

Sailor homes and missionary homes

The popular conception that crimps and boarding houses were deeply entangled with the criminal underworld was a key motivation for philanthropists and religious missionaries to set up their own sailor homes. These sailor homes were architecturally designed and intended to operate in a manner that was the antithesis of the 'crimp's criminal boarding house'. For philanthropists or missionaries who built new buildings, often converting them from notorious public houses, the resurrection of a sailor home was perceived as a victory for Victorian public morality over vice and criminality. However, as we shall discover, not all of the traditional sailor boarding house practices were jettisoned by philanthropists and missionaries as, after all, sailors were not compelled to patronise their new sailor homes. However, as Milne has noted, the founders of sailor homes were invested in the common idea that the sailor was child-like ashore and at the mercy of crimps and prostitutes. In the founders' view, then, sailor homes were places of protection and social and religious improvement. This inevitably meant that sailors were subject to the management's rules and often sailors were reluctant to patronise institutions that curtailed their freedoms.[53]

The earliest sailor society established in the capital was 'The Port of London Society' in 1818.[54] The end of the Napoleonic Wars led to large numbers of demobilised soldiers and sailors who were visibly destitute on the streets of East London. George Charles Smith, a sailor-turned-pastor, campaigned for the 'Seaman's Cause' and organised a public meeting to found the Society that set out to 'alleviate the worldly woes of sailors' and promote religion among merchant seamen. At first, seafarers received religious instruction from a sloop moored in the Thames, but by 1856 it had changed its name to the British and Foreign Sailors' Society and established an institute near the London docks.[55] The British and Foreign Sailors' Society home was grounded in the principles of religious and social improvement, and the institute employed agents to approach sailors on ships, and in the streets, pubs, and boarding houses, to bring the sailors into contact with the 'great truths of the gospel'. Henry Walker, a London Christian worker, estimated that in 1896 there were twenty-three churches or 'Mission Stations' on and around Ratcliffe Highway, with some religious organisations taking over infamous establishments such as Paddy's Goose and Wilton's Music Hall.[56]

Missionary pamphlets, annual reports, and memoirs of religious workers often gave detailed accounts of how sailors had been converted from drink and sin to religious observance through the persuasive power of their preaching. For example, in 1820 James Rosewall, a London preacher, claimed that at his dockside mission, he had successfully converted a notoriously irreligious sailor who had regularly practised in drink and vice. After just over a year of attending meetings, Rosewall reported that '*now* the things which before he delighted he despised, *and religion*, which he hated, he now esteemed and loved as his chief good'.[57] However, these celebrated successes were very much in the minority, and sailor missionaries were consistently faced with the problem of meaningfully attracting sailors to their societies and homes. Thus, in 1861 Mr Fieldwick, the British and Foreign Sailors' Society Secretary, reported that the newly built institute had reading and coffee rooms, navigation schools, a lecture hall, and temperance societies, and was well equipped to inspire 'intellectual and moral elevation'. However, tellingly, he also admitted that while the institution had provided patrons with a great social improvement, sailors' adoption of religion 'is not very considerable'.[58] Indeed, while the British and Foreign Sailors' Society was the largest and most successful religious mission, their impact upon London's sailor population appears minimal.[59] The Society's annual report for 1890 revealed that they had conducted 700 public meetings, visited 2,000 vessels, and spoken personally to 672 sailors. Despite all this activity, the society could only convert 118 sailors who claimed to have 'professed a faith in Christ'. The Society also offered free beds for sailors, and this initiative only netted on average four boarding sailors per night over the year.[60] Missionaries would blame the sailors' attachment to 'strange prejudices, fancies and beliefs' for their lack of religious conversions. Perhaps more accurately, Hugill believed that sailors attended missionary events simply for the free food and company.[61]

The relatively limited impact on sailors' behaviour could well be explained by the attempt to instill religious and social improvement into the residents of the missionary sailor homes. The security that missionary homes provided had to be balanced with the freedoms and related dangers that were associated with the sailor boarding houses. The more successful sailor homes appropriated elements of sailor boarding houses and were more relaxed with in-house rules. The Well Street Sailor Home was built in 1828 on the site of a former theatre through funds raised by a consortium of former sailors and philanthropists. The exterior of the home was designed to differentiate the institution from sailortown's run-down boarding houses in the notorious courts and alleys of the Ratcliffe Highway district. Indeed, philanthropists viewed the sailortown district as a space of chaos, disorder, and immorality, and they desired to construct an institution that would challenge these 'evils' through its aesthetics and scale.[62] The home was positioned among 'a great many public houses' with around nine or ten within a few hundred yards, while the infamous Wilton's Music Hall was situated in nearby Grace Alley.[63] Given its location, Well Street was designed to dominate and almost intimidate the small backstreet taverns that surrounded it.

Built in the style of a workhouse or, as one sailor complained, 'a prison', its large and imposing form was constructed to symbolise the values of order, discipline, and morality.[64] However, looks could be deceptive, as the Well Street Sailor Home institutionalised some key aspects of the sailor boarding house. Similar to some of the most successful sailor boarding houses, Well Street embedded a maritime material culture, as Mayhew noted that the dormitories 'consist of a series of handsome oak cabins, with a passage down the middle' while the top tier of cabins resembled the design of a steamboat.[65] As in sailor boarding houses, cabins allowed just enough space for a bed, washstand, and a sea chest for the sailor to stow his belongings.[66] The main meeting areas in the sailor home also followed the tradition found in many boarding houses of decorating the interior with nautical curiosities. Mayhew found 'model ships, Malay proas, Madras catamarans, maps, charts, and foreign curiosities', while the corridors were adorned with prints and pictures of ships.[67] Significantly, like the sailor boarding houses, the Sailors' Home also assumed a key role in the dissemination of employment and training opportunities and was networked into nautical news and services. Mayhew observed that 'on one side of the hall hang framed lists of "Ships to Sail", "Cancelled Mariners' Register Tickets," "Qualifications for Masters and Mates," cards of "Navigation Taught", placards of Tailors "Recommended by the Sailors' Home"'.[68]

There was fierce competition for sailors among boarding house keepers and philanthropic sailor homes, and, at times, the Well Street managers adopted some of the more dubious tactics to lure sailors to their institution. The boarding house 'runners' had become notorious for bullying, conning, and hassling sailors to lodge in their houses. It was a strategy appropriated by Well Street, and their 'runners' appeared to have been just as dishonest and threatening as their boarding house counterparts, which resulted in several complaints and the dismissal of the Well Street representatives in question.[69] However, forty-five years later, Booth noted that the home's 'runners system' was still in operation, and staff continued to meet sailors at the docks and 'bring men and luggage direct to the house'.[70] Similarly, sailor homes were supposed to protect seafarers from extortionate prices for services and goods in sailortown. However, Mayhew's investigation discovered that Well Street Home officials were bribed by traders to gain entrance into the institution and sell goods at inflated prices. In light of these revelations, Well Street changed the rules, and traders were no longer admitted into the home.[71] However, by far the most attractive element for the sailors was the relatively relaxed atmosphere that prevailed in the home. Indeed, the austere exterior belied a culture that had more in common with a sailor boarding house than an institution of social improvement. As Mayhew entered the Well Street Home, he was surprised at how informally it was managed and that sailors had comparative freedom to conduct their affairs. He noted that:

> Seated on the oaken forms besides the fires at each end of the hall are some twenty or thirty seamen, newly 'rigged out', some in their sleek and glossy blue clothes and clean straw hats, and others in bright red or dark-blue flannel shirts – all smoking and chatting together. Some stand apart in small groups, conversing upon matters of business; while others in couples, pace half across the hall, backwards and forwards, as if still upon the deck.[72]

One sailor informed Mayhew that they were free 'to smoke as we please all day in the hall', and although prayers were performed every morning and evening, 'we are not compelled to attend'.[73] Indeed, unlike some philanthropic sailor homes, alcohol was served, and sailors were permitted to return to the home even if they were 'worse for wear'.

While Mayhew was visiting Well Street, he recalled seeing a sailor in the main lounge who was 'gesticulating as only drunken men in a passion do', while his friends attempted to pacify him. The secretary of the home, who was showing Mayhew around, approached the sailor and 'kindly' said: 'my good fellow when I saw you this morning you were all I could wish to be. Now do quiet yourself, there's a good man, and above all, don't drink any more, I beg you'. The sailor was respectful to the Secretary but continued to wonder off muttering to himself.[74] The management's tolerance of alcohol and drunken patrons certainly set the Well Street Sailor Home apart from the more orthodox institutions that attempted to instill social improvement through teetotalism and ejecting drunken sailors. Siting the sailor home amid sailortown also ensured that sailors were able to sample 'low' entertainment on their doorstep. After visiting the Well Street Home in the late nineteenth century, Joseph Havelock Wilson, the seamen's union leader, recalled:

> At this time Well Street was one of the strangest places in the world; you could be accommodated with a fight at any hour of the day or night, and you could lose your watch and chain in the twinkling of an eye, and as for entertainment you need not go to the theatre or music hall, but could find it outside the door in Well Street. There were barrel organs galore with a variety of tunes, some good some terrible; there was the one legged dancer ... [who] could do an excellent clog dance ... with the aid of his crutch. Then there was the coloured gentleman who used to fill his mouth with some kind of spirit and blow out flames, and a stout lady with an accordion who had been singing the 'Moon behind the Hill' for about 20 years, and she was not a bad singer either ... not the least of the attractions was a gentleman who would swallow watches, swords, pieces of glass.[75]

Thus, by the 1880s, and despite its founders' intentions, the home's relatively relaxed house rules and its sailortown environment had helped foster something akin to a boarding house culture.

However, while Well Street was a relatively popular philanthropic home, the number of sailors using the institution was disappointing. In 1851 Well Street had a capacity of 300 beds, and yet on Census night, only fifty-two sailors were boarding. Most sailors were fairly young with 75 per cent under thirty and 48 per cent under twenty-five.[76] The absence of a significant number of sailors over thirty years of age implies that sailors new to Ratcliffe Highway moved out to boarding houses once they had familiarised themselves with the district. These figures concur with Kennerley's calculations as he determined that in 1879 the Well Street Sailor Home admitted on average thirty-two seafarers per day, which was well below the institute's increased 500-bed capacity. Significantly, the 1870s saw Well Street enjoy the most successful period in its history, and although there seems to have been a small core of regular returnees, most sailors tended to use the sailor home as a safe transitional place before patronising the less institutional regimes of the boarding house.[77]

By the 1890s, when Charles Booth visited Well Street, its capacity was 400 beds with an average of nineteen sailors admitted per day.[78] Thus, even Well Street's liberal regime could not compete with the freedom that boarding houses could facilitate, as it rigidly enforced the rule that prohibited patrons from entering the home after 11 pm. Sailors were particularly critical of the removal of this freedom as the curfew curtailed much of the entertainment that sailortown had to offer. They also complained of the rigid routines that sailor homes adopted that reminded them too much of working on a ship and favoured instead the relaxed familiarity that boarding houses had. One seafarer much preferred the boarding house as it was 'something resembling the comfort of a home'. He added that in lodging houses, 'we receive comfort with the proprietress to attend on us. In the homes we are restricted and bound down to be in dinner at a certain time'.[79] It was this personal touch that sailor homes could never deliver.

Finally, seafarers would often correct the misapprehension that sailor homes were benevolent charities and that they in fact operated in commercial terms just like the sailor boarding houses. A shipwrecked sailor, who had been rescued and taken to London, was advised to go to the sailor home but was refused admission and informed that his only option was the Asylum for Destitute Sailors or the 'straw house'. He told Mayhew: 'I didn't like to go there, because a decent man feels degraded in such a place – all the good men I have talked to are of the same opinion. It's like going to a workhouse, turning into the straw-yard and we would as lief starve'.[80] Another sailor reminisced that 'when Jack's money is gone', he is evicted from the sailor home 'just the same as if he was in the hands of the most grasping boarding house keeper at the East End'.[81] An additional seafarer informed Mayhew that when he ran out of money, the Well Street Sailor Home 'turned me in the streets without a piece of food to put in my mouth'. He was told that they would not offer him any help in finding a ship and that he should go to the Asylum for Destitute Sailors.[82]

Othering Indian and Chinese seafarers: moral panics, crime, and containment

Thus far, we have explored how sailor homes had been designed to 'save' the sailor from himself, the crimps, and the sex workers who they believed would ensnare him. As we have seen, sailor homes also made provision for foreign sailors, though some segregation between different nationalities was often attempted. By the late nineteenth century, the importance of race had begun to influence the thinking of social explorers and missionaries, and sailor homes became places of 'containment', particularly for 'Lascar', or Indian, and Chinese seafarers. As early as the nineteenth century, Chinese and Indian sailors had become destitute on the streets of London as they had effectively been abandoned by the East India Company. By 1815 sufficient pressure based on humanitarian concerns had been mounted to persuade the East India Company to build segregated barracks for up to 1,000 East and Southern Asian seafarers in London.[83] By the late nineteenth century, the narrative that had positioned the Indian seafarers as victims of neglect had been replaced by stories that placed them and Chinese seamen at the heart of criminal networks. Influenced by Dickens's fictional juvenile gangs, Joseph Salter, a London missionary, claimed that sailors from the east and local women were rearing 'feral' children who were born into crime. Salter alleged that Ratcliffe Highway and Shadwell had become the 'perfect pest spots' where 'a mixed population of half-castes began to spring up'. He added that 'these were too often utilised by men of the Fagin type to steal, or beg, or do both'.[84]

The changing perception of the Lascar during the nineteenth century has been noted by Jonathan Hyslop, who has shown that the name 'Lascar' was an imaginary term that was used to justify inequalities in employment and working conditions. As steam began to dominate British shipping, there became a demand for cheaper labour that had not acquired the skills of sail seamanship. Both the 'Lascars' and Chinese seafarers were employed by shipping companies at the expense of European labour, and they gained a reputation as not only being physically inferior but also lacking the moral fibre of their British counterparts. Moreover, shipping companies added to these stereotypes by viewing Lascars and the Chinese as a docile and sober workforce.[85] One journalist claimed a vessel safely crewed by twenty-five English sailors would require seventy-five to 100 Lascars and that the Indian sailor can 'not steer, nor face cold or storm'.[86] In 1895 Charles Booth's researchers interviewed a series of boarding house keepers and sailor home staff and concluded that 'the Lascars are a principally inferior race to the English. 3 Lascars are reckoned equal to two English sailors. They are most orderly, docile and temperate, and so are preferred'. Confirming their lack of seamanship and physical inferiority, the report continued: 'they are no use in sailing vessels, nor in cold climates'.[87] From the mid-nineteenth century, these racist stereotypes of their maritime weaknesses were transferred to their conduct while ashore.

The moral panic over Indian and Chinese seamen's involvement in criminal networks, low boarding houses, and opium dens was also underscored by a fear that these seafarers were also a drain on the public purse, as there were concerns that those who were destitute would resort to the workhouse. Issues were brought to a head during the mid-1850s when almost 100 Indian sailors died on the streets of London after being abandoned by shipping masters, and it was estimated that there were over 200 regular beggars in the city. Subscriptions for a sailor home were raised, with contributions from the Queen, Indian princes, nobles, and merchants, though there were objections made on the proposed location. The initial site selected was the disused Pig and Cabbage public house in the East End, but the publican feared that inmates would be disruptive. He claimed that they would be 'climbing on the wall, swinging on the railings, singing "Hallelujah!" and shouting "Amen" till midnight, relieved not infrequently by a free fight. No! he would not disgrace the locality with such a nuisance'.[88] Eventually in 1857, the 'Strangers' Home for Asiatics, Africans and South Sea Islanders' was opened in West India Dock Road, which significantly was part of the sailortown district whose population were familiar with the cosmopolitan seafaring community. The official objective of the institution was similar to other sailor homes or missions in that they desired to remove seafarers from the danger of sailortown and 'protect them from imposition'. It also aimed to provide copies of the bible in their own language and to teach 'the truths of the Gospel'.[89]

However, unlike the other sailor homes that were designed to cater to western sailors, the Strangers' Home acted as a repatriation centre for Indian and Chinese sailors as it would facilitate return voyages with shipping masters. The Strangers' Home aimed to provide shelter, subsistence, and employment and then for the seafarer to be 'sent home'. Moreover, unlike orthodox homes, the management actively procured destitute seafarers from government institutions. In the first fifteen years of operation, the *Daily News* reported that over 2,000 men had been taken from the hospitals, jails, or workhouses and returned to their country of origin.[90] The management also attempted to segregate inmates as there were separate Asiatic and European messes, with the latter offering better conditions albeit at a slightly higher cost.[91] The home in many ways reflected the growing legislation that successive governments introduced in an attempt to control the Lascar and Chinese population in British ports. Charles Booth's report on the Strangers' Home in 1895 noted that the legislation dictated that shipping masters must provide customs officers with a complete list of all Asiatics on board, and they would be issued with a £30 fine for any seafarers who became chargeable to the poor law. If a seafarer refused to sail home, a magistrate could force their return via the shipping company that he had previously worked for.[92]

Nevertheless, even within these controlling frameworks, Milne has argued that the home was a 'place of safe association where a diverse community of sojourners could build their own support networks'.[93] Indeed, there is ample evidence to suggest that patrons were able to carve out their own cultures and traditions within the home, despite the management's emphasis being placed on Christian learning. It was reported that 'no oriental reckons to have made a meal if he has not eaten curry and rice. For breakfast and supper, at which tea and bread and butter are also served, fish is added to the curry and rice'. The reporter added that they take their prayers regularly and 'much more so, for a sea life interferes with a rigorous observance of the injunctions of the Koran' and 'they spread their carpet out in the spacious back yard at the hours their faith enjoins'.[94] Walker noted that patrons would lodge at homes to 'renew the acquaintance of former years, or it may be to ask advice in a time of trouble. Some few indeed come to see the Koran or the sacred cities sketched by Mahommedans'.[95]

Moreover, informal networks among the Indian and Chinese communities alerted seafarers coming ashore of the merits of the home. The *Daily News* noted that 'the resort to it on part of the Asiatic seamen had now become habitual and universal, the men "passing the word" around to each other as to its merits, in the mysterious, far-reaching way that intelligence spreads among seafaring folk'.[96] Thus even under these rather limiting conditions, the Strangers' Home was an important cultural contact zone for East and South Asian seafarers.

The Strangers' Home, however, could not compete with the boarding houses, and like other sailor homes, the number of patrons was disappointing. In 1881 the Census recorded only twenty-two inmates: eleven from China, six from India, two from Arabia, two from Singapore, and one African. It was a figure that suggests that the institution was filling less than 10 per cent of its available beds. However, the cultural hostility to both Chinese and Indian sailors at sea and ashore ensured that they were isolated from sailor boarding houses' international maritime culture, and instead established their own separate boarding houses. For example, in the late nineteenth century, several Chinese boarding houses were established that only seemed to admit Chinese seafarers or workers. Indeed, Chinese boarding house keepers often doubled up as warehouse owners, shop keepers, and dealers, using their premises for lodgers. For example, in 1901, while Wang Shing was described as a Chinese warehouseman and dealer in Chinese goods, he also accommodated seven Chinese sailors lodging at his premises.[97] Likewise, social researchers observed that Chinese boarding houses were established in abandoned shops. In 1903 Count E. Armfelt, the social explorer, found that 'Asiatics' favoured private boarding houses over sailor homes and would stay for three or four nights. He noted that:

> There are any number of these lodging-houses yet anybody would be at a loss to find one, for they look half deserted, and there is nothing to show that rooms are let within. Usually the lodging-house is a disused shop; its shutters are up and barred, and it admits only a faint glimmer of light through a small aperture high up near the ceiling. The door is unlocked, but shut to so that it need only be pushed open.[98]

Armfelt also discovered that seafarers were attracted to boarding houses as they were able to engage in cultural and religious practices within a non-institutional environment and also purchase charms and amulets from the boarding house keeper.

The boarding house enabled patrons to escape surveillance from the authorities and meet and engage with local people. Armfelt noted that all of the Chinese men who had left seafaring and stayed in London had married English women, and he was somewhat surprised to find 'that in their case marriage has not been a failure, for they seem happy'. He also admitted that 'their children look healthy and are comfortably dressed, and most of them are very nice looking. These dark-haired, black-eyed boys and girls, with the rosy cheeks and happy looks, are real little pictures'.[99] These unorthodox boarding house premises led the authorities to cast Chinese boarding houses as dirty and disease-laden, and their contact with English women in particular triggered moral alarm bells. In one boarding house police raid, Indian sailors were found in bed with English women, which for the magistrate and police confirmed that this was a low common lodging house and brothel, which 'was frequented by Lascars, and other men of colour'. Indeed, it was common for the police to complain that boarding houses with Indian and Chinese lodgers were plagued with 'dirty and offensive smells'.[100] Thus, by the late nineteenth century, in their working environment at sea and in their living arrangements ashore, South and East Asian sailors were 'Othered' by both the maritime and civic authorities, and their engagement with an international maritime culture was severely curtailed.

Conclusion

Lodging houses provide us with an insight into the middle class's worst fears about a growing underground criminal network preying on the naïve and innocent. These fears were played out in Victorian social investigations and the popular press and have found their way into more scholarly accounts of sailortown. However, once we dig beneath the sensational rhetoric, it becomes clear that boarding houses were a central pillar in sailortown culture and provided seafarers with a degree of autonomy and freedom. Away from the rules and regulations of the sailor home, sailors tapped into an underground network of boarding houses offering local information, employment opportunities, and even concealment for deserting sailors. Seamen's boarding houses were also distinguished from common lodging houses by their maritime material culture. Indeed, sailor boarding houses provided a recognisable and welcoming maritime environment for the transnational sailor and were international contact zones at the heart of Ratcliffe Highway. Thus, boarding houses were not usually nationally exclusive institutions and instead were spaces in which cultural negotiation was learned and exercised. However, this international maritime fraternal culture had its limitations. The racist tropes directed at South and East Asian seafarers in their working environments were extended to their living arrangements ashore. Sailor homes built specifically for East and South Asian sailors aimed to 'repatriate' them, and legislation penalised shipping companies that allowed Chinese and Indian sailors to become dependent on the poor law. Under such hostile conditions, it is perhaps no surprise that Chinese seafarers established their own exclusive boarding houses in Limehouse towards the end of the nineteenth century. Moreover, while Chinese and Indian sailors were often compartmentalised from their western sailor counterparts, they too demonstrated their ability to shape their own cultures both within sailor homes and in their boarding houses in London's sailortown.[101]

Notes

1 Quoted in T. Crook, 'Accommodating the outcast: Common lodging houses and the limits of urban governance in Victorian and Edwardian London', *Urban History*, 35(3), 2008, 414–36, 423.
2 British Parliamentary Papers (hereafter BPP), 'Lodging houses of the metropolis: Report on the common and model lodging houses of the metropolis (with reference to epidemic cholera in 1854)', by George Glover, 1855, 5.
3 For a discussion on Indian repatriation, see H. Garcia, 'The Strangers' Home for Asiatics, Africans and South Sea Islanders: Inaugurating a hospitable world order in mid-Victorian Britain', *Global Nineteenth Century Studies*, 1(1), 2022, 81–90.
4 A. Kennerley, 'Writing the history of the merchant seafarer education, training, and welfare: Retrospect and prospect', *The Northern Mariner/Le Marin du Nord*, XLL(2), April 2002, 1–21, 21. See, for example, N. Churchill, M. Warman, C. Gibson, and J. Leslie, *Stories from the Sea, 1818-2018* (Southampton, Sailor's Society, 2018). While this is an interesting and informative book, it is not targeted at an academic readership.
5 Crook, 'Accommodating the outcast', 415.
6 1861 Census returns of 13 Palmers Folly, London.
7 The 1861 Census returns for boarding houses in the following streets were recorded: St George's in the East, Wellclose Square, Princes Square, High Street, Neptune Street, Ratcliffe Street, Ship Alley, Brunswick Street, Perseverance Place, Palmers Folly, and St Georges Street.
8 Crook, 'Accommodating the outcast', 429.
9 London Metropolitan Archives (LMA), LCC/PH/REG/1/02, 'List of licensed seamen's lodging houses', 1908.
10 In total, fifty-four of the boarding house keepers had their sex recorded.
11 'List of licensed seamen's lodging houses', 1908.
12 LMA, LCC/PH/REG/1/02, 'Common lodging houses, police proceedings', 1908.
13 Crook, 'Accommodating the outcast', 432.
14 G. Milne, *People, Place and Power on the Nineteenth Century Waterfront: Sailortown* (Basingstoke, Palgrave Macmillan, 2016), 109.
15 *Morning Chronicle*, 2 May 1850.
16 Sailors' Society Archive, Sailor Society, Southampton, *The Sailor* Magazine, Vol II, 1821, 513–14.

17 S. Hugill, *Sailortown* (London, Routledge and Kegan Paul, 1967), 84–5.
18 Milne, *People, Place and Power*, 104.
19 *Old Bailey Proceedings Online* (OBP) (www.oldbaileyonline.org, version 6.0, 17 April 2011), August 1850, trial of John Walker, Charles Wilcox, John Elliot, Sarah Clements, Eliza Wilson, Selina Langley, t18500819-1508.
20 *Morning Herald*, 26 August 1850.
21 *Morning Chronicle*, 2 May 1850.
22 *Morning Chronicle*, 2 May 1850.
23 *Morning Chronicle*, 2 May 1850.
24 See Chapter 6 on the women of Ratcliffe Highway.
25 *Morning Chronicle*, 3 November 1851.
26 *Morning Post*, 6 December 1854.
27 Find My Past: 1851 and 1861 Censuses.
28 *Morning Chronicle*, 2 May 1850.
29 *Morning Chronicle*, 2 May 1850.
30 *Morning Chronicle*, 2 May 1850.
31 Crook, 'Accommodating the outcast', 422.
32 *Chart and Compass* (London, T. Wilson Booth, 1881), 209.
33 Quoted in Milne, *People, Place and Power*, 151.
34 Old Bailey Papers online, October 1887, trial of Richard Marchant and John Frost, t18871024-1048. An Albert was a Victorian fob watch chain.
35 H. Mayhew, *London Labour and the London Poor*, Vol IV (London, Griffin, Bohn & Co., 1862), 230.
36 LSE, Charles Booth Archive (hereafter CBA), Booth notebook B/138, 26, 1895.
37 LSE, CBA, Booth notebook B/138, 26, 1895.
38 *Daily News*, 18 May 1853.
39 *Daily News*, 1 November 1852.
40 *Lloyds Weekly*, 7 August 1864.
41 *Daily News*, 18 May 1853.
42 *The Graphic*, 30 April 1881.
43 R. Rowe, *Jack Afloat and Ashore* (London, Smith, Elder & Co., 1875), 77, 83.
44 Mayhew, *London Labour*, 228.
45 Find My Past: Census 1861.
46 T. Beames, *The Rookeries of London: Past, Present and Prospective* (London, Thomas Boswell, 1850, 1970 edn), 101.
47 *Chart and Compass*, 209.
48 Beames, *The Rookeries of London*, 101.
49 *Chart and Compass*, 209.
50 Hugill, *Sailortown*, 85. A fo'c'sle is the forward part of a ship's deck, usually used as a crew's living quarters.
51 *Morning Chronicle*, 11 April 1850.
52 E. Cuming, 'At home in the world? The ornamental life of the sailors in Victorian sailortown', *Victorian Literature and Culture*, 47(3), 2019, 463–85, 471.
53 Milne, *People, Place and Power*, 153–4.

54 Churchill, Warman, Gibson, and Leslie, *Stories from the Sea*, 10.
55 Churchill, Warman, Gibson, and Leslie, *Stories from the Sea*, Preface, 8–10; A. Kennerley, 'British seamen's missions and sailor homes 1815 to 1970. Voluntary welfare provision for serving seafarers' (unpublished PhD thesis, University of Exeter, 1989), 96.
56 H. Walker, *East London Sketches of Christian Work and Workers* (London, The Religious Tract Society, 1896), 179.
57 Sailor Society Archives (hereafter SSA), *The Sailor's Magazine*, Vol II, 1821, 32.
58 East London Observer, 25 May 1861.
59 Milne's analysis of missionaries across the globe tends to confirm their inability to meaningfully engage sailors. See Milne, *People, Place and Power*, 161–2.
60 SSA, *The Port of London and Bethel Union Society*, the 73rd Annual Report (London, T. Wilson Booth, 1890–91), 23.
61 LSE, CBA, Booth notebook B/280, 246; Hugill, *Sailortown*, 280.
62 Milne, *People, Place and Power*, 155.
63 J. Havelock Wilson, quoted in A. Kennerley, 'Joseph Conrad at the Sailor's Home', *The Conradian*, 33(1), spring 2008, 69–10, 82.
64 Milne, *People, Place and Power*, 155.
65 *Morning Chronicle*, 11 April 1850.
66 Milne, *People, Place and Power*, 155.
67 *Morning Chronicle*, 11 April 1850; *Standard*, 26 December 1878.
68 *Morning Chronicle*, 11 April 1850.
69 Kennerley, 'British seamen's missions and sailor homes 1815 to 1970', 90.
70 LSE, CBA, Booth notebook B/138 1895, 35.
71 *Morning Chronicle*, 19 April; 2 May 1850.
72 *Morning Chronicle*, 11 April 1850.
73 *Morning Chronicle*, 11 April 1850.
74 *Morning Chronicle*, 11 April 1850.
75 Quoted in Kennerley, 'Joseph Conrad at the Sailor's Home', 81–2.
76 Find My Past: 1851 Census, Well Street Sailor Home.
77 Kennerley, 'Joseph Conrad at the Sailor's Home', 83.
78 LSE, CBA, Booth notebook B/138 1895, 35.
79 *Western Daily Mercury*, 5 January 1876.
80 *Morning Chronicle*, 19 April 1850.
81 C. Fox Smith (ed.), *The Man before the Mast: Being the Story of Twenty Years Afloat* (London, Methuen, 1929), 2.
82 *Morning Chronicle*, 19 April 1850.
83 Milne, *People, Place and Power*, 157.
84 J. Salter, *The East in the West; Or Work among the Asiatics and Africans in London* (London, S.W. Partridge & Co., 1896), 17.
85 J. Hyslop, '"Ghostlike" seafarers and sailing ship nostalgia: The figure of the steamship lascar in the British imagination, 1860–1960', *Journal of Maritime Research*, 16(2), 2014, 212–28, 213.
86 *The Examiner*, 2 January 1858.

87 LSE, CBA, Booth notebook 138, 'Interview with Mr M. Johnson, superintendent of the Home for Asiatics, 1895', 53.
88 Salter, *The East in the West*, 152.
89 LSE, CBA, Booth notebook B/138, 48.
90 *Daily News*, 29 May 1872.
91 *Daily News*, 29 May 1872.
92 LSE, CBA, Booth notebook B/138, 49–50.
93 Milne, *People, Place and Power*, 157.
94 *Daily News*, 29 May 1872.
95 Salter, *The East in the West*, 153.
96 *Daily News*, 29 May 1872.
97 Find My Past: 1901 Census, Limehouse Causeway.
98 G.R. Sims (ed.), *Living London* (London, Cassell & Co., 1902), 82.
99 Sims (ed.), *Living London*, 83–4.
100 *Morning Post*, 6 December 1854.
101 James Frey has demonstrated that Indian sailors also manipulated the law courts to their own advantage while ashore; see J.W. Frey, 'Lascars, the Thames police court and the Old Bailey: Crime on the high seas and the London courts, 1852–8', *Journal of Maritime Research*, 16(2), 2014, 196–211.

6

Sex work and Ratcliffe Highway: Brothels, crime, and matriarchal networks

> *Ratcliffe Highway by night! The head-quarters of unbridled vice and drunken violence – of all that is dirty, disorderly, and debased. Splash, down, down comes the rain; but it must fall a deluge indeed to wash away even a portion of the filth to be found in this detestable place. Like a drab, it lies side by side with the river, who holds it in a foul embrace, kissing its rottenness with slimy lips and receiving into its broad bosom a portion of the corruption it contains.*
>
> Watts Phillips, *The Wild Tribes of London* (1855), 19

Watts Phillips's description of Ratcliffe Highway was notable for his contention that the source of Ratcliffe Highway's vice, dirt, and rottenness was the Thames, a malign female presence that smothered and debased its victims. This analogy indicates that, for writers like Phillips, the women who worked in, or at the margins of, the sex trade were a significant agent of moral and physical corruption, and their prey was the naïve sailor ashore. This caricature of the women who associated with sailors on Ratcliffe Highway was replicated in the press and police courts and hides the broad range of sex work operating in the district, and the women's differing experiences of the industry. While acknowledging the complexity of sex work during this period, this chapter will first explore how the press's vivid derogatory descriptions of women engaged in prostitution represented a deeper anxiety about the proletarianisation of the modern city. The chapter will recover women's encounters with sailors, brothel keepers, and 'pimps'. It will contrast the experiences of sex workers locked into a cycle of exploitation and violence with other women who lived on the margins of the sex industry and were able to exert some agency in a hostile and bleak environment. Ratcliffe Highway was an important contact zone for sex workers to meet sailors, while its urban geography of secluded courtyards, streets, and alleys provided some peer-group surveillance and security. Finally, the chapter will also explore how philanthropic attempts to reform Ratcliffe Highway women were largely unsuccessful due to their inability to break their robust and independent matriarchal subculture. Sex workers were, by their very nature, on the margins of Victorian civil society, so their activities, associations, and behaviour are difficult to document. However, it is possible to piece together fragments of these people's lives by working through Old Bailey transcripts, police court reports, newspapers, and the Census.

From 'lusty Moll' to the wild 'Empress of Disorderlies': the growing anxiety of urban modernity

A number of historians have noted that mid-nineteenth century reforms to the criminal justice system were an important step in the state's attempt to pacify a gregarious urban subaltern culture. Reforms such as the introduction of professional magistrates and police courts were intended to 'civilise' working people by encouraging them to take their disputes through the courts rather than settle them on the street.[1] This move to 'civilise' and 'pacify' the poor was accompanied by a greater scrutiny of public urban spaces, aided and abetted by the newly formed Metropolitan Police force. Thus, street activities that would have been tolerated in Georgian London, such as heavy drinking, certain forms of prostitution, and sailors' excesses ashore, became the subject of public complaint, and police surveillance and intervention. Such was the intense fervour of magistrates to cleanse the Ratcliffe Highway region of depravity that the *East London Observer* complained in 1857 that 'the suddenly-found zeal of the public against immorality has led to an onslaught on nearly all of our East-end places of public entertainment, and many an old established and respectable place of entertainment has fallen victim'.[2] At the same time, Victorian anxieties about how the city had fostered a moral and physical decay had provoked fears about the long-term consequences of urban modernity.

These two mid-nineteenth century trends – the move to civilise the streets and an increasing anxiety about urban development – were important in influencing how women prostitutes were represented and perceived in the Victorian city. Indeed, the 'modern' prostitute symbolised the Victorian city's descent into moral and physical decay, and, to social commentators, nowhere was this decline more evident than on Ratcliffe Highway.[3] One reporter surmised that the number of prostitutes had increased on Ratcliffe Highway during the 1850s due to the demolition of the Lower Shadwell district for the enlargement of London Dock, which had driven the women 'from their old and comparatively obscure haunts to Ratcliffe Highway, Commercial Road, and East Smithfield'.[4] According to the local press, not only were there more women on the streets, but the modern prostitute was a savage imitation of her Georgian predecessors. Commentators looked back fondly to the stereotypical prostitutes 'Moll and Poll' of the late eighteenth and early nineteenth centuries. These women were cast as benign domesticated characters who were romantically involved with their sailors and cared for them while ashore.[5] For these commentators, the brutal condition of the modern city was reversing Darwin's theory of evolution and fostering a degenerate proletariat that had all the hallmarks of a primaeval and savage race.[6] Religious missionaries also adopted a similar narrative and were shocked at the women's brazen behaviour. Reverend Edward Thomas, a missionary, noted how Ratcliffe Highway women behaved and dressed differently from the other 'fallen women' in London. He wrote how women of all different ages did not attempt to conceal their profession. The young women were 'brazen-faced' and 'vicious to a painful degree', while the oldest included the 'inured harridan of the streets, coarse, and cunning, with countenance as low as vice could make it, and as hard in sin as flint'.[7]

These working-class women were accused of maternal culpability, described as incapable of friendship and exploitative to one another, which ultimately ended in mutual destruction. This lack of comradeship and altruism was explained by their 'child-like' mental capacity that led to spontaneous and violent irrational rages ending in women's street fights.[8] Their dress also surprised observers since 'the fashion of the women varied like the colours of the rainbow. Many were remarkably clothed as far as material went'.[9] Likewise, one reporter for the *Daily News* noted that the prostitutes of Ratcliffe Highway dressed differently to other women and flaunted 'apparel of the coarsest and gaudiest kind'.[10] Indeed, on almost every level, these women transgressed bourgeois feminine norms, and nowhere was this more apparent than on the public highways. Correspondents of the local press complained that due to the neglect of the police, Ratcliffe Highway had descended into a moral and cultural abyss. To the 'respectable' residents of Ratcliffe Highway, modern prostitutes openly mocked bourgeois-gendered codes of behaviour by loudly taking possession of the main thoroughfare. One correspondent in the *East London Observer* wistfully remembered how earlier on in the century, prostitutes found it quite sufficient to advertise their profession by walking the streets 'bare-headed, and with a red silk handkerchief – a bandanna – tied round their delicate shoulders', and a halfpenny cane in their hands. But now, things had changed:

> how many a modest woman is forced into the roadway to avoid the half a dozen caricatures of her sex, who, wildly drunk, are walking abreast, occupying the whole of the footway, and singing, or rather screeching, snatches of obscene songs at the very top of their voices.[11]

Correspondents frequently complained that on Ratcliffe Highway, respectable people were plagued by the 'audacity and obscenities of the hordes of prostitutes who congregated in the street'.[12] Not only did prostitutes, at times, dominate the pathways, they also took possession of the Highway itself. The reporter claimed that prostitutes would dress up in masquerade dresses and 'cram themselves into and on several cabs' and parade up and down Ratcliffe Highway in a noisy procession, stopping off on the many hostelries en route. According to the correspondent, other prostitutes hired donkeys and traps that raced through the Highway, intimidating passers-by 'in drunken hilarity in carts filled with screaming women and swearing sailors'. By the 1850s, then, prostitution on Ratcliffe Highway was not discretely confined to side streets and public houses but flagrantly exercised on the main thoroughfare in a gregarious and noisy fashion. One exasperated resident of Ratcliffe complained that the police were to be seen everywhere but the Highway itself. 'Where are the police? In your Kitchen sir! Flirting with your housemaid, madam! Chatting with your potman, or barmaid, mine host!'[13]

Street prostitution was undoubtedly the most dangerous, isolating, and brutalised form of sex work. It was also the most visible form of sex work, which to the bourgeois Victorian gaze further confirmed their sense that modern prostitutes had taken on masculine attributes. Thus, Zoe Alker has shown in nineteenth-century Liverpool that women who worked on the street were described as 'broad-set, loose girls with bloated faces and rough hair in bed-gowns and brawny arms'.[14] The disputes and fights that these women had with their clients and other women were played out on the streets, with some gaining infamous reputations for their unruly public behaviour. The local press identified several 'well known women of the town' who fitted this category, but by far the most notorious woman of Ratcliffe Highway during the mid-nineteenth century was Julia Mahoney. The press dubbed her, among other things, 'the Wild Irish Girl' and the East End 'Cannibal', but she was more widely known as the 'Empress of Disorderlies'. It is worth exploring her life in a little more detail as it illustrates how some women who fell into street sex work were troubled by mental health issues, lacked the security of social networks, and resorted to drink and violence to survive the harsh realities of their desperate environment.

Mahoney was born in Cork and first emerged in 1851 as a twenty-one-year-old woman in a 'low-lodging house' in Lambeth Street, Whitechapel. Within a year she had moved to another brothel in Whitechapel that was raided by the police in 1852.[15] This transitory life had continued moving further east to a similarly low-lodging house in Bluegate Fields near Ratcliffe Highway by 1853. She appeared to have made few friends or networks in the district and had become notorious for her brutality when fighting with women. In 1853, at the age of twenty-three, she was described as a 'dissipated and revolting-looking woman of the town' and labelled a 'cannibal' after biting the nose off a fellow sex worker in a row over a client.[16] A year later, Mahoney appeared in court for seriously assaulting and injuring Sarah Graham, another sex worker, with a poker, tongs, and a shovel. Mahoney was described as having arms 'covered in scars' which were the result of 'violent assaults on persons of her own sex over and over again'.[17] Having, it seems, few reliable acquaintances or a stable social network, Mahoney relied upon her aggression and fighting capabilities while working on the streets. She also turned to drink and, from the late 1850s, suffered from mental health issues, and she attempted to take her own life by throwing herself off the notorious Gravel Road Bridge and later tried once more while in her Millbank prison cell.[18]

In 1870 it was reported that she had over fifty convictions for drunkenness, assaults, and petty felonies, which in one instance resulted in an appearance at the Old Bailey. Thus, in 1864 Mahoney stood trial for feloniously wounding Elisabeth Germane, a neighbour, and was imprisoned for twelve months.[19] She served prison sentences throughout the 1860s and 1870s until she was released on licence in February 1883 at the age of fifty-three having been confined for seven years. She does not appear again in the newspapers or courts after this date as she conceivably moves from one institution to another. The Census recorded a Julia Mahoney, described as a pauper, in the Mill End Workhouse in 1891. While Mahoney's notoriety was infamous, her life history was far from unique, having become brutalised from an early age and living a precarious and dangerous existence on the streets and low brothels. While Mahoney cut a lonely figure living a perilous existence, tramping from one lodging house to another, other young women became caught up in 'low' brothels run by exploitative criminals in an era that was becoming increasingly intolerant to street disorder or sexual immorality.

Sanitising the streets: brothels and crime on Ratcliffe Highway

The shift from a Georgian tolerance of prostitution and sailor excess to Victorian attempts to root out vice and immorality during the mid-nineteenth century was incapsulated by the creation of the East London Association for the Suppression of Vice in 1857.[20] This was a small but very vocal organisation that was formed on the premise that the police and the criminal justice system were incapable and unwilling to quash vice in the district. In their inaugural meeting, it was stated that the Association was established with: 'the object of abating that class of public offences which consists in acts of indecency, profanity, drunkenness and prostitution, which unhappily, has of late years increased to an alarming extent throughout the various and densely populated parishes of the east end of London'.[21] The active members were upper class and solidly middle class with a strong religious element and included Whig politician Lord Ebury,

Reverend Lowder, who was head of the St Georges Mission, and Thomas Charrington, the prominent anti-vice campaigner in London.[22] Despite these leading figures, throughout its existence, the Association complained of a lack of members, public engagement, and funds. Nevertheless, during the 1850s and 1860s, the Association did succeed in shining a light on some of the worst brothel owners who presided over a network of bawdy houses and who were exploitative and violent to the women they employed.

In July 1858 the East London Association for the Suppression of Vice attended before the Thames Police Magistrate to obtain a warrant for the arrest of a notorious family who kept a chain of twenty-five 'common brothels' in the district that housed over 150 prostitutes. The family comprised Benjamin James, his wife Mary James, and Morris Speedy (her brother). They, along with Elizabeth Martin, Mary Martin, and Ann Gilmour, were all accused of running disorderly brothels and maltreating the women who worked in them. These brothels were described as 'short-rents', which allowed them to shut down their premises and move to others at short notice. They were based in the narrow streets that branched off Ratcliffe Highway such as Neptune Street, Neptune Court, and Glasshouse Street. The East London Association claimed that these brothels had been the sites of robberies, and fights with both men and women who had been maimed for life. It was alleged that the family charged women high rents and intimidated them into 'robbing captains, mates, and seamen'. According to the Association, the terrible conditions and fear that the women lived under had resulted in:

> repeated instances of suicide among the unfortunate females under the control of Mrs James and her husband. Some had cut their throats, others had drowned themselves in the London Docks, and not a few had hung themselves, or put an end to their existence by taking poison.[23]

While Benjamin and Mary James owned the brothel business, the press focused on Mary as her appearance, business, and shocking behaviour seemingly transgressed gendered norms. Whereas Benjamin James was hardly mentioned in any of the press coverage and described as an 'old and infirm gentleman', much greater attention was centred on Mary's appearance and morality.[24] The press noted that Mary was known as 'the bloater' and was 'a large, bloated, vulgar woman' who assailed the police with 'horrible and obscene language and threats'.[25] As we shall see, journalists, and also magistrates, often linked a woman's physical appearance to a perceived immorality. Despite the press's focus on Mary James, all five defendants pleaded guilty to living off immoral earnings and their short-leased premises were closed. No records appear to have survived that relate to their activities after 1858, though it is likely that they carried on working in brothel keeping under assumed names.[26]

The fierce families or individuals who owned a large network of brothels would often rely on violence, threats, and intimidation to keep young girls working for them. One observer told Bracebridge Hemyng of the brothel keeper's brutal treatment meted out to women to prevent their escape:

> When the forlorn, unfortunate wretch returns to her infamous abode, she is maltreated and kept nearly naked during the day, so that she cannot attempt to run away. She is often half starved, and at night sent again into the streets as often as she is disengaged, while all the money she receives goes to her keeper whether male or female. This is not an exaggerated picture, but a fact attested by myself. I have known a girl, aged fifteen years, who in one night knew twelve men, and produced to her keeper as many pounds.[27]

Furthermore, to earn sufficient money to pay the extortionately high rent, women had to resort to stealing from men who used the brothels. Women working in these brothels experienced little control over their lives and were constantly under surveillance by the brothel owners or their staff. For example, one journalist who visited a notoriously low brothel described how the proprietor had complete control over those who worked in the building:

> The door of each room in the house just named is fastened on the outside whenever occupied, and the key kept by the proprietor of the establishment, who has also a sliding panel in every door, through which to objurgate his or her tenants, to look down upon them when they are least prepared for observation.[28]

These were undoubtedly the worst and the most dangerous forms of sex work that women were subjected to.

Alongside larger-scale brothel ownership were the women and their partners who operated their businesses under the cover of beer shops or coffee houses. When these brothels were raided, they would shut down, move premises, and reopen under the pretence of a different business. The owners would also change their names, particularly if the brothels were associated with violence and robberies. For example, Mary Ann Sullivan led a life of brothel keeping and crime in the Ratcliffe Highway district during the middle years of the nineteenth century. In 1861 she was embroiled in the mysterious death of Thomas Hall, the Captain of the Brig Mary, North Shields. On the morning of 23 November, Hall left his ship with a considerable amount of money to go drinking with Ellen McCarthy and Julia Grieg, who were described as 'low prostitutes'. It was alleged that Hall and McCarthy spent the night in a brothel, after which he returned to his ship in the morning. However, he retired to bed feeling ill and died a few hours later.

At the coroner's inquest, Sullivan, who was described as a 'brothel-keeper', acknowledged that McCarthy had regularly brought men back to her house in Betts Street. However, she denied that McCarthy had slept with Hall in her brothel on the night of his death, claiming that he had never visited the premises. McCarthy also denied sleeping with Hall and claimed he had left the pub to return to his ship. The surgeon, Dr Arnold, detected opium in Hall's stomach, and it was suspected that he had been poisoned with the view of carrying out a robbery. However, the drug did not take full effect until he was on his ship, which explained why he had died with 11*l*. in gold still in his pocket.[29] Nevertheless, the inquest concluded that there was insufficient evidence to charge McCarthy with attempted robbery because there was uncertainty over how the opium had been administered.[30] There is good evidence that Sullivan and her associates continued to practise robbery in her brothel since she appeared in Clerkenwell Court three years later. In 1864 Mary Ann Sullivan, Frederick Sullivan, and Louisa Shannon were charged with a brothel robbery. Much to the outrage of the local newspaper, they were all acquitted by the jury.[31]

However, a year later, Sullivan moved to new premises, found a new partner, and changed her name. In June 1865 Daniel Evans and Mary Ann Evans were found guilty of keeping a disorderly house at 9 Wellington-Place, St George's in the East. It was reported that Mary Ann Evans, who had previously called herself Mary Ann Sullivan, had recently begun a relationship with Daniel Evans and both had routinely committed violence and robbery while operating the brothel. The magistrate remarked that sailors were their main victims as they were obliged to return to sea and often failed to report the crime. Mary Ann Evans was described as 'a most notorious character, having been the associate of thieves, and many robberies had taken place in the neighbourhood of this house'. Both were found guilty, and Mary Ann Evans was imprisoned for twelve months with hard labour and Daniel Evans for three months, after which Evans disappears from the criminal justice records.[32]

Perhaps one of the most notorious women who combined brothel keeping with robbery was Anne Gilligan. Such was her infamy, Gilligan did not attempt to hide her identity from the authorities or move her business each time she was convicted. Indeed, by the late 1860s her brothel in Angel Court, Shadwell, had become a celebrated 'den of thieves' and an inspiration for the authors of Penny Dreadfuls.[33] Her criminal enterprise, however, seems to have taken its toll as, at the age of thirty-six, she was described in the press as 'an elderly woman with white hair'.[34] The reporter at the Thames police court noted:

> Robberies and outrages of every kind had been perpetuated in the lodging house which she kept. She herself suffered a term of penal servitude for felony, and had been subsequently charged with murder; but capital accusation had not been brought home to her … to complete the charge of Ann's misdeeds, she was charged with the comparatively venial offences of selling malt liquors and spirits during prohibited hours.[35]

However, her years immersed in the criminal underworld and her numerous court appearances had taught Gilligan how to perform in court and where the loopholes were in the legal system. She was remarkably candid about herself and her business, but this was part of her strategy in court to avoid conviction. Gilligan was charged with breaches under the Common Lodging House Act. However, she explained to the court that in her defence, 'her house was, as she assured the magistrate with touching candour and in broader English, merely a low house of ill-fame. She confessed that she lived in an illicit union with a thief, and was a thief herself'.[36] She further claimed that the police sergeant of K division had arrested her due to her refusal to divide with him a bounty of ten shillings she had extorted from a sea captain for the return of his papers.

Watching her performance, the reporter remarked that Gilligan had 'the candour of the dove, but the wisdom of the serpent'. Gilligan's approach somewhat wrong-footed Mr Paget, the magistrate, who was 'at first sorely puzzled to tell whether he could convict; for he felt serious doubt whether such a house as the prisoner confessed hers to be was a common lodging-house'. However, after careful thought, he concluded that he could convict her in full, which merely amounted to £10, a sum that seemed to the press wholly inadequate. Moreover, after an investigation, Gilligan's claim of police extortion was found to be unsubstantiated.[37] The *Daily Telegraph and Courier* reporter noted how Gilligan had avoided imprisonment despite brazenly charting her criminal credentials and felonies in the Thames police court. He added that:

> Angel Court, Palmer's Folly, Bluegate-fields are all abominable dens of infamy and crime, and have been so at any time during these five-and-twenty years ... The whole neighbourhood of Shadwell and Ratcliff-Highway absolutely swarms with nuisance hovels, kept by bandits and procuresses, who harbour the lowest class of loose women, and whose business it is to drug drunken sailors; to hocus, rob, and maltreat them; and, for aught that can be known to the contrary, to murder them.[38]

The reporter lamented that fining criminals or even imprisoning them would do little to stop these dens of infamy continuing, and so he contended that 'to get rid of wasps it is usual to destroy the wasps' nest'. He urged the British authorities to follow Haussmann's Parisian model as he 'demolished the cité altogether, and built sumptuous boulevards instead'. He concluded that the 'breaking up of their haunts' and the destruction of their 'dens' was the 'only practical step towards destroying "habitual criminals" as a class'.[39]

The 1871 Census confirmed that Gilligan continued to live at number 2 Angel Court with Catherine Sullivan, Ann O'Brian, Annie Learney, and

Mary Ann McGimmil. These women were all in their twenties or early thirties and described as fallen women who, like Gilligan, had originated from Ireland. They shared the brothel with three labourers and a domestic servant.[40] However, the Census records indicate that Angel Court was subject to the piecemeal slum clearances in London during the 1870s and 1880s.[41] At the time of the 1881 Census, only number 1 Angel Court is listed with residents, while the 1891 Census records neither Angel Court nor Ann Gilligan.[42]

Women-run brothels and micro-community networks

In one of his many letters to the *Morning Chronicle*, Mayhew described the facilities and institutions available to the sailors who came ashore from London's port. After depicting the welfare homes and respectable boarding houses, he described the 'lower' lodging houses that were 'half brothel'. He noted that these were fairly small institutions sometimes run by a husband and a wife. In these brothels, the husband was usually a London dock stevedore whose casual work was an insufficient income for his household, so he hired rooms out to women. However, the most numerous type of brothel in this area was run entirely by 'girls on their own account'.[43] These half-brothel, half-lodging houses run solely by women were located away from the glare of Ratcliffe Highway and in the narrow side roads and courts that ran off it.[44] As we have seen in Chapter 1, the higher property rents pushed the low-paid and 'low' boarding houses, pubs, and brothels into the surrounding vicinity. Thus, while Ratcliffe Highway accommodated the largest and most infamous entertainment venues and was famed for the night-time 'parading' of prostitutes and sailors, most women sex workers lived and worked in the margins. These women gravitated to the liminal urban spaces and forged micro-communities that tolerated or endorsed divergent lives and identities. Indeed, the Reverend Charles Lowder recalled that when walking down the 'notorious streets' off Ratcliffe Highway, he witnessed women flaunting their 'sin and finery' and was shocked that 'public opinion against it there is none'.[45]

Small side streets and courts such as New Gravel Road, Perseverance Place, and Palmers Folly all shared similar characteristics in that these streets were dominated by women residents. For example, as Tables 6.1 and 6.2 illustrate, in Palmers Folly and Perseverance Place, there was usually over double the number of women than men living on these streets. Unlike the larger surrounding streets where 'general servant' was the most numerous occupation for women, in these two streets, the vast majority of women were classed as needlewomen. Significantly, sailors who were

Table 6.1 Sex and occupation of the residents of Palmers Folly, 1861 and 1871

Male occupations registering 10 or more of the total male occupations stated in Palmers Folly, 1861	Female occupations registering 10 or more of the total female occupations stated in Palmers Folly, 1861
Labourer: 12.5%	General servant: 13%
Sailor: 44%	Needlewoman: 45%
Miscellaneous trades numbering under 10: 43.5%	Miscellaneous trades numbering under 10: 43%
	Women recorded as head of the household: 31%
Total number of working men: 50	Total number of working women: 115
Male occupations registering 10 or more of the total male occupations stated in Palmers Folly, 1871	**Female occupations registering 10 or more of the total female occupations stated in Palmers Folly, 1871**
Sailor: 68%	'Unfortunates': 72%
Miscellaneous trades numbering under 10: 32%	Miscellaneous trades numbering under 10: 28%
	Women recorded as head of the household: 36%
Total number of working men: 20	Total number of working women: 50

visitors or temporary residents represented the largest occupational category in both Palmers Folly and Perseverance Place. Moreover, the greater independence that these matriarchal enclaves facilitated is demonstrated by the high number of women who were recorded as the head of household in these streets. Indeed, before the demolition of these streets in the late nineteenth century, these matriarchal areas seemed to have been growing in strength, with both streets recording rises in women-heading households, with Perseverance Place increasing from 0 to 82 per cent of women assuming the role in 1871. The formation of these matriarchal networks was aided by the relatively compact nature of these areas as these small streets consisted of only twenty-four properties in Palmers Folly and twenty in Perseverance Place.

As we shall see, all this made for a tight-knit neighbourhood that hosted a strong network of women involved in sex work. Both streets were known to house a string of 'low' brothels. For example, through searching reports that identified brothels in the London press between 1850 and 1880, it was revealed that 50 per cent of the addresses of Palmers Folly were at one point identified by the authorities as brothels.[46] Rooms and even whole properties

Table 6.2 Sex and occupation of the residents of Perseverance Place, 1861 and 1871

Male occupations registering in Perseverance Place, 1861	Female occupations registering in Perseverance Place, 1861
Seamen: 57%	Needlewoman: 50%
Miscellaneous trades numbering under 10: 43%	Laundress: 41%
	Miscellaneous trades numbering under 10: 9%
	Women recorded as head of the household: 0%
Total number of working men: 17	Total number of working women: 51
Male occupations registering in Perseverance Place, 1871	**Female occupations registering in Perseverance Place, 1871**
Labourer: 67%	'Unfortunates': 41% (78% of these women were recorded as head of the household)
Miscellaneous trades numbering under 10: 33%	Needlewoman: 9%
	Laundress/char women: 36%
	Servants: 14%
	Total women recorded as head of the household: 82%
Total number of working men: 15	Total number of working women: 22

were often rented out on a weekly basis, meaning that brothels tended to relocate further down the street to avoid police scrutiny.[47] The reputation of these areas was routinely castigated by magistrates for the 'daily assemblage of loose women' in the police courts from those 'horrible places' such as Palmers Folly. After one incident in which six women were charged with riotous behaviour, Mr Paget, the Thames police court magistrate, declared that he would 'restore peace in the district, and put an end to scenes which were a disgrace to a civilised country'.[48] Thus, the press, courts, and magistrates projected these streets as dangerous and immoral areas that were an affront to civilisation. Indeed, one journalist noted that the 'Bloodbowl Houses' and 'thieves kitchens' of the Penny Dreadfuls did not merely rest in the 'ferried imagination of the penny romancer or the "sensational" reporter' but were a feature of Palmers Folly and other 'abominable dens of infamy and crime'.[49]

This gothic portrait of Palmers Folly was replicated in other journalistic forays into the area and regularly in the police courts. However, these descriptions do not help us understand the micro-support networks that evolved precisely because of the dangerous and appalling conditions that these women were living in. As we have seen, Palmers Folly and Perseverance Place, which totalled just over forty buildings, had twice as many women living there as men. It was common for those who lived in the courts and 'rookeries', which were located behind major thoroughfares, to develop informal surveillance systems to identify and prevent entry to unwelcome visitors from the police or officialdom. The social campaigner George Sims discovered an elaborate password system in one court that confirmed the user was not a policeman, which thereby allowed the visitor to enter.[50] Indeed, like Sims, a journalist in the 1860s was treated by the local inhabitants of Palmers Folly with the same suspicion. As he made his way through Palmers Folly's gated entrance and down the street, he described how 'you are peeped at by untidy and dishevelled figures, who stand at slightly open doors or peer down from the shrouded windows'. As he progressed further down the street, the residents of Palmers Folly warned their neighbours that the police were in the vicinity. He noted 'shadowy figures flitting across our darkened pathway and whistling and other sounds signalling the presence of strangers and the imminent approach of the police'.[51]

The careful monitoring of strangers entering this gated community ensured that women were able to call upon assistance should they be confronted with dangerous situations. This informal support network emerged into view when violence against women occurred in the street. In 1855, after quarrelling with a woman outside a brothel, Peter Brock, an Italian sailor, drew a knife and threatened the woman and the brothel keeper. It was reported that 'a female named Bassett, living in one of the adjoining houses, with more courage than discretion, endeavoured to remove the prisoner [Brock], and pushed him'. After a struggle, Brock threw Bassett on the floor and stabbed her in the thigh. Despite this violence, Catherine Smith, another neighbour, 'attempted to seize the prisoner, and her temerity had nearly cost her her life, for the prisoner made an attempt to stab her in the belly. She avoided the blow, and the Italian fled'.[52] The sailor was pursued by Peter Ryan, another resident, who caught Brock and turned him over to the police. Brock was found guilty of unlawfully wounding Ann Bassett and sentenced to six months' imprisonment with hard labour.[53] Thus, while the Palmers Folly community were intensely suspicious of the police, it seems that they turned to the criminal justice system when it advantaged them.[54] Other examples of residents intervening in disputes include a case in 1858 when a Greek sailor attacked several women in Palmers Folly. Edward Mahoney, described as an Irish labourer, challenged the sailor who was 'beating some prostitutes in a den of infamy'. Antonio Pinner, the sailor, attacked Mahoney with a knife, leaving him with a badly cut arm. The magistrate had no sympathy with Mahoney's attempt to defend the women and fined him 10s while fining Pinner £5 and in default of payment two months' imprisonment.[55]

The foundation of this neighbourhood street surveillance was built on the micro-networks that had been fostered between women working in the brothels situated in Palmers Folly and Perseverance Street. The internal dynamics of these communities can be explored further through surviving court cases that reveal the relationships between the men and women who forged these networks. For example, in 1852 Joes Frutoso, a Spanish sailor, appeared at the Old Bailey charged with murdering James Almon, an English sailor, in a New Gravel Lane brothel. Like Palmers Folly, New Gravel Lane had an equally lurid reputation and was similarly populated with women residents and brothels.[56] During the trial, Mary Ann Kirwin, who described herself as a 'brothel keeper', explained that she had kept the house at 106 Gravel Lane for over three years, though after the death of Almon, she had moved her business to nearby premises. Kirwin, who was twenty-nine, described how she lived with Mary Ann Smith, Margaret Donovan, and Emily Willis, who were prostitutes, Sarah Slater, her cousin, and Ann Copas, the servant. However, these women had spent less than a year at the property as none of them were listed at Kirwin's address at the Census point in March 1851. As we have seen, this transitory life of young women moving from one boarding house or brothel to another fits into the larger work patterns of sex workers in 'low' brothels located on the side streets of Ratcliffe Highway. However, this transitory way of life should not obscure the real communal and familial networks that operated in these districts. In the trial, Kirwin indicated that she had built up a friendship with Smith as she had known her for some time before her moving in. She also had allowed her cousin to stay with her until she found another place to lodge, which may have reduced her earnings as Slater was not a prostitute.

Kirwin's account of her household in court also offers an insight into how young women entered sex work. In explaining her lodgers' roles, Kirwin stated that 'Slater was not a prostitute, nor yet Copas'.[57] The clear implication was that Copas, when she was sufficiently old enough, would relinquish her role as a house servant and become a sex worker. Given that Kirwin employed and housed her, Copas would have been left in an invidious position. Indeed, Kirwin's background suggests that she would have been a formidable woman to cross as she had been involved in numerous 'assaults and rows', had been fined for assaults, and imprisoned for six months for robbery on two separate occasions. In explaining her background story, Kirwin insisted that despite her criminal history, she was a respectable brothel keeper. Indeed, her evidence in court reveals how respectability was a fluid class and gendered construct that was influenced by the marginality of their urban location. This was a respectability forged from the realities of working in a precarious, poverty-stricken, and gendered environment. It is worth quoting Kirwin's testimony at length as, despite her criminal record, she steadfastly maintains that she is a respectable brothel keeper:

> I have kept this brothel going on for three years – during that time I have not been in any trouble about my place; I have been in trouble, but not on account of that – the last time I was in trouble was last April – I was charged with felony, with robbing a man, not in my brothel, in the same lane, but not in my own brothel – I got six months – I was not tried at this place, somewhere in Clerkenwell ... I was charged with stealing six sovereigns – the man I robbed was not hurt, he did not complain of being hurt – I came out of prison in April, I had been in six months – I have not been in trouble since April, I have had warrants out for me for assaults – two, not more; I paid the fines, 10s. and 12s. – it was for assaulting Sarah Foreman, a brothel keeper, the same as myself; she broke my windows, and I assaulted her – it was both times for assaulting her – she assaulted me and I assaulted her – that is the only thing since April – I was not tried on any other occasion, except in April, not since April – before that I was, eight years ago, that was the first time, that was on a charge of a gentleman's watch – I had six months for that, it was a charge of robbery – that was in the City – I was then on the streets – those are the only times; I was never convicted only those times – I have been in prison for assaults and rows, and that like, I am sure I cannot tell you how many times.[58]

Kirwin's respectability, like male working-class respectability, was not fixed but malleable and influenced by the environment.[59] Thus, for Kirwin, brothel keeping and respectability were not mutually exclusive activities. For women sex workers, their sense of self and respectability was governed by an awareness of their own spatial urban environment. The dark and secluded courts, back alleys, and side streets of Ratcliffe Highway were liminal spaces which allowed women to digress from moral norms to carry out their work and to maximise their safety.[60] Thus, Kirwin was keen to emphasise the *location* of her robberies and that they took place on the streets and not inside her brothel. Indeed, the rows and assaults she was also imprisoned for all took place on the streets rather than in her brothel. She also claimed that even her most serious robberies did not involve any violence against the clients she stole from. When violence did occur, it was meted out to fellow women in her trade. She indicated that these rows, often with fellow brothel keepers, were part and parcel of the job and did not detract from her own sense of respectability. Significantly, her testimony hints at a distinction between her behaviour when she was starting 'on the streets', where criminal activity was the norm, and her most recent period of keeping a brothel.

Besides this fluid sense of respectability, prostitutes also forged relationships with men that would not have been tolerated in more land-locked working-class communities. Alongside their regular clientele, women in waterfront communities would sometimes have four or five 'husbands', sailors whom they would see regularly on their return to port. These relationships were discovered by social researchers who interpreted this arrangement as a way for a prostitute to win favour with their sailor to cunningly steal the considerable earnings he had accumulated from his sea voyages. Indeed, they suspected that the 'husband' and 'wife' labels were merely a ruse for a purely cash-nexus interaction. In 1879 the Reverend Edward Thomas wrote that women would flock to the docks when a ship came in and trick the sailor into accompanying her until the money ran out. According to Thomas, ports gave prostitutes a unique opportunity to increase their earnings:

> Ratcliffe and Wapping have ways of their own, and in no particular could this be better illustrated than in the conduct of the sailors and women present. It was observed that each seaman had his own particular girl, and continued with her, and this is one of the customs of the place. For the time Jack remains constant, or should he fail to prove so, he is fought for by his paramour, and this continues as long as his money remains unexhausted.[61]

Likewise, in 1875 Reverend Harry Jones noted that prostitutes in his parish of St George's in the East claimed to have several 'husbands'. He wrote that there was an 'illegitimate sort of faithfulness between many individuals' that was recognised among women and men and that it was 'the poor sailors' who were the 'prey' for this sort of deception.[62]

Henry Mayhew also noticed these informal arrangements when one prostitute told him that 'I know very many sailors – six, eight, then oh! More than that. They are my husbands. I am not married, of course not, but they do think me their wife whilst they are on shore'. She added that she looked after their money as 'it [is] very bad for [a] sailor to keep his money himself; he will fall into bad hands'.[63] He noted that women who ran establishments that were half beer shop and half brothel 'act as the men's wives; and indeed, some have married in church three or four times'. He postulated that these marriages were because sailors 'marry such people for the spree of the thing', and their relationship was essentially based on a financial transaction as he noted that 'as soon as his money and clothes are gone (he very seldom saves his clothes), he must go'.[64] However, the police sergeant of H division hinted to Hemyng that these women developed longer-term relationships with their sailors, rather than simply financially exploiting them:

> when sailors landed in the docks, and drew their wages, they picked up some women to whom they considered themselves married pro tem, and to whom they gave the money they had made by their last voyage. They live with the women until the money is gone (and the women generally treat the sailors honourably). They go to sea again, make some more, come home, and repeat the same thing over again.[65]

Evidence from the trial of the murder of James Almon also suggests that a close and emotional relationship could evolve between 'wives' and their 'husbands'. Kirwin noted that Mary Ann Smith and James Almon had been sleeping together for some time before Smith moved into her brothel. When cross-examined on whether she cohabited with Almon, Smith replied that:

> Yes – I lived at 74, New Gravel-lane, before I went there – Almon came to me the Sunday before Christmas, and I had been sleeping with him every night since – I did not share the money I made with him – he lived at his boarding-house, and slept with me – he always paid me of a night.[66]

Although Almon had lodgings in a boarding house, he paid Smith and slept with her every night. Significantly, Smith did not give Kirwin a cut of Almon's payment, as she did with other clients, suggesting that a more emotionally intimate relationship had developed between them. Their conduct within the brothel also suggests a deeper personal bond as the trial heard how Smith and Almon were passing the time 'sky larking' together in the parlour before the stabbing. Indeed, Smith demonstrated a real concern for Almon after the attack and seemed to go through a grieving process as she visited Almon twice in the hospital, and, after his death, she paid her last respects to him with a visit to the mortuary. This friendship, however, did not preclude Smith from earning money from other men, as she made clear in the trial. She stated that Almon 'made no objection to my going up stairs on this night – he never spoke – I believe he knew I was going up stairs with the other man – there is no doubt about it'.[67] The social observers who discovered these 'husband' and 'wife' relationships immediately dismissed these arrangements as another method by which prostitutes exploited the naivety of sailors ashore. However, while these longer-term relationships undoubtedly provided women with some financial security, they were recognised within their close-knit community, and offered them friendship, protection, and an emotional bond.

One form of sex work that was hardly ever explored in social investigations was male prostitution. Hints were made by journalists like James Greenwood in relation to workhouses and lodging houses, but studies on the scale of Acton's work on women prostitution were never undertaken. As Matthew Cook's authoritative account of London's homosexual subculture has demonstrated, the paucity of sources creates difficulties for the historian when attempting to capture the everyday life of same-sex encounters. Cook's fascinating insight into this subculture is illuminated through the examination of various major and minor scandals covered in the press, along with an assessment of how the authorities became increasingly concerned about male homosexuality in the late nineteenth century.[68] However, in enclosed working-class subcultures such as sailortown, male homosexuality rarely came to light. Moreover, in the sensational press, sailortown was cast as a masculine, violent, and murderous district, and the reportage of sailors paying for homosexual sex did not conform to this narrative. However, on the odd occasion a male prostitute was charged and sent to trial, we can at least piece together some fragments of their life in sailortown.

The case of Elijah Scott, an American person of colour, caused a minor sensation in 1850 after he was accused of soliciting sailors and other men. Scott was a twenty-year-old, American-born runaway slave who assumed the name Eliza after claiming to have been abandoned in London by a ship's captain who had befriended him on a voyage to England. Having become destitute, Scott seemed to have entered sailortown's sex trade and was arrested for assault and attempted buggery in the autumn of 1850.[69] The Mansion House police court had attracted an 'immense crowd', and the reporter described Scott's appearance in court as 'dressed in a light cotton gown, with stripes, and a straw bonnet, and certainly had a most feminine appearance'.[70] Scott was charged with 'unlawfully assaulting Bennett James Martin, with intent to induce him to commit buggery'.[71] Martin, a merchant's clerk, explained that in the early hours of Friday morning:

> I was returning from a party towards my home in the Minories, the prisoner came up in his present dress of a female, and asked me if I was good natured. I of course thought he was a woman, and we walked together. As we went into a more retired place, the prisoner lifted a veil which was fastened to the bonnet, and then I for the first time observed that the face was that of a person of colour. I soon suspected from the growth of the beard that I was speaking to a man.[72]

Martin reported Scott to the police, and once arrested, the prisoner gave their name as Eliza Scott. According to J.W. Tanner, a policeman, 'I then asked him whether he was not a man. He denied most positively that he was a man, and positively called God to witness that he was telling the truth in denying the imputation'. After a medical examination, the police confirmed that Scott was biologically male.[73] Scott was found guilty and sentenced to one year's imprisonment, after which he disappeared from the historical record.[74]

Until his imprisonment, Scott seems to have been successful in attracting men and becoming accepted by the women sex workers of the area. Tanner had always considered Scott as a woman and believed 'he belonged to the wretched class who live by prostitution'.[75] Likewise, W.C. Potter, another policeman, noted that 'the prisoner walks the neighbourhood of the Thames Tunnel and Ratcliff-highway, and I have frequently seen him with sailors, and always considered him to be a woman'.[76] Indeed, the case provides us with an insight into how some sex workers who identified as female appeared to have associated with women sex workers in the area. Scott lived in Angel Gardens near Ratcliffe Highway, a notorious district, which like Palmers Folly was dominated by small brothels kept by women. In addition, several policemen in court testified that Scott was regularly seen in the company of 'Ratcliff-highway street-walkers' who, they claimed, like the police, were unaware 'of the fact that he was a man'.[77] This last claim by the police was, perhaps, rather far-fetched, since Scott seems to have lived in the same street as sex workers, associated and worked with them on the streets, and, more importantly, sported a rather obvious beard. Scott's trait of strongly resembling a woman in 'appearance' and 'manner', and asking potential clients if they 'were good natured' in an 'effeminate tone', replicated male sex work in other sailortowns. Hugill noted that in the sex work district of the seaport of Cebu in the Philippines, there were '*Maricones*, or men dressed as women, calling softly to the passing sailor, "Allow! What's yo' name?"'.[78] While matriarchal networks clearly played an important part in shaping female agency within the sex trade, one can tentatively suggest that they also facilitated male sex workers working in the Ratcliffe Highway district. The next section will explore how outside agencies sought to wrestle back control of the streets from the women who worked on them.

Saving souls from prostitution

Women, then, relied upon social networks and friendships forged within brothels and thoroughfares that ran off Ratcliffe Highway. Women also sought financial security and friendship with some seafaring men, or their 'husbands', whom they saw when they came ashore. However, while this social support operated largely within working-class cultural networks and communities, attempts were made by external bodies to help women by 'reclaiming' them back to God and 'civilisation'. Religious missionaries made regular forays into the East End to take women away from vice and their surroundings and place them in the suburbs or homes for fallen women. For example, the Whitechapel Magdalen Hospital and organisations such as the Moon Light Mission and the Midnight Meeting Movement were all active in the 1850s and 1860s.[79]

The Midnight Meeting Movement was a good example of how the religious zeal of the organisers transgressed the carefully choreographed temporal and urban bourgeois codes that segregated respectability from vice.

In its first meeting in 1859, the Movement sought to attract prostitutes to a midnight meeting held in one of the grandest restaurants in Regent Street. According to one observer, 'the spacious rooms were brilliantly lighted, the atmosphere warm and cheery; all the appointments indicated comfort and warmth'.[80] Thus, at the midnight hour when 'decent' women were at home, a space reserved for wealth and respectability during the day was populated by street people who indulged in 'sin and wickedness'.[81] The meeting was opened by the Reverend Baptist W. Noel, who was conscious that there should be 'no display of ministerial authority'. He addressed his 'strange' audience, asking them to turn their back on vice and embrace 'the Saviour's love in redemption'.[82] Light refreshments followed while other Christians in the room sat at tables advising women to relinquish their current lives and move to a house for fallen women. The event was deemed a great success as it attracted over 250 women, and, while some in attendance 'maintained a hardened bravado', at the close of the meeting, seventeen women declared that they wanted to leave prostitution and lodge in the home.[83]

This format was rolled out to other districts of London such as St Giles and, significantly, Ratcliffe Highway. However, while Thomas declared that 'youth and beauty were well represented' in the Regent Street meeting, he described the women of Ratcliffe Highway as 'ungainly and bloated' and 'of real feminine beauty there were but few good specimens'.[84] Repelled by his surroundings, Thomas's descent into the underworld of Ratcliffe Highway confirmed to him that urban degeneration and moral and physical degeneration were two sides of the same coin. Thus, he noted that 'I am bound to say that their looks indicated but very little intelligence'.[85] Nevertheless, Thomas considered these meetings a great success as 480 women responded to the invitation to the midnight meeting at the Ratcliffe Highway Sailor's Institute. Undoubtedly, the large numbers of women sex workers who attended midnight meetings in the metropolis during the 1860s and 1870s were impressive.

However, there is little evidence to suggest that women left their working-class networks that had been forged in the Ratcliffe Highway neighbourhoods to accept help from these external philanthropic initiatives. In 1872 an investigative journalist from the *Telegraph* shed further light on the social dynamics within the midnight meetings on Ratcliffe Highway which indicated that, despite the large attendance, women were manipulating proceedings to their own agenda. Indeed, the Midnight Meeting Movement's decision to take the message out into the 'darkest' suburbs undoubtedly emboldened the local women and conversely plunged those middle-class campaigners, unfamiliar with St George's, into a strange and alien environment. This unfamiliarity is captured by the reporter's experience of visiting Ratcliffe Highway for the first time. He noted that on his journey, 'I have a feeling as though I had passed beyond the haunts of civilisation into some strange desert'.[86] The anxiety that Ratcliffe Highway engendered within him was extended to the 'street-women' he met at the meeting in the St Matthew's School room on Princes Square. On entering the hall, he recalled that 'with the instinctive horror naturally experienced for what is new or strange, I felt myself shrinking from these poor girls in the dancing room, whilst my merry missionary shook each one by the hand and greeted her with his "well Lassie!"'. The reporter was clearly intimidated by the almost ninety women who filled the hall, from the 'brazen-faced harridan who had been "out" for long years' to the 'girl of fifteen, whose "outing" numbered only weeks'.[87]

Conversely, these women were familiar with both their surroundings and the fraternal networks they had developed in the district. Indeed, while the clergy and movement activists served tea and cake to their visitors, the women remained sitting at small tables and talking in their familiar social groups. After the light refreshments, attempts at 'reclaiming' the women took centre stage and a clergyman read aloud portions of the scripture to the women to persuade them to leave vice and live in a home for fallen women. However, the clergyman could have perhaps chosen his scripture a little more carefully as his parable of the Ten Virgins was 'received with a regular guffaw', and throughout the recitation, the girls giggled 'and quite lost the point of the allegory'.[88] Furthermore, the reporter noted that 'the noisiest and most troublesome' women 'did their best to disturb proceedings, leaving noisily as soon as they had disposed of a very heavy tea, and had a brief "lark" during the preliminary proceedings'.[89] Nevertheless, the clergyman pronounced the evening a success as of the eighty-eight women attending, four were 'reclaimed' and were taken in cabs to homes for fallen women. To the reporter's surprise, one of the 'noisiest' and most disruptive women of the cohort was one of the four who had pledged to reject a life of prostitution. However, he was later informed that the women who stayed behind in the hall to be 'reclaimed' often had ulterior motives:

> those who remain are often disappointing cases. Either they act on impulse, which cools down before the morning; or they sometimes go to the Home because it is late, and they may be locked out of their lodgings; or even they will go simply for the 'lark' of having a ride in a cab.[90]

The Midnight Meeting Movement had built a reputation of attracting large crowds of women to their meetings and successfully 'reclaiming' a proportion of the attendees from prostitution. The figures certainly look impressive and from an outside perspective, it appeared that the Movement had successfully supplanted the women's traditional support networks to draw them away from prostitution. However, the location, size, and timings of these meetings allowed women to transfer their social networks from the streets and into the meeting room, affording them a considerable degree of agency during the gatherings. Thus, women sex workers had developed robust social networks that were effective in protecting themselves in the sometimes perilous neighbourhoods in which they lived and worked, and were resilient in the face of urban missionaries who sought to remove them from their communities.

Conclusion

While the Victorian press painted a monolithic picture of dangerous, 'brazen-faced harridans', this portrayal obscured the wide range of working-class women engaged in, or at the margins of, sex work on Ratcliffe Highway during the nineteenth century. Thus, this chapter has argued that sex work took many different forms and was a fixed and almost tolerated feature of sailortown culture. It certainly allowed criminal networks to acquire a thriving business of exploitative and dangerous brothels that threatened both the sex workers and the sailors who used them. While we know more about the women who were constantly before the police courts who struggled with poverty, alcoholism, and mental health, the lives of the women effectively incarcerated in brothels run by male 'bullies' can only be speculated upon. These women found themselves trapped in the most desperate and unforgiving environments and were in the most abusive and dangerous sector of the sailortown sex trade. However, sailortown also provided opportunities for women to break free from this cycle of exploitation. Those women who had successfully provided themselves with some economic and social stability, and a degree of agency in their lives, were part of micro-matriarchal networks, facilitated by sailortown's urban geography and status as a contact zone. Not only did ports provide opportunities for women to meet sailors, but these districts also allowed sex workers to carve out an enclave in which their own safety and interests could be guarded. Moreover, as we have seen, there is some evidence to suggest that these women also facilitated some specific male sex workers to operate alongside them. Finally, while these matriarchal networks were resilient to police and missionary intervention, they were unable to stop the Victorian town planner who had bulldozed the likes of Palmers Folly and Angel Gardens by the late nineteenth century.

Notes

1. M. Wiener, *Men of Blood: Violence, Manliness and Criminal Justice in Victorian England* (Cambridge, Cambridge University Press, 2004), 289; J. Carter Wood, *Violence and Crime in Nineteenth Century England: The Shadow of Our Refinement* (London, Routledge, 2004), 141.
2. *East London Observer*, 24 October 1857.
3. For an example of how this narrative was used in other areas, see Hugh Miller's description of Manchester in H. Miller, *First Impressions of England and Its People* (Edinburgh, Adam & Charles Black, 1847, 1861 edn), 27.
4. *The Globe*, 18 May 1855.
5. *Daily Telegraph and Courier*, 16 October 1871. See Chapter 3.
6. For other commentators who shared similar views, see B. Beaven, *Visions of Empire: Patriotism, Popular Culture and the City, 1870–1939* (Manchester, Manchester University Press, 2012), 44–5.
7. E.W. Thomas, *Twenty-Five Years' Labour among the Friendless and Fallen* (London, Shaw & Co., 1879), 37.
8. A. J. Piper, '"Woman's special enemy": Female enmity in criminal discourse during the long nineteenth century', *Journal of Social History*, 49(3), 2016, shv049, 685, 671.
9. Thomas, *Twenty-Five Years' Labour*, 36.
10. *The Daily News*, 31 August 1864.
11. *East London Observer*, 10 October 1857.
12. *The Globe*, 18 May 1855.
13. *East London Observer*, 10 October 1857.
14. Z. Alker, 'Street violence in mid-Victorian Liverpool' (unpublished PhD, John Moores University, 2014), 131.
15. Census 1851: Julia Mahoney is located in Lambeth Street, Saint Mary, Whitechapel; *Morning Chronicle*, 20 October 1852.
16. *London Evening Standard*, 28 December 1853.
17. *Bell's New Weekly Messenger*, 26 March 1854.
18. *The Globe*, 18 April 1857; *The Sun*, 25 April 1870.
19. *The Sun*, 11 September 1858; for an account of drunken behaviour, see *Marylebone Mercury*, 3 November 1860; *Morning Advertiser*, 19 May 1864. See also the Old Bailey, 10 July 1871, trial of Julia Mahoney, Ref t18710710-504.
20. *East London Observer*, 9 April 1864.
21. *East London Observer*, 9 April 1864.
22. *East London Observer*, 9 April 1864; C.F. Lowder, *Ten Years in St George's Mission: Being an Account of Its Origin, Progress, and Works of Mercy* (London, G.J Palmer, 1867), 89.
23. *Morning Post*, 31 July 1858.
24. *East London Observer*, 19 June; 8 August 1868.
25. *East London Observer*, 7 August 1858.
26. *East London Observer*, 14 August 1858.

27 H. Mayhew, *London Labour and the London Poor*, Vol IV (London, Charles Griffin and Company, 1851), 225. At the time of writing, £12 in 1851 is the equivalent of approximately £1,400 in 2023.
28 *London Daily News*, 1 September 1864.
29 *Morning Advertiser*, 4 November 1861.
30 *East London Observer*, 7 December 1861.
31 *Clerkenwell News*, 12–13 August 1864.
32 *Morning Post*, 7 June 1865.
33 *Daily Telegraph and Courier*, 23 October 1869.
34 *Daily Telegraph and Courier*, 23 October 1869; Gillian is recorded as thirty-eight years old in the 1871 Census.
35 *Daily Telegraph and Courier*, 23 October 1869.
36 *Daily Telegraph and Courier*, 23 October 1869.
37 *Daily Telegraph and Courier*, 23 October 1869.
38 *Daily Telegraph and Courier*, 23 October 1869.
39 *Daily Telegraph and Courier*, 23 October 1869.
40 Find My Past: 1871 Census, 2 Angel Court, Shadwell.
41 L. Vaughan, pre-publication version of 'Mapping the East End "labyrinth", in *Jack the Ripper and the East End Labyrinth* (Museum of London and Random House, 2008), https://discovery.ucl.ac.uk/id/eprint/4844/1/4844.pdf, accessed 5 March 2021.
42 Find My Past: Censuses 1881 and 1891; street search: Angel Court.
43 *Morning Chronicle*, 2 May 1850.
44 *Morning Chronicle*, 2 May 1850.
45 C.F. Lowder, *Ten Years in St George's Mission*, 13.
46 A search was made using the *British Newspaper Archive* of newspapers published in London between 1850 and 1880. This was tabulated with searching the number of buildings located in Palmers Folly in the 1851, 1861, 1871, and 1881 Censuses in Find My Past.
47 *Evening Standard*, 20 November 1867.
48 *The Sun*, 17 May 1867.
49 *Daily Telegraph*, 23 October 1869.
50 G. Sims, *How the Poor Live and Horrible London* (London, Chatto & Windus, 1889), 4–5.
51 *The Daily London News*, 1 September 1864.
52 *Morning Post*, 2 April 1855.
53 *London Evening Standard*, 10 May 1855.
54 J. Davis, 'A poor man's system of justice: The London police courts in the second half of the nineteenth century', *Historical Journal*, 27(2), June 1984, 309–35, 308, 312.
55 *The Sun*, 26 January 1858.
56 OBP, 2 February 1852, case of Jose Frutoso Berdugo, Ref t18520202-253.
57 OBP, 2 February 1852, case of Jose Frutoso Berdugo, Ref t18520202-253.
58 OBP, 2 February 1852, case of Jose Frutoso Berdugo, Ref t18520202-253.

59 B. Beaven, *Leisure, Citizenship and Working-Class Men, 1850–1945* (Manchester, Manchester University Press, 2005), 66–7.
60 Alker has found similar forms of behaviour in women involved in crime in Liverpool; see Alker, 'Street violence in mid-Victorian Liverpool', Chapter 3.
61 Thomas, *Twenty-Five Years' Labour*, 36–7.
62 H. Jones, *East and West London: Being Notes of Common Life and Pastoral Work in Saint James's, Westminster and in Saint George's-in-the-East* (Smith, Elder & Co., London, 1875), 219–20.
63 Quoted in V. Burton, 'The work and home life of seafarers, with special reference to the port of Southampton, 1870–1921' (unpublished PhD thesis, London School of Economics, 1988), 285.
64 *Morning Chronicle*, 2 May 1850.
65 Mayhew, *London Labour*, 227.
66 OBP, 2 February 1852, case of Jose Frutoso Berdugo, Ref t18520202-253.
67 OBP, 2 February 1852, case of Jose Frutoso Berdugo, Ref t18520202-253.
68 M. Cook, *London and the Culture of Homosexuality, 1885–1914* (Cambridge, Cambridge University Press, 2003).
69 *The Sun*, 24 September 1850.
70 *The Sun*, 24 September 1850.
71 Rictor Norton (ed.), 'Eliza/Elijah Scott, the Black Man Woman, 1850', *Homosexuality in Nineteenth-Century England: A Sourcebook*, 15 July 2020, http://rictornorton.co.uk/eighteen/1850scot.htm, accessed 12 May 2023.
72 *The Morning Advertiser*, 25 October 1850.
73 *The Sun*, 24 September 1850.
74 Norton (ed.), 'Eliza/Elijah Scott, the Black Man Woman, 1850'.
75 *The Morning Advertiser*, 25 October 1850.
76 *The Morning Advertiser*, 25 October 1850.
77 *The Morning Advertiser*, 25 October 1850.
78 S. Hugill, *Sailortown* (London, Routledge and Kegan Paul, 1967), 336.
79 *Pall Mall Gazette*, 16 August 1865; *The Era*, 9 November 1889.
80 Thomas, *Twenty-Five Years' Labour*, 78.
81 Thomas, *Twenty-Five Years' Labour*, 78.
82 Thomas, *Twenty-Five Years' Labour*, 78.
83 Thomas, *Twenty-Five Years' Labour*, 79.
84 Thomas, *Twenty-Five Years' Labour*, 79.
85 Thomas, *Twenty-Five Years' Labour*, 79.
86 *East London Observer*, 1 January 1872.
87 *East London Observer*, 1 January 1872.
88 *East London Observer*, 1 January 1872.
89 *East London Observer*, 1 January 1872.
90 *East London Observer*, 1 January 1872.

7

Male violence, class, and ethnicity in sailortown

> *But for fully a century it enjoyed the reputation of being one of the toughest streets in the world ... All the dregs and offscourings of male and female humanity swarmed in the foul and filthy dens of the Highway, ready to prey on the lusts, the follies, and the trustfulness of the sailor.*
>
> C. Fox Smith, *Sailor Town Days* (1923), 27–28

Throughout the nineteenth century, sensational narratives of Ratcliffe Highway conveyed a sense that the district was menaced by an undercurrent of violence. As we have seen in the previous chapters, sensational writers delivered the consistent message that Ratcliffe Highway was the living embodiment of squalor, violence, and vice. For many who journeyed to the extremities of the east, the Highway felt both physically and morally isolated from civilised society, a place in which debauchery and viciousness reigned.[1] The large numbers of foreign sailors in traditional seafaring dress with knives strapped to their belts, along with numerous crimps and sex workers, gave the district a dangerous but also an exotic appeal. With its multi-ethnic space and transient sailortown character, Ratcliffe Highway provided the perfect copy for popular newspapers keen to attract readers with sensational and violent stories. The Highway was framed as a wild place in which the normal rules that governed fights between men were superseded by the ubiquitous use of the knife that had been introduced by the foreign sailor. The fear that foreign sailors had introduced a dangerous knife culture into port cities had, by the late nineteenth century, fed into a wider anxiety about race in Britain. By the 1880s, there was an increasing acceptance of scientific racism in wider society and a perception that 'Englishness' was being eroded by alien settlers with their own languages, customs, and religions.[2]

With its transient foreign sailor population living among a local working-class community, Ratcliffe Highway was one of the key areas of London which was investigated during the formulation of the Aliens Act of 1905.[3]

However, it will be argued that the moral panic that gripped the press did not correlate with the relatively low incidences of male-on-male knife assaults that were heard before the Old Bailey between 1850 and 1900.[4] Indeed, levels of serious knife wounding, manslaughter, or murder were very similar to other working-class areas of London. Nevertheless, London's sailortown was undoubtedly a tough masculine space in which seafarers and local working-class men stubbornly retained fighting traditions and rituals to defend their honour and challenge the local police force. Nevertheless, what marked Ratcliffe Highway out from other districts was its multi-ethnic urban space. Within the context of working-class masculinity and violence, sailortowns were international contact zones that enabled seafarers from different nationalities to engage with a diverse set of subaltern fighting rituals. It will be argued that the rituals that regulated violence were recognised by English, foreign, and local working-class men alike, ensuring that, while sometimes aggressive, the district did not fall into the anarchic violence that was imagined by the press. This chapter, then, will examine the moral panic that centred on Ratcliffe's violent and cosmopolitan reputation and explore why the foreign sailor was demonised. Moreover, in investigating street violence, the chapter advances our understanding of how working men from differing nationalities navigated ethnically diverse fighting rituals within an urban, working-class setting.

Sailor violence, the sensational press, and the national context *c.* 1850–1900

According to Henry Mayhew, the growth of the port increased Ratcliffe Highway's social problems and intensified levels of criminality due to 'the reckless and improvident character of sailors'.[5] Ratcliffe Highway's association with the foreign sailor meant that it became the focal point for this narrative and assumed an exotic and dangerous reputation. Indeed, the local press cast the district as a place of mystery and its people bereft of civilising influences. One reporter on the *East London Observer* noted that:

> On leaving the silent city to go eastward at night, I have a feeling as though I had passed beyond the haunts of civilisation ... past the postern gate of the Tower, and you are in the sailors' *quartier*; on into Ratcliff-highway – euphemistically termed St George's-street – where, amid frequent public houses and dancing rooms, low vice keeps perpetual saturnalia.[6]

Throughout this period, the *East London Observer* ran sensational articles on the district's crime and violence that were designed to spread fear among its readers. For example, in the 1857 article 'Down the Highway', the journalist discovered 'Italians and Greeks with stilettos – women screaming obscenity – men, wild with the 'vitriol madness'.[7] The newspaper also played on the fears of its readers as, amid the garrotting moral panics of the early 1860s, it reported of the dangerous 'strong masculine women' who would garrotte unsuspecting sailors on Ratcliffe Highway.[8]

Between the mid-nineteenth century and the early twentieth century, the newspaper offered plenty of coverage of how the people of Ratcliffe Highway consistently contravened society's norms.[9] Similarly, according to *Pearsons Weekly*, the 'Highway presented a scene of coarse debauchery which was probably unique in Europe' and where 'half the cut-throats and thieves of East London' gathered.[10] Due to transient sailors, Ratcliffe Highway was dubbed a 'lawless' district, and on entering the locality, the traditional codes of the 'fair knuckle-fight' were superseded by the 'hordes' of knife-wielding foreign seamen. The *Daily News* perpetuated the sense that crime was linked to the mysterious foreigner and proclaimed that the Highway was suitable for an 'ethnological study'. It noted that sailortown attracted 'Lascars, with their bushy locks and swarthy skins, contrast strangely with the solitary Chinaman'. The reporter went on to describe 'half a dozen other races', from 'hawk eyed New Zealanders, whose cheeks and forehead are fantastically tattoed [sic]' and 'full bloodied negroes from Gambia, and half caste Portuguese from Goa'.[11]

The presentation of the foreign sailor as an urban menace became a common theme in the popular press. For example, James Ritchie's accounts of the Highway in the 1850s conjured up a mysterious but also dangerously anarchic district of London. In one of his night-time adventures, he encountered:

> A row of foreign mariners pass me, seven abreast: swarthy, ear-ringed, black-bearded varlets in red shirts, light-blue trousers, and with sashes round their waists. Part of the crew of a Sardinian brig, probably. They have all their arms round each other's necks; yet I cannot help thinking that they look somewhat 'knifey,' 'stilettoey.' I hope I may be mistaken, but I am afraid that would be odds were to put an indefinite quantity of rum into *them*, they would put a few inches of steel into *you*.[12]

The dangerous reputation of the foreign sailor was cemented on Ratcliffe Highway in 1857 when a series of knife assaults involving seamen received widespread coverage. Under the heading 'The Use of the Knife by Foreign Seamen', one correspondent in the *East London Observer* complained that it had become unsafe to walk on Ratcliffe Highway after sunset for fear of the knife-bearing foreign 'blood-thirsty villains'. He added that in London this 'deadly weapon will soon be as freely used here as in Spain, Italy and other parts of the continent'.[13] The following week, the *East London Observer*'s editor denounced the poor policing of Ratcliffe Highway and complained that 'the Lascar, Chinese, or the Italian flash their sea knives in the air, or the American "bowies"', and attack innocent Englishmen by gouging them or indulge 'in some other of those innocent amusements in which his countrymen delight'.[14]

By 1859 the press and those in the criminal justice system were calling for laws to prohibit foreign sailors from carrying knives while ashore. When American sailors were brought before Mr Self in the Thames police court for stabbing an Englishman, the magistrate lamented that 'he was very sorry indeed there was no regulation to prevent American and Spanish seamen from wearing their knives and daggers when they came on shore'. He added that 'foreign seamen had too often used their knives and daggers upon Englishmen in the streets and in the houses of public entertainment'.[15] Likewise, in 1863 the *Express* called for legislation to prevent sailors carrying knives in London after a fatal stabbing that year. The reporter commented that:

> The frequent use of the knife by the foreign seamen, in one case terminating fatally a few days ago, has created great public alarm in the district. Numerous persons have been stabbed. The foreign seamen appear in the streets of the district every night with their large sheath knives at the side of them, and they are drawn without any provocation at all.[16]

Discussing the same incident, the *London Evening Standard* commented that 'the use of the knife, once almost unknown in this country, is making a progress that requires some more effectual check than is given to it by an individual stabber being now and then convicted and punished'.[17] Indeed, in 1864, on the back of the media campaign, MPs in the House of Commons pressed for new laws to prohibit sailors from carrying knives. However, the government dismissed the prospect of banning seafarers from carrying knives, as it would have been too difficult to enforce.[18] By the late nineteenth century journalists and commentators had painted a horrifying picture of Ratcliffe Highway in which foreign sailors had introduced the murderous knife on to the shores of Britain (see Figure 7.1).

As the nineteenth century evolved, the reputation of Ratcliffe Highway and that of its foreign sailors and settlers continued to feed into the national discourse on the 'problems' of 'alien communities' in British society. Between 1881 and 1905, it is estimated that approximately 100,000 Jewish immigrants from Russia, Poland, and Austria settled in Britain. This led racist organisations, such as the British Brothers' League, to claim that Britain was subject to an 'alien invasion'. It was within this political climate that the 1902 Royal Commission on Alien Immigration was established. This Royal Commission led to the 1905 Aliens Act which placed controls on

Male violence, class, and ethnicity 165

Figure 7.1 German and English sailors fighting, 1892 (depicted by a French newspaper – note that the tradition of the English fighting with their fists was recognised overseas since only the Germans are using knives)
(*Le Petit Journal*, 2 January 1892)

immigration to Britain for the first time. The Commission held 149 public meetings, interviewed 175 witnesses, and examined a large quantity of statistical data.[19]

A significant amount of attention was directed to London's Ratcliffe Highway as there were concerns that foreign sailors, and the foreign prostitutes who accompanied them, were not returning home and instead were settling in Britain. For Major William Evans-Gordon, one of the leaders of the British Brothers' League, foreign prostitutes corrupted British society to a far greater extent than their English counterparts:

> It was also shown that the foreign prostitutes are generally more depraved than the native women of the same class, and that their corruption takes the most deleterious forms. It is they who practise and perpetuate those extravagances of vice which, but for them, would hardly be known in this country except to readers of Horace and Catullus.[20]

Evans-Gordon was a member of the Royal Commission and was arguably its most active participant, and he heavily influenced the final report and its recommendations.[21] The committee comprised a range of Conservative and Liberal Members of Parliament, bankers, poor law guardians, and civic servants, and it was clear through their leading questions that they viewed the 'Anglo-Saxon race' as under threat from an 'alien invasion'.[22] Only, the banker and philanthropist Lord Rothschild and the liberal solicitor Sir Kenelm E. Digby refused to endorse the Commission's conclusions.[23]

Quantifying sailors' knife violence in St George's in the East and Whitechapel, 1850–1900

In the late eighteenth century, London was at the nation's forefront in creating new law enforcement agencies designed to deal with a rapidly growing metropolis. The development of prisons and the introduction of a new police force followed the creation in 1772 of a paid magistracy who sat in newly formed police courts. The police courts were designed to replace the amateur justices of the peace and dealt with less serious offences such as drunkenness and assault. Magistrates passed more serious indictable offences to the Quarter Sessions or Assizes where a judge and jury would sit. For the City of London and Middlesex, the court of Assize was the Old Bailey. However, from 1855 magistrates were empowered to convict and punish offenders for common assault, small theft, and embezzlement.[24] By the 1850s there were thirty-eight paid magistrates presiding over thirteen police courts in Metropolitan London.[25] The Victorian police courts in London were extremely busy places with approximately 100,000 annual cases heard during the mid-nineteenth century.[26] The records generated by this more professionalised judicial process have provided historians with a wealth of evidence to examine types and levels of crime in Victorian London.

However, the attempt to quantify and analyse nineteenth-century urban crime is fraught with methodological difficulties. As Wiener has pointed out, there is usually a significant gap between actual and recorded low-level violence.[27] In the case of Ratcliffe Highway, the problem is magnified as the

Male violence, class, and ethnicity 167

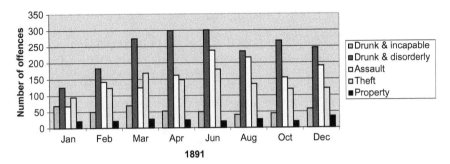

Figure 7.2 Monthly categories of offences: Thames Magistrates Courts, 1891
(*London Metropolitan Archive*: PSTH/A1/20–24, surviving Thames
Magistrates Records for 1891 – the court books for May, July, September,
and November are missing)

Thames police court archive, which had jurisdiction for this area, is missing records for the middle years of the nineteenth century. These records would have captured the more low-level varieties of crimes such as assaults, drunkenness, and petty theft. The *East End Observer* was the principal newspaper that covered the district and, as we have seen, it undoubtedly singled out Ratcliffe Highway as a dangerous and violent area. However, despite its interest in crime, the *East London Observer* did not carry a regular and comprehensive report of the Thames police courts, rendering any quantitative analysis unreliable. Nevertheless, the Thames police court records do exist for the late nineteenth century and they provide us with a guide to the *types* and *levels* of violence that occurred in the Thames region.

An analysis of the offences for the available months of 1891 revealed that criminal activity generally fell into one of five categories, with most people being charged with the offence of being drunk and disorderly. Figure 7.2 illustrates that the crime of being drunk and disorderly was consistently the highest category throughout the year. The number of arrests peaked in June, which recorded an average of ten people per day charged with the offence. The charge of assault was the second largest category, while cases related to theft and, to a lesser extent, property damage appeared monthly at the Thames police court.

Figure 7.3 demonstrates that the most numerous assaults recorded were between men, though most were not considered 'brutal assaults' or 'excessively violent', as magistrates made a special point of noting this category of offence. Indeed, throughout 1891, brutal assaults by males on males stood at only 4 per cent for the year.

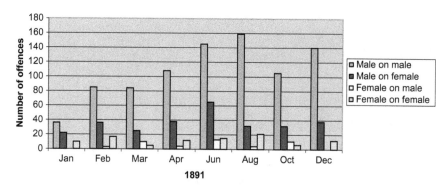

Figure 7.3 The sex of offenders and victims of assault: Thames Magistrates Courts, 1891
(*London Metropolitan Archive:* PSTH/A1/20–24, surviving Thames Magistrates Records for 1891)

The daily sitting of Thames Magistrates Courts, then, comprised a routine mix of drunkenness, low-level assaults, theft, and property crime and was not, as social commentators would often claim, overrun with murders, knifings, and brutal assaults.[28] This pattern of Ratcliffe Highway crime revealed in the Thames police records is supported by evidence retrieved from the Old Bailey papers. While the Thames police courts dealt with routine and fairly low-level crime, the most serious criminal cases in London were heard at the Old Bailey, and the online database provides comprehensive coverage of the period 1850–1900.

Although the Old Bailey online project used modern categories to facilitate statistical analysis, they reflect, as closely as possible, the descriptions of offences found in the proceedings. Using the statistical search facility, a search of the Old Bailey database can identify the location of the crime, the perpetrator's and victim's genders and occupations, and whether a prosecution was successful. In searching for serious knife crime for the whole of London during this era, it was possible to contrast knife crime in the Ratcliffe Highway district with the rest of the metropolis. A search was made of cases under the offence categories of 'breaking the peace' and 'killing' that were 'male on male' and involved a 'knife' between 1850 and 1900.[29] While the place of the incident was usually documented, the occupation of the assailant was recorded in only 20 per cent of the cases. Of this 20 per cent, over half were identified as sailors. However, it was more likely that a sailor's livelihood was stated during the trial, as seafarers would often be questioned about the nature of their shore leave.[30]

Once duplicate transcripts and assaults situated on the high seas were removed, there were 645 cases brought before the Old Bailey involving male-on-male knife assaults and killing using a knife in London during these fifty years. Significantly, 87 per cent of these knife crimes were committed between 1850 and 1880, indicating that, despite the fears of the sensational press, serious knife crime across London was in decline. Of crucial importance to this study is the location of the male knife assaults. Two neighbouring civil parishes, Whitechapel and St George's in the East, recorded the most cases of serious knife fights and accounted for 11 per cent of the total number of cases brought before the Old Bailey between 1850 and 1900. These were both solid working-class districts of similar size. Ratcliffe Highway was situated in the St George's in the East district, stretching across from west to east and dominating the area with its numerous boarding houses, public houses, and brothels.

However, if we examine the Old Bailey data annually, there is no evidence that male-on-male knife assaults were increasing year on year in either Whitechapel or St George's in the East. Between 1851 and 1856, there were only two or three cases recorded a year spread between St George's in the East and Whitechapel. However, in 1857 seven cases were tried at the Old Bailey, of which five were located on Ratcliffe Highway. Of these five sailors, one was English and the others were from Spain, Chile, the US, and Sweden. The fact that the two assailants in Whitechapel that year were also foreign (a German musician and an Italian cook) only served to heighten fears about how 'alien' forms of knife crime were being imported on to the English streets.[31] It was from this year that the Highway gained a widespread reputation for harbouring knife-wielding foreign sailors in newspaper reports and sensational journalism.[32] Even so, 1857 was very much an aberration since the number of serious knife assaults heard at the Old Bailey remained relatively low in Whitechapel and St George's in the East between 1858 and 1880. The one exception was 1866 in which six cases were documented. Table 7.1 reveals that between 1850 and 1900, St George's in the East recorded lower levels of knife crime than Whitechapel. Moreover, while sailors feature prominently as the assailants, the court's decision not to routinely record the assailant's or victim's occupations undoubtedly underestimates the number of labourers involved in knife assaults.

Table 7.2 illustrates that after 1880, the number of knife crimes in St George's in the East and Whitechapel plummeted and between them accounted for only 3 per cent of the total serious knife crimes in London. Other working-class districts recorded higher totals such as Holborn and Tottenham, a North London suburb that grew rapidly after 1880, each registering 5 per cent of metropolitan knife crime.[33]

While quantifying criminal statistics in the nineteenth century is fraught with problems, the evidence suggests that Ratcliffe Highway did not differ dramatically from other port cities.[34] The common forms of violence that came before the local magistrates' court were only officially counted in the

Table 7.1 Male-on-male knife fights in St George's in the East and Whitechapel between 1850 and 1900 (T. Hitchcock, R. Shoemaker, C. Emsley, S. Howard, J. McLaughlin, et al., *The Old Bailey Proceedings Online*, 1674–1913)

Location	Total number of incidents between 1850 and 1880	Percentage of total male-on-male knife assaults in London	Assailant		Victim	
St George's in the East	40	5	Sailor	25	Sailor	23
			Semi-skilled labourer	0	Semi-skilled labourer	3
			*Other	15	Policeman	4
					*Other	10
Whitechapel	36	6	Sailor	3	Sailor	3
			Semi-skilled labourer	3	Semi-skilled labourer	8
			*Other	33	Policeman	1
					*Other	27

*Other includes individuals where occupation was not given.

Table 7.2 Districts with the most serious knife crime compared with St George's in the East and Whitechapel between 1881 and 1900 (T. Hitchcock, R. Shoemaker, C. Emsley, S. Howard, J. McLaughlin, et al., *The Old Bailey Proceedings Online*, 1674–1913)

District	Percentage of total cases (167)
St George's in the East	0
Whitechapel	3
Holborn	5
Westminster	4
Tottenham	5

nation's crime figures from 1857, and even then this data omits the sex of the victims.[35] The government, between 1870 and 1874, did compile statistics on 'brutal assaults' in Britain, which provide a snapshot by region of the numbers and types of serious offences committed. In this data set, the victim was recorded but the sex of the perpetrator was omitted, and there was no official definition of what constituted a 'brutal assault'. Neither the police nor the courts distinguished 'brutal' from common assaults so they had to rely on the severity of the sentences and 'the memory of the officers connected in the cases' to complete their statistics.[36] However, Metropolitan Police Commissioner G.N.W. Henderson indicated that relative to other crimes, the brutal assault was fairly rare as he believed that 'this peculiar offence was confined to a very limited class of persons'.[37]

To summarise, evidence drawn from the Thames police courts and the Old Bailey online database indicates that the number of serious male-on-male knife assaults in St George's in the East was relatively low between 1850 and 1900 during the period in which Ratcliffe Highway flourished as London's principal sailortown. Moreover, the data suggests that the number of incidents in St George's in the East did not significantly differ from that of its neighbouring district of Whitechapel. Thus, while the use of knives in serious male-on-male assaults was relatively rare, they were not confined to London's sailor quarter but featured in the predominately working-class district of Whitechapel.

The spike in incidents in 1857 may also explain why, in the popular imagination, the Highway became notorious for knife assaults. Indeed, the Old Bailey data indicates that foreign sailors were concentrated on Ratcliffe Highway, which, to the anxious middle-class observer, gave the street an exotic, dangerous, and anarchic reputation.[38] However, as we have seen, the press's lurid depiction of the Highway did not correlate with the relatively low incidents of *serious* crime. The next section will argue that sailortown facilitated a means of regulating male violence since, as an international contact zone, ethnically diverse sailors were able to familiarise themselves with the rituals of masculinity and conflict. Thus, English and foreign sailors navigated their way through differing customs of subaltern fighting as there was a recognition that these rituals upheld one's masculinity. Significantly, it will be argued that there was a multitude of fighting rituals that were not only shared by sailors of different nationalities but also by the wider English working-class community. Thus, while from the outside the subaltern community appeared addicted to impulsive violence, they actually enacted forms of violence that were self-regulated by ritual and rarely ended in serious assault or manslaughter.

Subaltern and multi-ethnic violence in a port city contact zone

The transient nature of sailortown and the notorious reputation of the sailor led many opinion formers to believe that seaports lay outside of the justice system's quest of 'civilising' the English streets.[39] In one opinion piece, the

London Evening Standard noted that fighting traditions in sailortown were very difficult to eradicate:

> We do not expect Jack to have the polish, the self-control, the etiquette which prevent gentlemen when they quarrel from knocking each other about. Nay more, if persons of the grade of sailors do quarrel (and quarrelling in some form or other is a clear human institution) we do not object to their settling a quarrel on the spot, with the abundantly sufficient materials for pounding afforded by closed fists and very hardened knuckles.[40]

Indeed, in the police courts, it was common for magistrates to take a keen interest in the way the men fought. Anything other than a 'clean fight' was frowned upon, as magistrates considered the use of knives as an unwelcome foreign import and often described such incidents as 'foul' murders.[41] As Robert Shoemaker has shown, the 'clean English fight' in working-class districts shared common features as they were usually 'provoked by insults which called into question the honour and honesty of one of the participants, leading to a challenge'.[42] Both parties recognised and accepted rules designed to ensure the fight was conducted on equal and fair terms, that the fighters carried no weapons and were ready before combat began. Indeed, these fights attracted large crowds who played an active role in organising and monitoring the contest. It was this type of scene that confronted Dr Linklater as he made his way down Ratcliffe Highway in the 1880s. He complained that 'I saw a fight in broad daylight in the open street between two sailors who were stripped for the combat, and no policeman was to be found to stop it'.[43] The absence of the police was not unusual even though such fights could draw large crowds that blocked major thoroughfares.

The 'fair' fight was a public spectacle, watched by the fighters' peers to ensure fair play, and, importantly, the two combatants could confirm that honour had been restored before their own community. Though fights often broke out spontaneously, this ritualised form of pugilism evolved a remarkable level of organisation, as Robert Thimbleby, an East End police constable, testified. On a Sunday afternoon in October 1863, he was strolling through Commercial Road East when he chanced upon Samuel Morris, a boilermaker, and another man fighting in the middle of the street. He recalled that: 'Both were stripped to the waist. A ring had formed. Lovell was acting as a second to one of the combatants. There were 300 or 400 persons surrounding the two men fighting, and the road was completely blocked up with omnibuses, cabs, and carts.'[44] When he attempted to separate the two men, Thimbleby 'was assailed with a volley of abuse and threats' while 'the mob' responded by becoming 'very disorderly'. After sending for help from the local police station, Thimbleby attempted to arrest both fighters and 'their seconds', only to be thwarted by the angry crowd who rescued Morris's combatant and his second. In total, nine police officers were required to quell the resultant disturbance. The fight had broken out after a man had allegedly attempted to steal Morris's dog, insulted him and his wife, and spat in their faces. After he was struck by his assailant, Morris declared in court that he was 'compelled to fight'.

The Thames police court magistrate, Mr Partridge, stated that 'it was most disgraceful for two men to be stripped to the waist and fighting on a Sunday afternoon while people were on their way to their respective places of worship and prayer and he thought officer Thimbleby had acted very properly'.[45] Significantly, a recognition that by participating in a 'fair fight' a man could restore his honour still lingered on in the upper echelons of Victorian society as the fight was not in *itself* criticised but more that it had occurred on a day of worship. In addition, Partridge felt obliged to defend Thimbleby on the accusation that his intervention had prevented a man regaining his honour on the grounds that the fight had occurred on a Sunday. Morris was fined 20s, and in default twenty-one days' imprisonment, and Lovell was fined 10s, or ten days' imprisonment.[46] This case also sheds light on the type of violence adopted to restore honour in English working-class communities and how quickly the event was coordinated after the initial quarrel erupted. Once the fighters had stripped to their waists, a code of conduct was enacted in which 'seconds' came forward to support their combatants, which, in the process, blocked vehicles from passing through.

In addition, the animated crowd not only oversaw 'fair play' but also intervened to rescue the combatants when they adjudged that the police had unjustly broken the informal codified rules of a 'fair fight'. The 'fair fight', and attacks on policemen who attempted to stop them, continued into the late nineteenth century. In 1881, the Thames police court heard how Thomas Youngman, a dock labourer, and Henry Skinner, a labourer, both in their early twenties, attempted to resist arrest after the police intervened in their fight. It was reported that Constable Samuel Dutch was on duty in the Ratcliffe Highway district when 'he saw a large crowd collected at the corner of Star-Street. He went there and saw the prisoners stripped to the waist fighting'. Skinner attacked Constable Dutch who had attempted to arrest him but was eventually overpowered by another officer.[47] Youngman was sentenced to prison for one month and Skinner for two months with hard labour. Not only did the 'fair fight' persist into the late nineteenth century but also its tradition seems to have cut across generations. In 1889 at the Thames police court, Henry Newby, fifty-eight and a shopkeeper, was charged with breaking James Smith's leg after a disagreement between the two men led to a fight. Newby, of Ratcliffe Highway, called upon Smith of Poplar and said:

> 'If you're a man you'll take your coat off'. Both men went into the road and put themselves in a fighting attitude. Prisoner punched Smith in the mouth, and he fell. Prosecutor called out, 'my leg is broken' and Newby helped him up ... when arrested, prisoner said 'I'm sorry if I've broken your ankle'.[48]

Newby was bound over to answer the charge when called upon. Not only does this suggest that recognition of the 'fair fight' was intergenerational but also that working-class communities endorsed what they considered an acceptable level of violence to preserve one's honour, manhood, and status. In helping his opponent up and apologising, Newby acknowledged that in breaking Smith's ankle he had overstepped the mark. Furthermore, magistrates seemed to recognise that the 'fair fight' was a legitimate way to settle disputes.

As late as 1888, Charles Cumming, who was described in the Thames police court as a sailor with 'no coat, waistcoat or hat', was charged with being drunk and disorderly. It was reported that Cumming was seen running up and down the Whitechapel Road like a 'mad man' and offering to fight everyone he met. In answering the charge, Cumming explained that while ashore: 'Some "landsharks" set to him. He pulled off his coat and waistcoat to fight them like a man, when some "varmint" ran away with his things – Mr Saunders [the magistrate] said he was sorry for the defendant's loss, and allowed him to go away.'[49] For the magistrate, then, Cumming's drunken and violent behaviour on the streets was forgivable as upholding one's honour and fighting like a man took priority.

Far from being a lawless district, these incidents suggest that within the Ratcliffe Highway vicinity, there were informal rules governing the 'English fair fight' that labourers, sailors, and the working-class community in general recognised. As we have seen, alongside British sailors and the local working-class community, there were a significant number of foreign sailors residing in boarding houses or ships who had very different codes of fighting to uphold male honour, status, and manhood. The most common complaint about the foreign sailor was their propensity to carry knives.[50] While contemporaries stereotyped certain ethnicities with deviancy, as Gallant has shown, Southern European subaltern cultures traditionally used knives to settle disputes between men and knife fights that were governed by a code of conduct 'as rule-bound as the aristocratic duel'. This knife fight followed a 'known script' and the combatant aimed to cut and scar rather than kill and slay. Here, the watching crowd played an important role as once a man drew blood, men from the gathering would step into the breach and pull the fighters apart.[51]

Significantly, the East End police roundly contradicted the claim of the sensational press that foreign sailors used their knives indiscriminately on Englishmen. Sir Richard Mayne, the Chief Commissioner of the Metropolitan Police, observed that foreign sailors tended to use knives on each other rather than on the police or the English.[52] Ethnic-specific fighting rituals were part of wider traditions such as language, food, and dancing that seafarers preserved on English soil through a network of pubs and boarding houses.[53] As we have seen, pubs, singing saloons, and boarding houses were key cultural contact zones that often exposed English and foreign sailors to a variety of ethnic traditions and rituals. Ethnic-specific rituals came into play once the violence had occurred, and it was important for sailors to recognise the different codes of combat and establish the rules of any conflict before the fight began. In a multi-cultural space such as Ratcliffe Highway, it was not uncommon for foreign seamen to adopt the 'English fair fight' code, given that they would face the English justice system if they were caught.

In 1864 two Spaniards, Juan Du Luca and Raymond Rodrigues, argued over a woman they had both been seeing, with Du Luca demanding that 'if you have any spite against me, come out and fight me English fashion. If I beat you, I beat you; if you beat me, you beat me'.[54] However, with sailors from different ethnicities schooled in a variety of fighting traditions, it is perhaps unsurprising that individuals would unscrupulously capitalise on the uncertainty of fighting rules in disputes to gain an advantage. For example, in 1857, George de Matras, a Greek sailor, remonstrated with Jose de Rosario, an Italian sailor, accusing him of cowardice for striking Alice Whitehead, in Neptune Street, just off Ratcliffe Highway. Rosario responded by shouting that 'I'll fight you, English, Italian, or Greek fashion'.[55] At the Old Bailey trial, George Peters, a Greek sailor and witness, testified that:

> I understood the deceased [Matras] to say that if he had any wish to fight, he would fight in English fashion – the prisoner [Rosario] had his hand constantly in his breast – he told the deceased he should like to fight in the English fashion, but he was constantly telling him to come away from the light, beckoning with his finger – the deceased accused him of having a knife, and the prisoner said, 'I have no knife about me' – the deceased laid hold of the prisoner by the elbow; the prisoner then lowered himself, took a knife out, and gave the deceased three stabs on the abdomen, and when he went to arrest him from stabbing any further, he gave him one on the breast; that made four stabs – I put the prisoner between my legs, and then took the knife away from him – this is the knife (produced).[56]

Rosario's use of a knife in a fight which both parties had agreed would be fought 'in the English fashion' had thrown the 'whole of the East End' into 'a state of excitement in consequence of the perpetration of a very cold-blooded murder'.[57] The high degree of consternation that the incident had generated in the locality would indicate that this type of deception was fairly rare, though it certainly added to Ratcliffe Highway's reputation as a place of fear and danger. Rosario was found guilty of manslaughter and sentenced to fifteen years of penal servitude.

Du Luca's offer to fight in 'English' and Rosario's offer to fight in 'English, Italian, or Greek fashion' illustrate how sailors were conversant with the different ethnic traditions of fighting to uphold one's honour. These cases also demonstrate that in multi-ethnic contact zones, it was necessary to establish a mutually agreed code of conduct before embarking in combat. However, while it appears that sailors understood differing fighting codes of conduct, how did they engage with the local working-class sailortown community?[58]

In the parliamentary enquiry on alien immigration, a central theme that had pervaded many of the questions and responses was the eruption of racial conflict between the 'native' working class and the foreign sailors and settlers. One witness had described how some working-class communities in the East End had driven out foreign settlers by smashing their windows and beating down their doors.[59] However, on Ratcliffe Highway, witnesses gave a very different picture of the relationship between foreign sailors, foreign settlers, and the local working class. The witness John Harris, of the port sanitary authority, drew on his experience of working and living in the sailortown district and declared that:

> I must say the English and the aliens live on the most friendly terms together. There is hardly a charity, whether it is to build a mission room to a church or any other thing, that we find the aliens who can afford it do not contribute their amounts to these institutions. If it was not for the aliens and the sons of aliens, who have large factories in the district, and who employ a great number of Christian girls and men, there would be no employment for them at all.[60]

Despite Harris's evidence, members of the Commission were keen to confirm that the foreign sailor and prostitute were instrumental in shaping Ratcliffe Highway's notorious reputation.

However, the Commission were somewhat surprised when Chief Superintendent John Mulvaney stubbornly resisted their assumptions about the district. Mulvaney had patrolled the district for over six years and knew intimately the relationship between sailors and the local population. Lord James then questioned Mulvaney on a number of issues which tried to draw out the extent of racial tensions in St George's in the East district:

> Is there any strong feeling growing up between the aliens and the British subject? [JM] The feeling has shown itself in isolated cases in the streets I have observed, by carmen shouting at the foreigners when they see them, and that sort of thing; but not to any extent.

This district has become, in fact, a foreign colony? [JM] It has practically.

With regard to this question of breaches of the peace, you say you do not apprehend any immediate breach of the peace? [JM] No.

What breaches of the peace have there been ... as showing the feeling of the British against the alien immigrant? [JM] I think two or three years ago, in 1899, there was a little disturbance in Cornwall Street, but nothing of any moment.

I think you hold the opinion that immorality is certainly increasing among the alien population? [JM] No, I would not say that immorality is increasing among them. I think their morality compares favourably with any other section of the community.[61]

Despite repeated leading questions from the panel, Mulvaney consistently presented a community in St George's in the East which was relatively harmonious. Significantly, he also referred to the incident in Cornwell Street, which a previous witness had described as 'a perfect riot', as 'nothing of any moment'. Indeed, while it is difficult to capture the testimonies of sailors and sex workers in St George's in the East, those who worked closely with these communities consistently implied an interdependence between the sailors and the local population.

In his memoirs based on his work in St George's in the East, Reverend Harry Jones provided nuanced accounts of how these working-class communities functioned. For Jones, it was the maritime trade that dominated the St George's district which integrated sailors into the urban population:

> We are among the first to receive and handle the riches of the earth which are poured into London. Our contact with distant places is fresh, our people are related to sailors, our estimate of commerce is formed before the wholesale importation of goods is divided into the many rills of retail trade. The main stream of business, like the Thames which carries it, flows through our midst.[62]

Thus, instead of being a peripheral actor ashore, the sailor was pivotal in how the community of Ratcliffe Highway perceived and engaged with the wider world. His was the key trade in the district and he had established familial and social networks in the area. This interdependence between sailors and the wider working-class sailortown community was embodied in their shared hostility to the police.

In both St George's in the East and Whitechapel, the police were hindered in their work by groups of sailors and local men attempting to rescue arrested prisoners from the police. For example, in 1861 at the Middlesex Sessions, William Reagan was sentenced to two years of hard labour for endeavouring to rescue a prisoner from being taken to the magistrate's court and assaulting a policeman.[63] Reagan and 'a mob' of men surprised the policemen transporting the prisoner, beat the police with their own staffs, released their companion, and made their escape. Reagan was arrested the following day and described by the police as keeping company with 'some of the worst thieves in the neighbourhood'.[64] This attack upon the police and the rescue appears to have been planned in advance and conducted by a well-orchestrated 'mob' of several men who knew the arrested man. However, on other occasions, it seems that much of the neighbourhood, including foreign sailors, spontaneously came out to prevent the police from arresting suspects.

In 1854, Orlando Mosulany, a twenty-year-old Austrian sailor, was charged at the Thames police court with endeavouring to rescue John Macarthy, a ticket of leave convict, from the police. As soon as the police arrived on Ratcliffe Highway, a crowd of between 400 and 500 people gathered to prevent the arrest of Macarthy. Constable Hart explained that 'the street was quite full, the noise and shouts were fearful, and many took part in the disturbance'. The court heard that 'the mob attempted to rescue the prisoner and the police were compelled to draw their truncheons and drive then back'. Mosulany and Macarthy were committed to trial at the Middlesex Quarter Sessions.[65] Just as sailors attempted to rescue locals from the police, working men in St George's and Whitechapel also endeavoured to prevent the arrest of seafarers. In 1863 two sailors fought the police to avoid arrest in Leman Street, Whitechapel. It was reported at the Thames police court that 'an up-and-down fight took place, and the roughs of Whitechapel encouraged the sailors in the resistance to the police officers'. The two sailors, William Conway and Edward Ashe, were fined five pounds each and in default two months imprisonment.[66] Thus, despite drinking some distance away from London's sailortown, these sailors were spontaneously supported by Whitechapel's 'roughs' in their altercation with the police. Similarly, in 1878 a violent incident at the East and West Indian Dock Company revolved around an attempted rescue of a sailor from the police. John Kelley, a labourer, was charged with assaulting David Jones, a police constable. The *East End Observer* reported that:

> Whilst the sailor was being taken to a police box, a rush was made to rescue him by a mob of labourers who were there. The prisoner in the dock was at the head of the gang and came up to the witness [Jones] and struck him in the chest, and followed this up by kicking him at the top of the thigh.[67]

Despite protesting his innocence and claiming that it was the large crowd that injured the police constable, Kelley was sentenced to one month's hard labour at the Thames police court.[68] Perhaps the most interesting feature about these cases is that sailors and local working-class people combined to obstruct the police. Despite being a foreign seaman, Mosulany was clearly familiar with the local community's antipathy towards the police, while Kelley, a labourer, along with the rest of 'the mob', risked arrest and punishment to rescue a sailor. English and foreign sailors, then, were participants in working-class street culture and active in attempting to thwart police intervention.

Conclusion

Ratcliffe Highway was often conveyed in the sensational press as one of several city ports that had been subject to an invasion of dangerous foreign sailors who had imported the use of knives into the fighting culture of Britain. However, the evidence heard at Parliament's select committees and the figures generated from the Thames police courts and Old Bailey papers testify that there were relatively few incidents of serious knife crime. Indeed, the evidence strongly indicates that knife crime was not exclusive to London's port and that, by the end of the nineteenth century, new working-class suburbs in the north of the metropolis were recording more cases than St George's in the East.[69] However, the genuine cosmopolitan nature of Ratcliffe Highway's sailortown meant that they were more important as contact zones than places of conflict and violence. Ratcliffe Highway helped foster a cosmopolitan space where cultural contact and exchange occurred through leisure institutions and sailor boarding houses. Thus, sailortown culture cultivated a streetwise sailor, adept in recognising the different customs of upholding masculinity in densely populated, working-class districts. As we have seen in the preceding chapters, the proletarian sailor was cast as immoral, prone to drunkenness and impulsive violence. The English sailor was also exposed to the 'unfair' fighting traditions of foreign sailors, which fuelled the belief that there was a deadly knife contagion on the shores of Britain. These stereotypes do not stand up to closer scrutiny as sailors were very much part of a subaltern community, facilitated by a sailortown's contact zone qualities. Their mutual suspicion of the authorities was extended to the police, as the subaltern community sometimes combined to rescue people from arrest. In addition, while middle-class observers presented Ratcliffe Highway as a chaotic environment that was splintered by random acts of gratuitous violence, the relatively low levels of serious male-on-male knife crime demonstrate that this was a *functioning* community. Despite sailortown's often tough reputation, its cosmopolitan subaltern culture was self-regulated through recognised fighting customs enacted by a fiercely independent community of sailors and working people.

Notes

1. *East London Observer*, 10 October 1857.
2. J.M. MacKenzie, 'The press and the dominant ideology of Empire', in S. Potter (ed.), *Newspaper and Empire in Ireland and Britain* (Dublin, Four Courts Press, 2004), 23–38.
3. British Parliamentary Papers (BPP), *Royal Commission on Alien Immigration*, Vol II, 1903, 81.
4. For moral panics in a historical context, see P. King, 'Moral panics and violent street crime 1750–2000: A comparative perspective', in B. Godfrey, C. Emsley, and G., Dunstall (eds), *Comparative Histories of Crime* (London, Routledge, 2003), 53–71; D. Lemmings and C. Walker (eds), *Moral Panics, the Media and the Law in Early Modern England* (Basingstoke, Palgrave Macmillan, 2008).
5. L.U. Scholl (ed.), *Research in Maritime History Merchants and Mariners: Selected Maritime Writings of David. M. Williams* (Newfoundland, International Maritime Economic History Association, 2000), 215.
6. *East London Observer*, 1 January 1872.
7. *East London Observer*, 10 October 1857.
8. *East London Observer*, 10 October 1857; Sindall, R. 'The London garrotting panics of 1856 and 1862', Social History, 12(3), 1987, 351–9.
9. *East London Observer*, 3 October 1857, 6 August 1859, 8 October 1864, 26 August 1882, 20 May 1911.
10. *Pearsons Weekly*, 6 February 1902.
11. *Daily News*, 29 May 1872.
12. *Household Words*, 6 December 1851.
13. *East London Observer*, 3 October 1857.
14. *East London Observer*, 10 October 1857.
15. *Morning Chronicle*, 13 May 1859.
16. *Express*, 31 January 1863.
17. *London Evening Standard*, 10 January 1863.
18. *Shipping and Mercantile Gazette*, 4 March 1864.
19. J. Thomas, 'Alien immigration and the London School of Economics: Some early connections' (unpublished paper, 2017), 6.
20. W. Evans-Gordon, *The Alien Immigrant* (London, Chas Scribner's Sons, 1903), 263.
21. Thomas, 'Alien immigration', 8.
22. The commission was largely concerned with Jewish immigration from Eastern Europe that had begun in the late nineteenth century.
23. Thomas, 'Alien immigration', 6, 8.
24. J. Davis, 'A poor man's system of justice: The London police courts in the second half of the nineteenth century', *Historical Journal*, 27(2), June 1984, 309–35.
25. Davis, 'A poor man's system of justice', 308, 312.
26. Davis, 'A poor man's system of justice', 308, 312.

27 M. Wiener, *Men of Blood: Violence, Manliness and Criminal Justice in Victorian England* (Cambridge, Cambridge University Press, 2004), 8.
28 Only one murder was recorded in the period covered here which did not involve the sailor population. Brutal assaults included the use of weapons such as knives and clubs.
29 *Old Bailey Proceedings Online*; we searched for all offences where the transcription matched 'knife', and offence categories of breaking the peace and killing, defendant male, victim male, between 1850 and 1880. The category of 'breaking the peace' included the offences of assault, riot, threatening behaviour, and wounding. The category of 'killing' included murder and manslaughter. Cases that were duplicated were omitted from the statistics.
30 If we assume that in the vast majority of cases a seafarer's occupation was revealed in court, only seventy-nine (14 per cent) of the 558 men brought to trial for knife assault were sailors.
31 *Morning Chronicle*, 10 August 1857; *East London Observer*, 26 September 1857; *Evening Standard*, 20 October 1857.
32 See, for example, J.E. Ritchie, *The Nightside of London* (London, William Tweedie, 1857), 104; *Era*, 2 February 1862; *East London Observer*, 8 October 1864; *The Metropolitan*, 14 September 1872; J. Greenwood, *In Strange Company: Being the Experiences of a Roving Correspondent* (London, Henry S. King and Co., 1883).
33 www.british-history.ac.uk/vch/middx/vol5/pp317-324, accessed 21 June 2023.
34 J.E. Archer, '"Men behaving badly?": Masculinity and the use of violence, 1850–1900', in S. D'Cruze (ed.), *Everyday Violence in Britain, 1850–1950: Gender and Class* (Oxford, Routledge, 2000), 42.
35 Archer, '"Men behaving badly?"', 42.
36 BPP, *Reports to the Secretary of State for the Home Department: The State of the Law Relating to Brutal Assaults* 1875, 149.
37 BPP, *The State of the Law Relating to Brutal Assaults* 1875, 149.
38 Archer has found similar exaggerated stories of 'notorious' districts of Liverpool's port communities; see J.E. Archer, *The Monster Evil: Policing and Violence in Victorian* Liverpool (Liverpool, Liverpool University Press, 2011), 8.
39 Wiener, *Men of Blood*, 289.
40 *London Evening Standard*, 10 January 1863; John E. Archer has found a similar resistance among working men in abandoning the fair fight for the courts. He argues that the 'civilising process, although evident from the late 1860s and early 1870s, had not been successfully accomplished in Liverpool by the end of the century'. See Archer, *The Monster Evil*, 92.
41 *Illustrated Police News*, 8 June 1867.
42 R.B. Shoemaker, *The London Mob: Violence and Disorder in Eighteenth Century England* (London, Bloomsbury, 2004), 178. See also Andrew Davies's important body of work on working-class gangs, which demonstrated the longevity of the traditional working-class 'fist fight' in the industrial north of Britain. Even in the late nineteenth century, Davies noted that the police were

reluctant to intervene when a 'fair fight' had been organised to uphold the combatants' honour. Indeed, in Manchester, it seems prosecutions were only pursued when fighting codes had been breached such as when men had kicked or used weapons against an opponent. See, for example, A. Davies, 'Youth gangs, masculinity and violence in late Victorian Manchester and Salford', *Journal of Social History*, 32(2), 1998, 349–69.

43 Winchester College Archive, D2/58 Envelope J, 'St Landport, Winchester College Mission', Dr Linklater diary, 16.
44 *Morning Advertiser*, 20 October 1863.
45 *Morning Advertiser*, 20 October 1863.
46 *Morning Advertiser*, 20 October 1863.
47 *East London Observer*, 27 August 1881.
48 *East London Observer*, 21 September 1889.
49 *East London Observer*, 4 February 1888. A 'landshark' or Crimp was a common name for someone who would take advantage of sailors ashore, charging them high interest rates for loans or expensive lodgings; see G. Milne, *People, Place and Power on the Nineteenth Century Waterfront: Sailortown* (Basingstoke, Palgrave Macmillan, 2016), 107–8.
50 *Morning Post*, 6 January 1899. Clive Emsley has shown that when foreign sailors appeared in Victorian courts charged with knife offences, their defence counsel would stress the defendants' 'foreignness', which would usually lead to a more lenient sentence as they were not familiar with the more 'civilised' English fighting traditions: C. Emsley, *Hard Men: Violence in England since 1750* (London, Hambledon Press, 2005), 87.
51 T.W. Gallant, 'Honor, masculinity, and ritual knife fighting in nineteenth-century Greece', *American Historical Review*, 105(2), April 2000, 359–82, 361.
52 BPP, *Select Committee on Theatrical Licenses and Regulations*, 1866, Minutes of Evidence, Qs 1072–4.
53 A good example is the Prussian Eagle entertainment venue that offered German food and dancing. See *Illustrated Police News*, 4 March 1871.
54 *East London Observer*, 8 October 1864.
55 *East London Observer*, 26 September 1857.
56 *Old Bailey Proceedings Online*, October 1857, trial of Jose de Rosario killing (t18571026-1058), 26, accessed 8 August 2017.
57 *East End Observer*, 26 September 1857.
58 For a wider discussion on sailors and working-class communities, see J. Davey, 'A higher class of men? Sailors and working-class communities in Bristol 1850–1914' (unpublished PhD thesis, University of Portsmouth, 2019).
59 BPP, *Royal Commission on Alien Immigration*, 80.
60 BPP, *Royal Commission on Alien Immigration*, 82.
61 BPP, *Royal Commission on Alien Immigration*, 281.
62 Harry Jones, *East and West London: Being Notes of Common Life and Pastoral Work in Saint James's, Westminster and in Saint George's-In-The-East* (London, Smith, Elder & Co., 1875), 168.

63 There is some confusion as to whether Reagan was a sailor or a tailor, with different newspapers providing conflicting accounts of his employment. The *East London Observer*, 12 October 1861, and *The Morning Advertiser*, 8 October 1861, referred to Reagan as a sailor, while the *London Evening Standard*, 8 October 1861, and the *Morning Post*, 8 October 1861, recorded that he was a tailor.
64 *East London Observer*, 12 October 1861.
65 *Morning Advertiser*, 4 October 1854.
66 *Lloyds Weekly*, 4 October 1863.
67 *East End Observer*, 26 January 1878.
68 *East End Observer*, 16 January 1878,
69 The Old Bailey data indicates that the new working-class district of Tottenham, North London, had by the end of the nineteenth century recorded more levels of serious knife crime than Whitechapel or St George's in the East. For Tottenham, see www.british-history.ac.uk/vch/middx/vol5/pp317-324, accessed 9 August 2023.

Conclusion

There is nothing particularly inviting – nothing but dirt and disease, drunkenness and vice – to be seen in a walk through St George's-in-the-East. But to the man of thought, a vast expanse of almost untrodden wilderness opened, in working out the problem as how the poor live – or rather die, for in but too many cases their existence is nothing better than a living death.

East London Observer, 1 March 1884

The journalist who wandered through Ratcliffe Highway and pondered on how the poor lived and died could have replicated their walk in any poverty-ridden city in Britain during the 1880s. This begs the question as to whether the experience of living in sailortown was any different to living in the slums of Manchester, Leeds, or Birmingham. Sailortowns were, after all, working-class districts that were subject to the same middle-class scrutiny and social exploration of the land-locked urban slum. The residents of slums and sailortowns were both the focus of civilising missions that often inflated moral panics and sensational press stories to even greater levels by the late nineteenth century. If slums and sailortowns were similarly treated by journalists and social observers, the districts' social demography also had important overlaps. Indeed, one of the key findings in this book is that sailors were very much part of the working-class community, having cultural and familial roots in sailortown districts.[1] Like slums, sailortowns were also subject to moral panics that centred on vice, debauchery, and violence, but with the added villainous caricature of the 'foreign devil' seafarers. However, as we will discuss below, sailortown differed from the classic slum in two important ways. First, contemporaries developed a specific narrative as to why sailortown had become a moral abyss, which was undoubtedly forged from their anxieties about the onset of urban and industrial society. Second, the highly cosmopolitan and transient nature of sailortown introduced a more complex cultural landscape than the traditional land-locked slum.

With the arrival of rapid urbanisation and the steam revolution in the shipping industry, contemporaries troubled by modernity began to yearn nostalgically for a lost maritime world. Ratcliffe Highway commentators were convinced that Dibdin's loyal, benign sailors and women had been replaced by a more degenerate, subversive, proletariat class of people who had no understanding of maritime traditions. As we have seen, this nostalgia for a mythical maritime past was employed repeatedly between 1850 and 1914. Indeed, no matter the decade the author was writing in, the classic Jack Tar and Moll characters were always described as in their pomp twenty years previously. However, these disparaging narratives of sailortown and its people did not go uncriticised, and these challenges provide an insight into the internal cultural dynamics of Ratcliffe Highway. On the occasions that residents and sailors pushed back on the judgemental descriptions of their district, we can glimpse a robust working-class community in which an urban–maritime culture shaped a sense of themselves and the traditions and conventions that governed subaltern behaviour in the district. Certainly, while it is almost impossible to recover what subaltern communities thought, an understanding of the material lives they lived, their behaviour, and what they would and would not tolerate moves us closer to retrieving a more authentic experience of sailortown. Indeed, this book argues that sailortown was a *distinctive* and *functional* working-class community that was self-regulating and self-moderating. This is perhaps even more remarkable given that the sheer size of the international seafaring workforce that stepped ashore on Ratcliffe Highway placed sailortown's transient nature on a different level to the traditional slum. While the bourgeois observer viewed the district as chaotic and dangerous, to the international sailor, Ratcliffe Highway exhibited the recognisable characteristics of an urban–maritime culture associated with sailortown. This culture infused the locality and informed sailortown's own micro-economy of the merchant shipping industry, sailor leisure, and boarding facilities.

In understanding *how* sailortown functioned, this book has viewed Ratcliffe Highway through the prism of a contact zone. Pratt's definition of contact zones as 'spaces where cultures meet, clash and grapple with each other' captures the complex cultural exchanges within these waterfront cosmopolitan communities.[2] Sailortown was undoubtedly a transient district and a space of 'heightened interaction' that you would struggle to find in any other urban context.[3] Its compact district fostered a space in which differing subaltern cultures met, sometimes negotiating and at other times clashing with one another. With its plethora of former international seafarers running boarding houses and entertainment venues, sailortowns exuded a 'stateless' quality and were in stark contrast to the wealth of leisure venues in Britain that carried imperial names or décor. Indeed, this book has argued that we should not underestimate sailortown's capacity to provide important cultural networks to the international seafarer.

The Victorian image of the sailortown crimp exploiting the naïve sailor and entangling him into vice and debt was often propagated by missionaries who wanted to generate charitable funds, and newspapers keen to improve their circulation. As we have seen, through the seamen's lodging house system, sailors stepping ashore into an unfamiliar port often forged good relations with boarding house keepers who were a source of shipping employment intelligence and, for some, were a means of deserting poor employers. Indeed, both the lodging houses and entertainment venues carried symbols of maritime material culture that distinguished themselves from the common lodging houses and contributed to a vibrant urban–maritime culture. Indeed, the sailor was the supreme subaltern transnational worker who regularly crossed borders and connected cultures. He appropriated and reproduced a range of subaltern cultures and was an important agency in shaping an international urban–maritime culture that seafarers could recognise as they stepped ashore. In viewing sailortown through a contact zone lens, the experience of sailors, women, and the broader working-class community is put into sharp focus. It explains why sailors were attracted to the district despite the horror stories that rolled off the press, and it also clarifies the relationship they had with other sailors and the sailortown working-class community. For example, in some contexts, these differing subaltern cultures joined and understood a shared mutual hostility to the police, while in other scenarios, conflicts could arise in which participants would negotiate the method of combat adopted. In unpacking these differing subaltern cultures, we are also able to shed light on the significant role that women played in sailortown. For example, the overabundance of small sailor lodging houses and brothels afforded women an opportunity to carve out matriarchal enclaves in sailortown that enabled them a degree of agency in an otherwise relentlessly poverty-stricken and, at times, dangerous environment. It also reveals the complex relationship that women had with sailors, ranging from women who were exploited and abused to those who forged genuine long-term companionship with seafarers.

Recovering the experience of women in sailortown also showed the limits of their agency, given that they were living in a patriarchal and sometimes brutal working-class district. Similarly, sailortown did not escape the growing racism and industrial discipline that characterised British society towards the end of the nineteenth century. By the 1880s, the rigid onboard hierarchies imposed on sailors by shipping companies, and campaigns by British trade unions to cease the employment of foreign labour, began to foster a stratified life ashore for some seafarers.[4] Scientific racism underpinned institutional policies or campaigns that sought to divide seafarers into cheap Chinese or Indian labour on the one side, and the skilled British sailor on the other.[5] These racial stereotypes became influential in how the crew was structured and how sailors were perceived. For example, Joseph Conrad claimed that aboard ship, no one spoke to or looked at the Chinese stokers and that they never acknowledged the rest of the crew. He added that 'their appearances in the light of day were very regular, and yet somewhat ghostlike in their attachment and silence'.[6] As a consequence, Chinese labourers in particular forged their own communities further east and away from Ratcliffe Highway.

Finally, how representative was Ratcliffe Highway as an international sailortown? What cannot be denied is that in the middle of the nineteenth century, London's port was the largest in the world and at the centre of a global network of trade that attracted seafarers from around the globe. However, it is argued here that the traits of sailortown that we have discussed in this book were present in other smaller international sailortowns. Sailortowns the world over were castigated for their vice and crime, but, like Ratcliffe Highway, they were spaces of heightened interaction. These urban–maritime spaces evolved boarding houses and entertainment venues that were conducive to a flourishing cultural contact zone. Indeed, Ratcliffe Highway was not peculiar in this respect since its urban–maritime culture was a product of the transnational sailor, a worker who appropriated and reproduced this culture in the streets, lodging houses, and entertainment venues he patronised.

Notes

1 L. Kosok, 'Pleasurescapes on the edge: Performing modernity on urban waterfronts (1880–1960)', *Journal of Urban History*, 48(6), 2022, 1199–210, 1203.
2 J.R. Isaacs and A. Otruba, 'More-than-human contact zones', *Environment and Planning*, 2(4), December 2019, 697–711, 697.
3 M. Fuhrmann, *Port Cities of the Eastern Mediterranean: Urban Cultures in the Late Ottoman Empire* (Cambridge, Cambridge University Press, 2018), 24.
4 See, for example, M. Daunton, 'Jack ashore, seamen in Cardiff before 1914', *Welsh History Review*, 9(2), 1978, 176–203, 176.
5 J. Hyslop, '"Ghostlike" seafarers and sailing ships nostalgia: The figure of the steamship lascar in the British imagination, c. 1880–1960', *Journal of Maritime Research*, 16(2), 2014, 212–28, 217.
6 Quoted in Hyslop, '"Ghostlike" seafarers and sailing ships nostalgia', 212.

Bibliography

Newspapers and journals

All the Year Round
Argus
Bell's New Weekly Messenger
Chambers's Journal of Popular Literature, Science and Arts
Chart and Compass
Clerkenwell News
The Daily London News
Daily News
Daily Telegraph and Courier
East London Observer
East End Star
The Eclectic Review
The Examiner
Express
The Globe
Good Words
The Graphic
Household Words
Illustrated Police News
Kings County Chronicle
Leisure Hour
Lloyds Weekly
London Evening Standard
Metropolitan
Morning Advertiser
Morning Chronicle
Morning Post
Northern Whig
Our Corner
Pall Mall Gazette
Pearsons Weekly
Reynolds Newspaper
Saturday Review
Seaman
Shipping and Mercantile Gazette

Sun
Temple Bar
Western Daily Mercury

Archives

Censuses for 1861 and 1891

London Metropolitan Archives

(LMA), LCC/PH/REG/1/02, 'List of licensed seamen's lodging houses', 1908
PSTH/A1/20–24, surviving Thames Magistrates Records for 1891

London School of Economics

LSE, Charles Booth Archive (hereafter CBA), B/138, 26, 1895
LSE, CBA, Booth notebook B/280
LSE, CBA, 'Missionaries on Ratcliffe Highway', notebook B/224, 1896–98

Modern Record Centre, University of Warwick

MSS.175/3/14/1-2, 1913, National Union of Seamen Archive

Old Bailey Papers online

OBP, 2 February 1852, case of Jose Frutoso Berdugo, Ref t18520202-253
OBP, 10 July 1871, the trial of Julia Mahoney, Ref t18710710-504
OBP, October 1887, trial of Richard Marchant and John Frost, Ref t18871024-1048

University of Oxford

Broadside Ballads online; Roud Number V4683, 'Rolling down Ratcliffe Highway' (imprint London, 1877), collected between 1863 and 1885

Sailor Society Archives, Sailor Society, Southampton

SSA, *The Sailor's Magazine*
SSA, *The Port of London and Bethel Union Society, the 73rd Annual Report* (London, T. Wilson Booth, 1890–91)

Tower Hamlets Library

Ref LC 6244, A. Sherran, 'Blackwall Pier and Sailor Memories of Sixty Years Ago', 1916, unpublished manuscript

Winchester College Archive

D2/58 Envelope J, 'St Landport, Winchester College Mission', Dr Linklater diary

State papers

British Parliamentary Papers, *Select Committee on Public Houses*, 1853
British Parliamentary Papers, *Lodging Houses of the Metropolis: Report on the Common and Model Lodging Houses of the Metropolis* (with reference to Epidemic Cholera in 1854), 1855
British Parliamentary Papers, *On the Means of Devine Worship in Populous Districts*, 1858
British Parliamentary Papers, *Select Committee on Theatrical Licences and Regulations*, 1866
British Parliamentary Papers, *Reports to the Secretary of State for the Home Department: The State of the Law Relating to Brutal Assaults*, 1875
British Parliamentary Papers, *Royal Commission on Alien Immigration*, Vol II, 1903
Old Bailey Proceedings Online

Contemporary pamphlets, articles, and books

Acton, W. *Prostitution, Considered in Its Moral, Social, and Sanitary Aspects in London and Other Large Cities and Garrison Towns* (London, John Churchill and Sons, 1857, 1870 edn)
Anon, *The Swells Guide; Or a Peep through the Great Metropolis under the Dominion of Nox* (London, H. Smith, 1849)
Anon, *Wonderful London: Its Lights and Shadows of Humour and Sadness* (London, Tinsley Bros, 1878)
Baedeker, K. *London and Its Environs* (Leipsic, OH, Baedeker Publishing, 1902)
Beames, T. *The Rookeries of London: Past, Present and Prospective* (London, Thomas Boswell, 1850, 1970 edn)
Besant, A. 'How London amuses itself in the East', *Our Corner*, August 1886
Besant, W. *East London* (London, Chatto & Windus, 1901)
Booth, C. *Life and Labour of the People of London*, Vol VII (London, Macmillan, 1896)
Bullen, F. T. *The Men of the Merchant Service* (London, Murray, 1900a)
Bullen, F. T. *The Palace of Poor Jack* (London, James Nesbit and Co, 1900b), 17
Clayton, J. Father Dolling: A Memoir (London, Wells Gardner, Darton and Co., 1902)
De Quincey, T. 'On Murder Considered as One of the Fine Arts', in *The Works of Thomas De Quincey*, Riverside Edition, Vol IV (Boston, Houghton, Mifflin and Co., 1876)
Dickens, C. 'On duty with Inspector Field', *Household Words*, 64, 14 June 1851
Dickens, C. *The Uncommercial Traveller* (London, Chapman & Hall, 1905)
Dickens, C. *Our Mutual Friend* (London, Penguin, 1998, original publication 1864–65)
Egan, P. *Tom & Jerry: Life in London; Or the Day and Night Scenes* (London, John Camden Hotten, 1820, 1868 edn)
Evans-Gordon, W. *The Alien Immigrant* (London, Chas Scribner's Sons, 1903)
Ewing Ritchie, J. *The Night Side of London* (London, William Tweedle, 1857)
Fox Smith, C. *Sailor Town Days* (London, Houghton Mifflin, 1923)
Fox Smith, C. (ed.), *The Man before the Mast: Being the Story of Twenty Years Afloat* (London, Methuen, 1929)

Greenwood, J. *In Strange Company: Being the Experiences of a Roving Correspondent* (London, Henry S. King and Co., 1873)

Hood, T. 'The Bridge of Sighs', in A. Quiller-Couch (ed.), *The Oxford Book of English Verse: 1250–1900* (Oxford, Clarendon Press, 1900, 1912 edn)

Jones, H. *East and West London: Being Notes of Common Life and Pastoral Work in Saint James's Westminster and in Saint George's-in-the-East* (London, Smith, Elder & Co., 1875)

Knapp, A. *The New Newgate Calendar: Being Interesting Memoirs of Notorious Characters, Who Have Been Convicted of Outrages on the Laws of England, during the Seventeenth Century, Brought down to the Present Time* (London, J. and J. Cundee, 1826)

Levi, L. (ed.), *Annals of British Legislation: Being a Brief Digest of the Parliamentary Blue Books* (London, Smith, Elder & Co., 1866)

London, J. *The People of the Abyss* (New York, Grosset & Dunlap, 1903)

Lowder, C.F. *Ten Years in S. George's Mission: Being an Account of Its Origin, Progress, and Works of Mercy* (London, G.J Palmer, 1867)

Masterman, C.F.J. *The Heart of the Empire: Discussion of the Problems of Modern City Life in England* (London, T.F. Unwin, 1901)

Mayhew, H. *London Labour and the London Poor* (London, Griffin, Bohn, and Company, 1861, Vol I; 1862, Vol IV)

McKee, C. *Sober Men and True: Sailor Lives in the Royal Navy 1900–1945* (London, Harvard University Press, 2002)

Miller, H. *First Impressions of England and Its People* (Edinburgh, Adam & Charles Black, 1847, 1861 edn)

Mitchell, G. *Down in Limehouse* (London, Stanley Martin and Co., 1925)

Morrison, A. *The Hole in the Wall* (London, Methuen, 1902)

Phillips, W. *The Wild Tribes of London* (London, Ward and Lock, 1855)

Ritchie, J.E. *The Nightside of London* (London, William Tweedie, 1857)

Robinson, F.W. 'A night on the Highway', *Belgravia*, May 1879

Rowe, R. *Jack Afloat and Ashore* (London, Smith, Elder & Co., 1875)

Salter, J. *The East in the West; Or Work among the Asiatics and Africans in London* (London, S.W. Partridge & Co., 1896)

Sims, G.R. *How the Poor Live and Horrible London* (London, Chatto & Windus, 1889)

Sims, G.R. *Living London*, Vol 3 (London, Cassell and Co., 1902)

Thomas, E.W. *Twenty-Five Years' Labour among the Friendless and Fallen* (London, Shaw & Co., 1879)

Trench, M. *Charles Lowder: A Biography* (London, Kegan Paul, Trench & Co., 1882)

Walker, H. *East London Sketches of Christian Work and Workers* (London, The Religious Tract Society, 1896)

Walsham, W. 'The East End', *The Contemporary Review*, December 1888

Wright, T. *The Great Army of London Poor: Sketches of Life and Character in a Thames-Side District* (London, Charles H. Kelly, 1875, 1890 edn)

Secondary sources

Andrew, D.T. 'The code of honour and its critics: The opposition to duelling in England, 1700–1850', *Social History*, 5(3), October 1980, 409–34

Archer, J.E. '"Men behaving badly?": Masculinity and the use of violence, 1850–1900', in S. D'Cruze (ed.), *Everyday Violence in Britain, 1850–1950: Gender and Class* (Oxford, Routledge, 2000)

Archer, J.E. *The Monster Evil: Policing and Violence in Victorian Liverpool* (Liverpool, Liverpool University Press, 2011)

Arnold, D. 'Race, place and bodily difference in early nineteenth-century India', *Historical Research*, 77(196), 2004, 141–288

Barton, M. 'Duelling in the Royal Navy', *The Mariner's Mirror*, 100(3), July 2014, 282–306

Beaven, B. *Leisure, Citizenship and Working-Class Men, 1850–1945* (Manchester, Manchester University Press, 2005)

Beaven, B. *Visions of Empire: Patriotism, Popular Culture, and the City, 1870–1939* (Manchester, Manchester University Press, 2012)

Beaven, B. 'The resilience of sailortown culture in English naval ports, c. 1820–1900', *Urban History*, 43(1), 2016, 72–95

Beaven, B. and Griffiths, J. 'Creating the exemplary citizen: The changing notion of citizenship in Britain, 1870–1939', *Contemporary British History*, 22(2), 2008, 203–25

Beaven, B. and Seiter, M. 'Regulating sin in the city: The moral geographies of naval port towns in Britain and Germany, c.1860–1914', *Britain and the World*, 13(1), 2020, 27–46

Bell, K. '"They are without Christ and without hope": "Heathenism", popular religion, and supernatural belief in Portsmouth's maritime community, 1851–1901', in B. Beaven, K. Bell, and R. James (eds), *Port Towns and Urban Cultures: International Histories of the Waterfront, c. 1700–2000* (Basingstoke, Palgrave Macmillan, 2016)

Betts, O. '"Knowing" the late Victorian East End', *The London Journal*, 42(3), November 2017, 257–72

Brown, J. 'Charles Booth and labour colonies, 1889–1905', *Economic History Review*, 21(2), August 1968, 349–61

Burton, V. 'Boundaries and identities in the nineteenth century English port: Sailortown narratives and urban space', in S. Gunn and R.J. Morris (eds), *Identities in Space: Contested Terrains in the Western City since 1850* (Aldershot, Ashgate, 2001)

Burton, V. '"As I wuz a-rolling down the Highway one morn": Fictions of the 19th century English sailortown', in B. Klein (ed.), *Fictions of the Sea: Critical Perspectives on the Ocean in British Literature and Culture* (Oxford, Routledge, 2002)

Carter Wood, J. *Violence and Crime in Nineteenth Century England: The Shadow of Our Refinement* (London, Routledge, 2004)

Churchill, N., Warman, M., Gibson, C., and Leslie, J. *Stories from the Sea, 1818–2018* (Southampton, Sailor's Society, 2018)

Cook, M. *London and the Culture of Homosexuality, 1885–1914* (Cambridge, Cambridge University Press, 2003)

Cotsell, M. 'The uncommercial traveller on the commercial road: Dickens's East End', *Dickens Quarterly*, 3(3), September 1986, 115–22

Crook, T. 'Accommodating the outcast: Common lodging houses and the limits of urban governance in Victorian and Edwardian England', *Urban History*, 35(3), 2008, 414–36

Crone, R. *Violent Victorians: Popular Entertainment in Nineteenth Century London* (Manchester, Manchester University Press, 2012)

Cuming, E. 'At home in the world? The ornamental life of sailors in Victorian sailortown', *Victorian Literature and Culture*, 47(3), 2019, 463–85
Daunton, M. 'Jack ashore, seamen in Cardiff before 1914', *Welsh History Review*, 9(2), 1978, 176–203
Davies, A. 'Youth gangs, masculinity and violence in late Victorian Manchester and Salford', *Journal of Social History*, 32(2), 1998a, 349–69
Davies, A. 'Street gangs, crime and policing in Glasgow during the 1930s: The case of the Beehive Boys', *Social History*, 23(3), 1998b, 251–67
Davies, A. 'Glasgow's "Reign of Terror": Street gangs, racketeering and intimidation in the 1920s and 1930s', *Contemporary British History*, 21, 4 December 2007, 405–27
Davies, A. 'Police violence and judicial bias in the age of mass democracy: Glasgow, 1933–1935', *Social History*, 44(1), 2019, 57–85
Davis, J. 'A poor man's system of justice: The London police courts in the second half of the nineteenth century', *Historical Journal*, 27(2), June 1984, 309–35
Dietze, A. and Naumann, K. 'Revisiting transnational actors from a spatial perspective', *European Review of History: Revue européenne d'histoire*, 25(3–4), 2018, 415–30
Dixon, C. 'The rise and fall of the crimp', in S. Fisher (ed.), *British Shipping and Seamen, 1630–1960: Some Studies* (Exeter, University of Exeter, 1984)
Driver, F. (ed.), *The Geography Militant: Cultures of Exploration and Empire* (Oxford, Blackwell, 2001)
Dyos, H.J. 'The slums of Victorian London', in D. Cannadine and D. Reeder (eds), *Exploring the Urban Past: Essays in Urban History by H.J. Dyos* (Cambridge, Cambridge University Press, 1982)
Eaton, J. and Gill, C. *The Trade Union Directory* (London, Pluto Press, 1981)
Emsley, C. *Hard Men: Violence in England since 1750* (London, Hambledon Press, 2005)
Fingard, J. *Jack in Port: Sailortowns of Eastern Canada* (Toronto, University of Toronto Press, 1982)
Flanders, J. *The Invention of Murder: How the Victorians Revelled in Death and Detection and Invented the Modern Crime* (London, Harper Press, 2011)
Frey, J.W. 'Lascars, the Thames police court and the Old Bailey: Crime on the high seas and the London courts, 1852–8', *Journal of Maritime Research*, 16(2), 2014, 196–211
Fuhrmann, M. *Port Cities of the Eastern Mediterranean: Urban Cultures in the Late Ottoman Empire* (Cambridge, Cambridge University Press, 2018)
Gallant, T.W. 'Honor, masculinity, and ritual knife fighting in nineteenth-century Greece', *American Historical Review*, 105(2), April 2000, 359–82
Garcia, H. 'The Strangers' Home for Asiatics, Africans and South Sea Islanders: Inaugurating a hospitable world order in mid-Victorian Britain', *Global Nineteenth Century Studies*, 1(1), 2022, 81–90
Ginn, G. 'Answering the "bitter cry": Urban description and social reform in the late Victorian East End', *The London Journal*, 31(2), November 2006, 179–200
Haggerty, S., Webster, A., and White, N.J. (eds), *Empire in One City? Liverpool's Inconvenient Imperial Past* (Manchester, Manchester University Press, 2008)
Heere, C. '"That racial chasm that yawns eternally in our midst": The British Empire and the politics of Asian migration, 1900–14', *Historical Research*, 90(249), 2017, 591–612

Heerten, L. 'Mooring mobilities, fixing flows: Towards a global urban history of port cities in the age of steam', *Journal of Sociology*, 34, 2021, 350–74

Hitchcock, T. 'The new history from below', *History Workshop Journal*, 57, spring 2004, 294–8

Hugill, S. *Sailortown* (London, Routledge and Kegan Paul, 1967)

Hugill, S. *Sea Shanties* (London, Barrie and Jenkins, 1977)

Hyslop, J. '"Ghostlike" seafarers and sailing ship nostalgia: The figure of the steamship lascar in the British imagination, 1860–1960', *Journal of Maritime Research*, 16(2), 2014, 212–28

Isaacs, J.R. and Otruba, A. 'More-than-human contact zones', Environment and Planning, 2(4), December 2019, 697–711

Jackson, G. 'Ports 1700–1840', in P. Clark (ed.), *The Cambridge Urban History of Britain: Volume II, 1540–1840* (Cambridge, Cambridge University Press, 2000)

James, P.D. and Critchley, T.A. *The Maul and the Pear Tree: The Ratcliffe Highway Murders, 1811* (London, Faber and Faber, 1971)

Kennerley, A. 'Writing the history of the merchant seafarer education, training, and welfare: Retrospect and prospect', *The Northern Mariner/Le Marin du Nord*, XLL(2), April 2002, 1–21

Kennerley, A. 'Joseph Conrad at the Sailor's Home', *The Conradian*, 33(1), spring 2008, 69–102

King, P. 'Moral panics and violent street crime 1750–2000: A comparative perspective', in B. Godfrey, C. Emsley, and G. Dunstall (eds), *Comparative Histories of Crime* (London, Routledge, 2003)

Kirkland, R. 'Reading the rookery: The social meaning of the Irish slum in nineteenth century London', *New Hibernia Review*, 16(1), 2012, 16–30

Kosok, L. 'Pleasurescapes on the edge: Performing modernity on urban waterfronts (1880–1960)', *Journal of Urban History*, 48(6), 2022, 1199–210

Koven, S. *Slumming: Sexual and Social Politics in Victorian London* (Princeton, NJ, Princeton University Press, 2005)

Kwint, M. 'The circus and nature in late Georgian England', in P. Tait and K. Lavers (eds), *The Routledge Circus Study Reader* (Oxford, Routledge, 2016)

Land, I. *War, Nationalism and the British Sailor, 1750–1850* (Basingstoke, Palgrave Macmillan, 2009)

Land, I. 'The humours of sailortown: Atlantic history meets subculture theory', in G. Clark, J. Owens, and G. Smith (eds), *City Limits: Perspectives on the Historical European City* (Montreal, McGill-Queen's University Press, 2010)

Lee, J. 'Mutual transformation of colonial and imperial botanizing? The intimate yet remote collaboration in colonial Korea', *Science in Context*, 29(2), 2016, 179–211

Lemmings, D. and Walker, C. (eds), *Moral Panics, the Media and the Law in Early Modern England* (Basingstoke, Palgrave Macmillan, 2008)

Lincoln, M. *Trading in War: London's Maritime World in the Age of Cook and Nelson* (New Haven, CT, Yale University Press, 2018)

MacKenzie, J.M. 'The press and the dominant ideology of Empire', in S. Potter (ed.), *Newspaper and Empire in Ireland and Britain* (Dublin, Four Courts Press, 2004)

Maidment, B.E. *Reading Popular Prints, 1790–1870* (Manchester, Manchester University Press, 1996)

Marriott, J. *The Other Empire: Metropolis, India and Progress in the Colonial Imagination* (Manchester, Manchester University Press, 2003)

Marriott, J. *Beyond the Tower: A History of East London* (New Haven, CT, Yale University Press, 2011)

Mayne, A. *The Imagined Slum: Newspaper Representation in Three Cities 1870–1914* (Leicester, Leicester University Press, 1993)

McLaughlin, J. *Writing the Urban Jungle: Reading the Empire in London from Doyle to Elliot* (Charlottesville, VA, University Press of Virginia, 2000)

McWilliam, R. 'Man about town: Victorian night life and the Haymarket Saturnalia, 1840–1880', *History*, 103(358), 2018, 758–76

Milne, G. *People, Place and Power on the Nineteenth Century Waterfront: Sailortown* (Basingstoke, Palgrave Macmillan, 2016)

Morris, D. and Cozens, K. *London's Sailortown 1600–1800: A Social History of Shadwell and Ratcliff, an Early-Modern London Riverside Suburb* (London, East London History Society, 2014)

Murphy, A. 'The rise of the working class Shakespeare reader', in P. Bickley and J. Stephens (eds), Shakespeare, Education and Pedagogy: Representations, Interactions and Adaptations (London, Routledge, 2023)

Nilson, T. 'Hey sailor, looking for trouble? Violence, drunkenness and disorder in a Swedish port town: Gothenburg 1920', in B. Beaven, K. Bell, and R. James (eds), *Port Towns and Urban Cultures: International Histories of the Waterfront, c. 1700–2000* (Basingstoke, Palgrave Macmillan, 2016)

Nuttall, S. *Entanglement: Literary and Cultural Reflections on Post-Apartheid* (Johannesburg, Wits University Press, 2009)

Piper, A.J. '"Woman's special enemy": Female enmity in criminal discourse during the long nineteenth century', *Journal of Social History*, 49(3), 2016, shv049

Poole, S. 'More like savages than men: Foreign sailors and knife crime in nineteenth century Bristol', in S. Poole (ed.), *A City Built upon the Waterfront* (Bristol, Redcliffe Press, 2013)

Pratt, M.L. *Imperial Eyes: Writing and Transculturation* (London, Taylor & Francis, 2007)

Prince, K. 'Shakespeare in the early working-class press', in A. Krishnamurthy (ed.), *The Working-Class Intellectual in Eighteenth and Nineteenth-Century Britain* (Farnham, Ashgate, 2009)

Prins, A.H.J. *Sailing from Lamu: A Study of Maritime Culture in Islamic East Africa* (Assen, Netherlands, Van Gorcum, 1965)

Quennell, P. (ed.), *H. Mayhew and Others: The London Underworld in the Victorian Period* (New York, Dover Publications, 2012)

Reinwald, B. 'Space on the move: Perspectives on the making of the Indian Ocean seascape', in J. Deutsch and B. Reinwald (eds), *Space on the Move: Transformations of the Indian Seascape in the Nineteenth and Twentieth Century* (Berlin, Klaus Schwarz, 2002)

Rice, R. 'Sailortown: Theory and method in ordinary people's history', *Acadiensis*, 13(1), 1983, 154–68

Roper, M. and Tosh, J. *Manful Assertions: Masculinities in Britain since 1800* (Oxford, Routledge, 1991)

Seed, J. 'Did the subaltern speak? Mayhew and the coster-girl', *Journal of Victorian Culture*, 19(4), 1 December 2014, 536–49

Scholl, L.U. (ed.), *Research in Maritime History Merchants and Mariners: Selected Maritime Writings of David. M. Williams* (Newfoundland, International Maritime Economic History Association, 2000)

Schneer, J. *London 1900: The Imperial Metropolis* (New Haven, CT: Yale University Press, 1999)

Shoemaker, R.B. *The London Mob: Violence and Disorder in Eighteenth Century England* (London, Bloomsbury, 2004)

Shore, H. *London's Criminal Underworlds, c. 1720-c.1930: A Social and Cultural History* (Basingstoke, Palgrave Macmillan, 2015)

Sindall, R. 'The London garrotting panics of 1856 and 1862', *Social History*, 12(3), 1987, 351–9

Thomas, J. 'Alien immigration and the London School of Economics: Some early connections' (unpublished paper, 2017)

Wiener, M. *Men of Blood: Violence, Manliness and Criminal Justice in Victorian England* (Cambridge, Cambridge University Press, 2004)

Willis, C. 'From voyeurism to feminism: Victorian and Edwardian London's street-fighting slum viragoes', *Victorian Review*, 29(1), 2003, 70–86

PhD theses

Alker, Z. 'Street violence in mid-Victorian Liverpool' (unpublished PhD thesis, John Moores University, 2014)

Burton, V. 'The work and home life of seafarers, with special reference to the port of Southampton, 1870–1921' (unpublished PhD thesis, London School of Economics, 1988)

Chamberlain, T. 'Stokers – the lowest of the low? A social history of Royal Navy stokers, 1850–1950' (unpublished PhD thesis, University of Exeter, 2013)

Davey, J. 'A higher class of men? Sailors and working-class communities in Bristol 1850–1914' (unpublished PhD thesis, University of Portsmouth, 2019)

Kennerley, A. 'British seamen's missions and sailor homes 1815 to 1970. Voluntary welfare provision for serving seafarers' (unpublished PhD thesis, University of Exeter, 1989)

Moon, L. '"Sailorhoods": Sailortown and sailors in the port of Portsmouth circa 1850–1900' (unpublished PhD thesis, University of Portsmouth, 2015)

Blogs and websites

Londonist, https://londonist.com/2011/12/200th-anniversary-of-the-ratcliffe-highway-murders, accessed 30 September 2022

The Mass Gallery, William James Grant, 'The Bridge of Sighs', www.maasgallery.co.uk/component/joomgallery/british-pictures-2014/48-william-james-grant-1829-1866-1011, accessed 2 March 2022

Norton, R. (ed.), 'Eliza/Elijah Scott, the Black Man Woman, 1850', *Homosexuality in Nineteenth-Century England: A Sourcebook*, 15 July 2020, http://rictornorton.co.uk/eighteen/1850scot.htm, accessed 12 May 2023

Schwarz, L. 'London and the Sea', www.history.ac.uk/ihr/Focus/Sea/articles/schwarz.html, accessed 6 February 2014

Vaughan, L. Pre-publication version of 'Mapping the East End "Labyrinth"', in *Jack the Ripper and the East End Labyrinth* (London, Museum of London and Random House, 2008), https://discovery.ucl.ac.uk/id/eprint/4844/1/4844.pdf, accessed 5 March 2021

Index

Acton, William 100
Admiral Hope 90
Aliens Act 1905 164
Alker, Zoe 139
All the Year Round 46
American racial segregation 96
amusements *see* Ratcliffe Highway leisurescape
Angel Court 34
anti-modernist writing 23
Archer, John. E 8
Archer, Thomas 50
Armfelt, E. Count 130
assault 167
Asylum for Destitute Sailors 127

Baedeke, Karl 48
ballads 17, 20, 23
Barnett, Samuel 88
Beames, Thomas 41, 87, 94
Bell, Karl 21
Beresford, B.W. 69
Besant, Annie 52, 93, 94, 98, 101
Besant, Walter 44, 50, 54, 88
Betts, Oliver 7
Bishop of London 86
Bitter Cry of Outcast London 56, 81
Blackwood's Magazine 18
Bluegate Fields 12, 30, 34
boarding houses
    Chinese establishments in Limehouse 112
    comradeship 7
    as contact zones 117
    crime 114
    cultural benefits 111
    doubling as brothels 115
    exaggerated crime 116
    keepers 117
    living arrangements 121
    location of 30
    nationality of sailors 30, 112, 120
    nautically themed 121
    perceived criminality 111
    regulation of 112
    runners 124
    sinophobia 111
Booth, Charles 24, 25, 33, 45, 54, 67, 71, 128
Booth, William 7
Bridge of Signs (poem) 75
Bristol 9, 26
British Brothers' League 164
British Empire 71, 95
British and Foreign Sailor's Society 123
British press 11
brothels
    accusation of police corruption 144
    clandestine and transient businesses 142
    half-brothel, half-lodging house 145
    living arrangments 149
    low and exploitative 141
    managed by women 145
    relationships with sailors 152
    respectability within the profession 149
    robbery 142
Brunswick Street 30, 34
brutal assault 171
Bullen, Frank 65, 68, 72

bullies 66, 157
Burton, Valerie 2, 22

Cable Street 93
canabalism, accusations of 139
Carter Wood, John 8
census 11
Charrington, Thomas 141
Child of the Jago (novel) 49
Chinese boarding houses in Limehouse
　cultural and religious practices 130
　integrated within working-class
　　communities 130
　multipurpose buildings 130
Chinese sailors 6, 70, 127
Chinese sailors repatriation 129
Chinese-Anglo families 131
circus, Ratcliffe Highway
　audience 104
　entertainment 104
　structure of building 103
citizenship, Victorian ideals 67
Commercial Road 137
Common Lodging Houses Act 1851
　111, 144
contact zone 5, 8, 17, 26, 29, 36,
　86, 162
containerisation 35
Cook, Matthew 153
criminal justice system
　civilising the working class 8
　incorporation of working-class
　　people 78
　performance of working-class
　　defendants 79
　professionalisation of 166
　raising of working-class
　　subscriptions for defendant 79
　rescuing prisoners from the
　　police 177
　and the sensational press 79
crimping 113
Crook, Tom 7, 42
Cuming, Emily 4

dancing rooms 91, 93, 95, 96, 100
dancing styles 98
Deptford 28
De Quincey, Thomas 16, 18
desertion from ship 119

Dibdin, Charles 10, 25, 63, 64, 75, 102
Dickens, Charles 42, 52, 87
Dietz, Antje 4
Digby, Kenelm, E 166
dock labourers 34
dockers strike 1899 34
Douglas, Rosina 102
Doyle, Conan 7
drunk and disorderly 167
Duckworth, George 25, 54

East End Music Hall 101
East End Star 87
East India Company 127
East London Association for the
　Suppression of Vice 140
East London Defence Alliance 81
East London Music Hall 89, 93, 100
East Smithfield 137
East and West Indian Dock
　Company 178
Ebury, Lord 140
Egan, Pierce 63, 95
Empress of Disorderlies, Julia
　Mahoney 139
Emsley, Clive 8
Evans-Gordon, William Major 165

fair knuckle fight 163, 172
Femenio, Pedro 97
Fielding, John 45
fighting rituals 162
Fingard, Judith 2
flâneurs 63
folklore 22
foreign sailors
　descriptions of 49, 163
　dress 161
　repatriation 128
　replacing English sailors 70
　use of knives 49, 54, 161, 163
Fox Smith, Cicely 22, 44, 54, 82, 92
Fuhrmann, Malte 3, 6

Gallant, Thomas W. 174
gambling 89, 90
garrotting panic 77
Ginn, Geoff 88
gin-palaces 93
Glasgow 111

Grace Alley 93
Grant, William James (artist) 75
green rooms *see* dancing rooms
Greenwood, James 64, 76

Haussmann, Georges-Eugène 144
Hay, William 110
Heerten, Lasse 4
Hemyng, Bracebridge 142, 151
Hole in the Wall (novel) 49
Hood, James 75
Hoop and Grapes 93
horn-pipes 94, 102
Household Words 44
How, Walsham 56
Howard, John Reverend 96
Hugill, Stan 2, 20, 92
Huxley, Thomas Henry 55
Hyndman, H.M. 53
Hyslop, Jonathan 128

Indian sailors 127
Indian sailors' repatriation 129
industrial action *see* sailors' industrial action
informal seamen's trade union 73

Jack the Ripper 20
Jackson, Gordon 2
Jamrach menagerie 47
Jamrach, Charles 47
Jewish community 34
Jewish immigrants 164
Jolly Sailor 93, 97
Jones, Harry Reverend 35, 56, 89, 177

Kennerley, Alston 111
knife crime
    attempt to ban seafarers from carrying knives 164
    estimates in Ratcliffe Highway 166
    moral panic 162
    profession of assailant and victim 168
    Ratcliffe Highway contrasted with London districts 169
    Southern European fighting rituals 174
    stilettos 163

Koran 129
Koven, Seth 7

Land, Isaac 2, 63
landsharks *see* crimping
Lascar *see* Indian sailors
Lee, Jung 6
libertines 63
Life in London 64
Limehouse 112
Linklater, Robert Reverend 172
Liverpool 8, 22, 25, 26, 112, 139
lodging house *see* boarding houses
London County Council 112
London docklands 35
London docks 27
London port 26
London, Jack 7, 67
Lowder, Charles Reverend 87, 141

male homosexuality 153
male homosexual sex workers 154
male violence 8
male violence, regulation of 162
maritime material culture
    boarding houses 121
    public houses 94
    Ratcliffe Highway 46
Marrs family 19
masculinity 22, 23, 162
matriarchal networks 30, 146
Mayhew, Henry 52, 67, 115, 151
Mayne, Alan 43
Mayne, Richard 91, 94, 175
McKee, Christopher 69
McLaughlin, Joseph 7
McWilliam, Rohan 1
Mearns, Andrew 56, 80, 86
Melloy, Peter 103
Middlesex, the court of Assize *see* Old Bailey
Midnight Meeting Movement 154
Milne, Graeme 2, 4, 7, 35, 92, 114
Mitchell, George 21, 22, 35
Moon Light Mission 154
Morrison, Arthur 49
music hall audience
    race 100
    sex workers 100
    women 100

music hall performance
    nautically themed 102, 103
    relationship with the audience 102, 103
music hall performers
    women 102

Napoleonic Wars 122
Naumann, Katja 4
Neptune Street 30, 35, 175
New Gravel Lane 149
New York 95
Newgate Calendar 17
Norwich 19
Nuttall, Sarah 4

Old Bailey 166
Old Bailey records 12
Old Mahogany Bar *see* Wilton's Music Hall
Our Mutual Friend 43

Paddy's Goose 28, 31, 93
Palmer's Folly 30, 51, 145
Palmer's Folly, gothic descriptions 148
Paris 144
Parkinson, Joseph, C 25, 46, 51, 52, 89
Pearsons Weekly 163
Penny Dreadfuls 143, 147
penny gaffs 105
People's Palace 55, 88
philanthropy
    critical working-class reception of 56
Phillips, Watts 46, 95, 100, 101
police courts 78, 166
Polly of Wapping Stairs 65
Poole, Steve 9
Port of London Society 122
Portsmouth 18
Pratt, Mary 5
Pre-Raphaelites 76
Prince Regent 94
Prince's Square 156
prize money 95
prostitutes *see* sex workers
Prussian Eagle 93, 97, 99
public house
    art work 94
    people of colour 95
    portrayal as a thieves den 90
    racially exclusive institutions 96

Ratcliffe Highway 46
    complaints about public houses 90
    cosmopolitan nature 179, 184
    demography 28
    dullness 25
    Georgian libertines 63
    gothic descriptions of 50
    imperial gaze 105
    leisurescape 93
    local vernacular 53
    male violence 161
    maritime influence 94
    nostalgia 62
    in the popular imagination 16
    retailers 46
    song 23
    soundscape 52
Ratcliffe Highway Murders 17
rational recreation 88
Rawlinson, Robert 110
Regent Street 155
Register-General of Seamen 119
Reinwald, Brigitte 5
religious missionaries 87, 113, 154
Reynolds Newspaper 65
Ritchie, James 44, 48, 87, 163
river Thames
    associations with contamination 42
    associations with death 42
    Dickens, Charles 42
robbery 116
Robinson, F.W. 50, 97
rookeries 41
Rookeries of London 41
Rose and Crown 93, 96
Rosewall, James 123
Rothschild, Lord 166
Rowe, Richard 120
Royal Commission on Alien Immigration 1902 164
Russian pogroms 34
Ryder, Richard 17

sailing ships
    impact of sail on steam 24
    nostalgia 23
sailor homes

attempts to instill religious and self-improvement 123
entertainment 125
nautically themed 124
navigation classes 124
occupancy 126
philanthropic founders 122
shipping intelligence 124
style of architecture 124
sailor missionaries 123
sailors
   collecting animals at sea 47
   collecting exotic animals 47
   cultural capital 92
   culture ashore 45
   destitute 67
   entanglement with sailortown 92
   honour 162
   industrial action 72, 73
   intoxication 90
   as a member of the proletariat 62, 66, 69, 74
   nostalgia of 64
   professional beggars 67
   racial stereotypes 128
   relationship with the working class 162
   respectability 72
   self-improvement 72
   spendthrift 67
   stokers or firemen 69
   as subaltern transnational actors 4, 186
   as a symbol of national identity 63
   trimmers 69
   as victims of crime 87
sailors' homes
   racial segregation 129
Sailors' and Firemen's Union 70
sailortown
   economy 2
   as a functional working-class community 1, 185
   sites of urban cultural production 3
Salter, Joseph 127
San Francisco 22
Saturday Review 55
'Saucy Sailor Boy' (song) 105
Schneer, Jonathon 7
Schwarz, Leonard 26

scientific racism 6, 161, 163
Scott, Elijah 153
seafarers' sick benefit clubs 24
Seaman 70
Select Committee on Public Houses 1853 90
sensational press 161
sex workers
   as agents of moral and physical corruption 136
   dress code 138
   foreign 166
   Georgian tolerance 140
   mental health 139
   multiple 'husbands' 151
   philanthropic attempts to save fallen women 154
   pimps 136
   police surveillance 137
   possession of the streets 138
   rejection of philanthropic help 156
   street parading 139
   street walkers 139
   transvestites 154
   Victorian stereotypes 138
Ship Alley 96, 120
shipping masters 129
shipwrecked seamen 127
Shoemaker, Robert 172
Sims, George 67, 86, 89, 148
singing saloons 93
skinning *see* boarding houses crime
slum boundaries 41
slum clearance 34, 144
slum explorers 7
slums 30, 31, 40, 41
slums tourism 53
Smith, George Charles 122
social Darwinism 33, 48, 70, 78, 96
St George's in the East *see* Ratcliffe Highway
St Giles 41, 155
Steed, James 90
Strangers' Home 128
straw house *see* Asylum for Destitute Sailors
street entertainment
   performers 104
   surveillance 104

Sulvyne, Bettina Madame 102
Swell-mobsman 79

Thames police court 167
Thames police court extant records 167
Thomas, Edward Reverend 76, 93, 138, 151
Thompson, Peter Reverend 96
Tiger Bay 30, 31
trade winds 26
Trafalgar, Battle of 95
transculturation 5
transportation 114

urban-maritime culture 5, 48

Wapping 3, 26, 31, 35, 44, 45
Well Street Home scandal 125
Well Street Sailor Home 124
Wellclose Square 30, 35, 97
Whitechapel 169
Whitechapel Magdalen Hospital 154
Whitechapel murders 18, 19, 56, 81
Wiener, Martin 8, 166
Williams, John 17
Willis, Chris 74
Wilson, Havelock 70, 126
Wilton's Music Hall 28, 31, 93, 102
women of Ratcliffe Highway
   as a casulty of urban decay 78
   as members of the proletariat 76
   nostalgia of Moll and Poll 75
   as predators 77
   relationship with sailors 151
Wright, Thomas 79

EU authorised representative for GPSR:
Easy Access System Europe, Mustamäe tee 50,
10621 Tallinn, Estonia
gpsr.requests@easproject.com

www.ingramcontent.com/pod-product-compliance
Lightning Source LLC
LaVergne TN
LVHW050048200525
811683LV00004B/65